T0206182

Communications in Computer and Information Science   2143

Editorial Board Members

Joaquim Filipe⑩, *Polytechnic Institute of Setúbal, Setúbal, Portugal*
Ashish Ghosh⑩, *Indian Statistical Institute, Kolkata, India*
Lizhu Zhou, *Tsinghua University, Beijing, China*

Rationale

The CCIS series is devoted to the publication of proceedings of computer science conferences. Its aim is to efficiently disseminate original research results in informatics in printed and electronic form. While the focus is on publication of peer-reviewed full papers presenting mature work, inclusion of reviewed short papers reporting on work in progress is welcome, too. Besides globally relevant meetings with internationally representative program committees guaranteeing a strict peer-reviewing and paper selection process, conferences run by societies or of high regional or national relevance are also considered for publication.

Topics

The topical scope of CCIS spans the entire spectrum of informatics ranging from foundational topics in the theory of computing to information and communications science and technology and a broad variety of interdisciplinary application fields.

Information for Volume Editors and Authors

Publication in CCIS is free of charge. No royalties are paid, however, we offer registered conference participants temporary free access to the online version of the conference proceedings on SpringerLink (http://link.springer.com) by means of an http referrer from the conference website and/or a number of complimentary printed copies, as specified in the official acceptance email of the event.

CCIS proceedings can be published in time for distribution at conferences or as post-proceedings, and delivered in the form of printed books and/or electronically as USBs and/or e-content licenses for accessing proceedings at SpringerLink. Furthermore, CCIS proceedings are included in the CCIS electronic book series hosted in the SpringerLink digital library at http://link.springer.com/bookseries/7899. Conferences publishing in CCIS are allowed to use Online Conference Service (OCS) for managing the whole proceedings lifecycle (from submission and reviewing to preparing for publication) free of charge.

Publication process

The language of publication is exclusively English. Authors publishing in CCIS have to sign the Springer CCIS copyright transfer form, however, they are free to use their material published in CCIS for substantially changed, more elaborate subsequent publications elsewhere. For the preparation of the camera-ready papers/files, authors have to strictly adhere to the Springer CCIS Authors' Instructions and are strongly encouraged to use the CCIS LaTeX style files or templates.

Abstracting/Indexing

CCIS is abstracted/indexed in DBLP, Google Scholar, EI-Compendex, Mathematical Reviews, SCImago, Scopus. CCIS volumes are also submitted for the inclusion in ISI Proceedings.

How to start

To start the evaluation of your proposal for inclusion in the CCIS series, please send an e-mail to ccis@springer.com.

Go Irie · Choonsung Shin · Takashi Shibata ·
Kazuaki Nakamura

Editors

Frontiers of Computer Vision

30th International Workshop, IW-FCV 2024
Tokyo, Japan, February 19–21, 2024
Revised Selected Papers

 Springer

Editors
Go Irie
Tokyo University of Science
Tokyo, Japan

Choonsung Shin
Chonnam National University
Gwangju, Korea (Republic of)

Takashi Shibata
NEC Corporation
Kawasaki, Kanagawa, Japan

Kazuaki Nakamura
Tokyo University of Science
Tokyo, Japan

ISSN 1865-0929   ISSN 1865-0937 (electronic)
Communications in Computer and Information Science
ISBN 978-981-97-4248-6   ISBN 978-981-97-4249-3 (eBook)
https://doi.org/10.1007/978-981-97-4249-3

© The Editor(s) (if applicable) and The Author(s), under exclusive license
to Springer Nature Singapore Pte Ltd. 2024

This work is subject to copyright. All rights are solely and exclusively licensed by the Publisher, whether
the whole or part of the material is concerned, specifically the rights of translation, reprinting, reuse of
illustrations, recitation, broadcasting, reproduction on microfilms or in any other physical way, and transmission
or information storage and retrieval, electronic adaptation, computer software, or by similar or dissimilar
methodology now known or hereafter developed.
The use of general descriptive names, registered names, trademarks, service marks, etc. in this publication
does not imply, even in the absence of a specific statement, that such names are exempt from the relevant
protective laws and regulations and therefore free for general use.
The publisher, the authors and the editors are safe to assume that the advice and information in this book
are believed to be true and accurate at the date of publication. Neither the publisher nor the authors or the
editors give a warranty, expressed or implied, with respect to the material contained herein or for any errors
or omissions that may have been made. The publisher remains neutral with regard to jurisdictional claims in
published maps and institutional affiliations.

This Springer imprint is published by the registered company Springer Nature Singapore Pte Ltd.
The registered company address is: 152 Beach Road, #21-01/04 Gateway East, Singapore 189721, Singapore

If disposing of this product, please recycle the paper.

Preface

It is our great pleasure to publish these post-workshop proceedings of the 30th International Workshop on Frontiers of Computer Vision (IW-FCV 2024), which was held in Tokyo, Japan, during February 19–21, 2024.

The history of IW-FCV dates back to 1995. It was first held in Daejeon, Korea as the Japan-Korea Joint Workshop on Computer Vision with the aim of promoting research activities and exchanges between the computer vision communities in Japan and Korea. Since then, this workshop series has been held every year alternately in Korea and Japan, and since 2017, it has evolved into an international workshop that welcomes researchers from more diverse countries, mainly from Asia. This year's version, IW-FCV 2024, finally celebrated its 30th anniversary and was held in Tokyo with great success.

The primary focus of the workshop is on fundamental theories, techniques, and algorithms related to computer vision and image signal processing, with particular emphasis on practical applications. Given the rapid progress in this technical field, this year's call for papers especially highlighted topics including: Fundamentals and Theory (e.g., image filtering/enhancement/restoration, color and illumination analysis, and image coding), Computer Vision and Image Analysis (e.g., shape from-X, object detection and tracking, and deep learning for computer vision), Applications (e.g., image/video search and retrieval, surveillance, AR/VR/MR/HR, and bio-medical image analysis), and Recognition and Learning (e.g., 2D/3D object recognition, face and gesture recognition, and human pose estimation). Eventually, we received 61 submissions this year, by authors from more than six countries. Each paper was reviewed by three Program Committee members in a single-blind manner. Following the workshop presentations, only 12 high-quality full papers were selected for publication in the post-workshop proceedings, resulting in a quite low acceptance ratio of 19.7%.

We would like to thank all the participants in this workshop and each member of the committee for their great efforts in planning and organizing the workshop. Finally, we thank the organizer, The Institute of Electrical Engineers of Japan (IEEJ), for their continuous support.

May 2024

Go Irie
Choonsung Shin
Takashi Shibata
Kazuaki Nakamura

Organization

General Chairs

Kazuhiko Sumi   Aoyama Gakuin University, Japan
Yongduek Seo   Sogang University, South Korea

Program Chairs

Go Irie   Tokyo University of Science, Japan
Choonsung Shin   Chonnam National University, South Korea

Program Vice-chairs

Takashi Shibata   NEC Corporation, Japan
Kazuaki Nakamura   Tokyo University of Science, Japan

Secretary General

Naoshi Kaneko   Tokyo Denki University, Japan

Secretary Deputy

Seiya Ito   National Institute of Information and
            Communications Technology, Japan

Finance and Liaison Chairs

Hirooki Aoki   Chitose University, Japan
Eiichiro Momma   Nihon University, Japan

Web and Publicity Chair

Takayuki Fujiwara   Hokkaido Information University, Japan

Steering Committee

Yoshimitsu Aoki   Keio University, Japan
Junichiro Hayashi   Kagawa University, Japan
Kanghyun Jo   University of Ulsan, South Korea
Soon Ki Jung   Kyungpook National University, South Korea
Kunihito Kato   Gifu University, Japan
Hiroyasu Koshimizu   Chukyo University/YYC-Solution, Japan
Takio Kurita   Hiroshima University, Japan
Kiryong Kwon   Pukyong National University, South Korea
Chilwoo Lee   Chonnam National University, South Korea
Inseop Na   Chonnam National University, South Korea
Makoto Niwakawa   Meidensha, Japan
Weon-Geun Oh   ETRI, South Korea
Jong-Il Park   Hanyang University, South Korea
Yongduek Seo   Sogang University, South Korea
Choonsung Shin   Chonnam National University, South Korea
Kazuhiko Sumi   Aoyama Gakuin University, Japan
Rin-ichiro Taniguchi   Kyushu University, Japan
Kazuhiko Yamamoto   Gifu University, Japan

Technical Program Committee

Hiroaki Aizawa   Hiroshima University, Japan
Shuichi Akizuki   Chukyo University, Japan
Hideki Aoyama   Panasonic Holdings Corporation, Japan
Kyoung Ho Choi   Mokpo National University, South Korea
Keisuke Doman   Chukyo University, Japan
Hironobu Fujiyoshi   Chubu University, Japan
Hitoshi Habe   Kindai University, Japan
Atsushi Hashimoto   Omron Sinic X Corporation, Japan
Akinori Hidaka   Tokyo Denki University, Japan
Yuki Hirose   Osaka University, Japan
Maiya Hori   Tottori University of Environmental Studies,
                                       Japan
Ichiro Ide   Nagoya University, Japan

Chika Inoshita	Canon, Japan
Rui Ishiyama	NEC Corporation, Japan
Masakazu Iwamura	Osaka Metropolitan University, Japan
Motoi Iwata	Osaka Metropolitan University, Japan
Moon-Ho Jeong	Kwangwoon University, South Korea
Yusuke Kameda	Sophia University, Japan
Takuya Kamitani	Toshiba Tec Corporation, Japan
Hyun-Deok Kang	UNIST, South Korea
Marc A. Kastner	Kyoto University, Japan
Marie Katsurai	Doshisha University, Japan
Yasutomo Kawanishi	Riken, Japan
Jaeil Kim	Kyungpook National University, South Korea
Soo Hyung Kim	Chonnam National University, South Korea
Wonjun Kim	Konkuk University, South Korea
Kazuya Kitano	Nara Institute of Science and Technology, Japan
Takahiro Komamizu	Nagoya University, Japan
Kazuhiro Kono	Kansai University, Japan
Takio Kurita	Hiroshima University, Japan
Chul Lee	Dongguk University, South Korea
Jae-Ho Lee	ETRI, South Korea
Suk Hwan Lee	Tongmyong University, South Korea
Jianquan Liu	NEC Corporation, South Korea
Tetsu Matsukawa	Kyushu University, Japan
Tsubasa Minematsu	Kyushu University, Japan
Yu Mitsuzumi	NTT Corporation, Japan
Takaya Miyamoto	NEC Corporation, Japan
Tomo Miyazaki	Tohoku University, Japan
Yoshihiko Mochizuki	Saitama Institute of Technology, Japan
Minoru Mori	Kanagawa Institute of Technology, Japan
Katsuyuki Nakamura	Hitachi Co Ltd., Japan
Masashi Nishiyama	Tottori University, Japan
Naoko Nitta	Mukogawa Women's University, Japan
Wataru Ohyama	Tokyo Denki University, Japan
Takahiro Okabe	Kyushu Institute of Technology, Japan
Yuji Oyamada	Tottori University, Japan
Soon-Yong Park	Kyungpook National University, South Korea
Hideo Saito	Keio University, Japan
Atsushi Shimada	Kyushu University, Japan
Yongqing Sun	Nihon University, Japan
Satoshi Suzuki	NTT Corporation, Japan
Tomohiro Takahashi	Tokai University, Japan
Toru Tamaki	Nagoya Institute of Technology, Japan

Hiroshi Tanaka   Fujitsu Limited, Japan
Kenji Terada   Tokushima University, Japan
Kengo Terasawa   Future University Hakodate, Japan
Diego Thomas   Kyushu University, Japan
Masato Tsukada   University of Tsukuba, Japan
Hiroyuki Ukida   Tokushima University, Japan
Xiaomeng Wu   NTT Corporation, Japan
Yota Yamamoto   Tokyo University of Science, Japan
Takayoshi Yamashita   Chubu University, Japan
Yukiko Yanagawa   Omron, Japan
Keiji Yanai   University of Electro-Communications, Japan

Contents

Tackling Background Misclassification in Box-Supervised Segmentation: A Background Constraint Approach

Zhicheng Zhang🆔 and Takio Kurita(✉)🆔

Hiroshima University, Higashihiroshima 7398511, Japan
{m223446,tkurita}@hiroshima-u.ac.jp
https://www.hiroshima-u.ac.jp

Abstract. In contrast to the well-established paradigm of supervised instance segmentation, the emerging weakly supervised methodology encounters numerous challenges. One significant difficulty lies in the absence of pixel-wise labels, making it challenging for the model to learn a mapping from the input image to instance masks. For box-supervised instance segmentation, previous method encouraged similar neighboring pixels to share identical labels, yielding reasonably successful outcomes. Yet, such method does not perform well when differentiating highly similar background and foreground pixels, often misclassifying background as foreground due to methodological limitations. To address this problem, our proposed Background Constraint Approach (BCA) introduces a background-specific loss function to reduce misclassification of background pixels, while a complementary foreground loss function mitigates potential negative effects on foreground pixel classification. Our approach has outperformed the baseline by improving the Average Precision (AP) by 1.09% on the COCO val 2017 dataset. Visualization of the inference images confirms that our method more accurately classifies pixels previously mislabeled as foreground by the baseline.

Keywords: Instance Segmentation · Weekly Supervised · Deep Learning

1 Introduction

For deep learning models, the data used to train the model is vital, researchers hold their views that the more data used for training, the better the generalization of the trained model will be. In real world, researchers can easily collect a large amount of data, whereas facing a great challenge against labeling the data. Though there are some people proposed methods to label data by deep learning models, the accuracy of deep learning models is still far from that of humans, therefore labeling data still heavily relies on humans, and for some complex data sets, experts with specialized skills are needed to label, for example, find the lesion areas in an x-ray image. This makes labeling data very expensive,

© The Author(s), under exclusive license to Springer Nature Singapore Pte Ltd. 2024
G. Irie et al. (Eds.): IW-FCV 2024, CCIS 2143, pp. 1–13, 2024.
https://doi.org/10.1007/978-981-97-4249-3_1

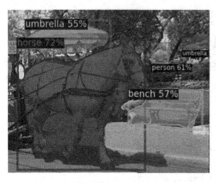 

Baseline   Ours

Fig. 1. The baseline incorrectly identified the pixels under the horse as part of the foreground, as it confused them with the road pixels that share a similar color to the white horse. However, with the integration of our background constraint method, there was a notable improvement in the accuracy of background pixel classification. **It should be noted that the model were trained using only box annotations**

and designing a method for models to learn certain features from insufficient label is a prospective research topic. Within the scope of instance segmentation, most methods are fully supervised which depends significantly on datasets annotated with pixel-wise precision. Labeling every single pixel in an image to show what object it belongs to gives us a very detailed picture which is beneficial for precision-dependent tasks. However, this method is time-consuming and costly due to its intricacy. An alternative approach involves segment objects within basic bounding box, which is more time-efficient and cost-effective. Although this method lacks the same level of detail, it is potentially sufficient for numerous applications.

Despite the difficulty of training a network for instance segmentation using only box annotations, previous researchers have suggested various methods to make the most of the limited information provided by bounding boxes. SDI [1] for creating mask labels for semantic segmentation operates through a sequential method. In the first step, it categorizes all pixels lying outside the perimeter of any bounding box as the background, effectively isolating the foreground elements. Next, when dealing with intersecting bounding boxes, the SDI [1] algorithm gives precedence to the bounding box with a smaller surface area, treating it as the primary semantic region within the overlap. DSRG [2] draw on classical seeded region growing methods for image segmentation. They propose a novel approach where a semantic segmentation network is trained beginning with these specific regions, and the level of pixel-wise supervision is gradually expanded through a process akin to seeded region growing. The MIL [3] approach divides the image into different bags using various lines, which consist of rows or columns of pixels within the image. Since an instance will intersect with the bounding box, those lines that at least cover an instance within a box are designated as positive bags, while lines not crossing any box are considered negative bags. Utilizing the labels of these bags to compute the loss for the predicted mask, MIL [3] facilitates an end-to-end method for both instance and semantic segmentation. This methodology has surpassed state-of-the-art models on the PASCAL VOC dataset [4]. Nevertheless, when applied to large-scale datasets such as MSCOCO [5], the model exhibits unsatisfactory performance. Boxinst [10] proposed a projection loss and a pairwise loss to alternate supervised mask loss, converting fully supervised method to box supervised method. The projection loss encourages the projection of predict mask close to the projection of bounding box, mean while the pairwise loss encourage neighboring pixels to have same pixel label if they are similar in color space. BoxInst [10] demonstrates strong performance on the MSCOCO [5] dataset, achieving a 10% increase in average precision (AP) compared to previous methods. This improvement brings the model's performance closely in line with its supervised counterpart.

A lot of previous studies have demonstrated favorable results in instance segmentation only using box annotations, with methods like Boxinst [10] delivering promising performance on the MSCOCO [5] dataset. However, it fell short in scenarios where the background and foreground colors are similar(e.g., Fig. 1). To tackle this problem, **the main contribution of our proposed method is:**

* **We introduced a background loss function to address the incorrect classification of background pixels.**
* **Additionally, we proposed a foreground loss function to mitigate the negative effects of the background loss on the foreground pixels.**
* **With the integration of our proposed method, there was a notable improvement in the accuracy of background pixel classification.**

2 Related Work

2.1 Condinst

CondInst [9] is an advancement built on the foundations of FCOS [6], which is recognized as a one-stage object detection framework. The evolution from object detection to instance detection in CondInst [9] is achieved by integrating a mask branch into the architecture, as depicted in Fig. 2. Features derived from the mask branch are fed into a mask FCN to create instance-specific masks. Furthermore, the introduction of a controller in the detection phase enhances the network's capability. The controller governs a head that produces an instance-aware mask FCN head, assigning a unique mask head to each instance. This mask head is capable of encoding various attributes of the instance, such as shape and size, allowing the mask heads to accurately discern the foreground and background details of each instance within the overall mask feature landscape. Unlike Mask R-CNN [7], which relies on Region of Interest (ROI) pooling with its associated drawbacks, CondInst [9] avoids these limitations. The drawbacks of using ROI include the potential inclusion of irrelevant information from other instances or

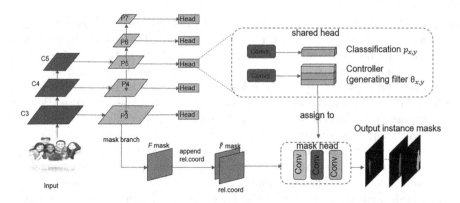

Fig. 2. The main structure of CondInst includes feature maps from the backbone network (e.g., ResNet-50). P3 to P7 are the FPN [8] (Feature Pyramid Network) feature maps. The mask branch output is $Fmask$. $\tilde{F}mask$, is created by concatenating relative coordinates to $Fmask$. The classification head determines the class of each instance based on its position (x, y), similarly to FCOS [6]. The controller makes the filter parameters θ_{xy} of the mask head for each instance. Like in FCOS [6], there are also center-ness and box heads that work together with the controller, but they are not shown in the diagram for simplicity. The dashed box shows that the heads are used repeatedly for P3 to P7. The shared head is repeatedly applied, corresponding to the number of instances present in the image.

the background, the need for a larger receptive field in the mask head to incorporate sufficient contextual information, and an overall increase in computational complexity. By not depending on ROI pooling, CondInst sidesteps these issues, potentially leading to more efficient and accurate instance segmentation.

The training approach of CondInst [9] for handling positive and negative samples follows the same strategy as FCOS [6], utilizing center region sampling to determine these samples. In addition to the loss functions used by FCOS [6], CondInst [9] incorporates an instance mask loss, which is an additional component specifically for the instance segmentation task.

$$L_{total} = L_{FCOS} + L_{mask} \tag{1}$$

2.2   Boxinst

Boxinst [10] builds upon Condinst [9], utilizing the same network architecture while introducing two new loss functions calculating to L_{mask} transition from supervised learning to box supervised learning.

$$L_{total} = L_{FCOS} + L_{proj} + L_{pairwise} \tag{2}$$

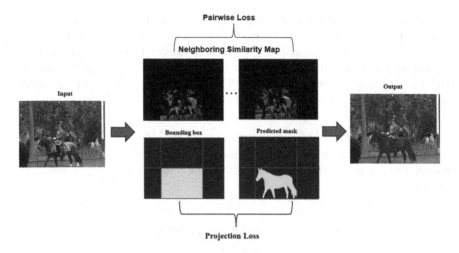

Fig. 3. presents an overview of Boxinst, where projection loss serves to ensure that the projection of predicted mask corresponds with the projection of the bounding box. Additionally, pairwise loss is derived from an 8-neighboring similarity map, which is created by calculating the similarity between each pixel and its eight surrounding pixels. (The architecture of Boxinst [10] is the same with Condinst [9], the details are omitted for brevity.)

2.3 Projection Loss

The projection loss encourages the predicted masks to share a similar projection along the x and y axes with the Ground Truth bounding box. The projection loss term is defined as:

$$
\begin{aligned}
L_{proj} = {} & L\left(\mathrm{Proj}_x(\tilde{m}), \mathrm{Proj}_x(b)\right) \\
& + L\left(\mathrm{Proj}_y(\tilde{m}), \mathrm{Proj}_y(b)\right),
\end{aligned} \tag{3}
$$

where $\tilde{m} \in (0,1)^{H \times W}$ is the network predictions of instance mask, $b \in (0,1)^{H \times W}$ is the mask generated by assigning 1 to the locations in the ground-truth box and 0 otherwise (Fig. 3).

2.4 Pairwise Loss

Boxinst [10] represent each pixels within the image, along with its neighboring images, as an undirected graph. Each vertex within the graph represents a pixel, and an edge exists between a pixel and its 8 neighbors if their similarity exceeds a specified threshold. The threshold is a hyperparameter set arbitrarily.

$$
G(V, E) \tag{4}
$$

Consider two neighboring pixels located at (i, j) and (p, q) within the image. Using y_e to represent the edge between them, where y_e equals 1 if there is an edge and 0 otherwise. The network prediction mask, denoted as $\tilde{m}_{ij} \in (0, 1)$, falls within the range (0, 1) and can be interpreted as the probability that the pixel (i, j) belongs to the foreground. The probability $y_e = 1$ can be defined using the following equations

$$P(y_e = 1) = \tilde{m}_{ij} * \tilde{m}_{pq} + (1 - \tilde{m}_{ij}) * (1 - \tilde{m}_{pq}) \tag{5}$$

To enforce similarity in prediction mask for pixels with the same labels and dissimilarity for pixels with different labels, the pairwise loss can be defined as follows:

$$L_{\text{pairwise}} = -\frac{1}{N} \sum_{e \in E_{in}} y_e \log P(y_e = 1)$$
$$+ (1 - y_e) \log P(y_e = 0) \tag{6}$$

As only box annotations are available and lack the actual values of y_e, they consider two neighboring pixels to have the same labels if their color similarity exceeds a predefined threshold t.

$$L_{\text{pairwise}} = -\frac{1}{N} \sum_{e \in E_{in}} 1_{\{s_e \geq t\}} \log P(y_e = 1)$$
$$+ 1_{\{s_e < t\}} \log P(y_e = 0) \tag{7}$$

A noteworthy point is that when two pixels exhibit closely matching colors, they are likely to carry the same labels, indicating that the edge connecting them is assigned a label of 1. Therefore, one can set a color similarity threshold t. If the color similarity exceeds t, the edge's label is probably 1. Color similarity is quantitatively defined in this context.

$$S_e = S(c_{i,j}, c_{l,k}) = \exp\left(-\frac{\|c_{i,j} - c_{l,k}\|}{\theta}\right) \tag{8}$$

The label of y_e can only be inferred as 1 when the similarity surpasses the threshold, but the label remains agnostic if it is less than the threshold. Consequently, the loss exclusively focus on positive edges and disregard negative edges.

$$L_{\text{pairwise}} = -\frac{1}{N} \sum_{e \in E_{in}} 1_{\{s_e \geq t\}} \log P(y_e = 1) \tag{9}$$

3   Proposed Method

Our method is driven by the observation that the Boxinst [10] model does not perform well on certain images (e.g., Fig. 1). This inadequacy arises particularly in scenarios where the foreground pixels closely resemble the background, leading to incorrect classification due to the model's tendency to assign the same label to these similar foreground and background pixels. For instance, in Fig. 1, a white horse against a grey road presents a challenge; despite the road being the background and the horse the foreground, their similar color tones can result in parts of the road being misclassified as foreground. Hence, we proposed a loss function called background loss L_{bg} to constrain these misclassified background pixels.

$$L_{mask} = L_{projection} + L_{pairwise} + \lambda L_{bg} \tag{10}$$

In our experiments, we observed that when combining pairwise loss, projection loss, and background loss, the model tends to fail (e.g., Fig. 6). This happens because some foreground pixels, influenced by the background loss, are mistakenly classified as part of the background. Then, the pairwise loss further exacerbates this issue by encouraging adjacent pixels, similar to those misclassified, to be wrongly labeled as background as well. As a result, most of the foreground pixels end up misclassified as background, with only a few remaining correctly identified as foreground to maintain a semblance of accuracy in the mask projection relative to the box projection. To mitigate the impact of background loss on foreground pixels, we introduced a foreground loss component into the model. This addition aims to balance the influence of background loss, ensuring a more accurate classification of foreground pixels.

$$L_{mask} = L_{projection} + L_{pairwise} + \lambda L_{bg} + \beta L_{fg} \tag{11}$$

3.1 Background Similarity

Our observation shows that for a given bounding box, the majority of pixels on the bounding box edge typically belong to the background. Additionally, most background pixels inside the bounding box closely resemble the edge pixels on the bounding box. For instance, as shown in Fig. 1, there are road pixels misclassified as background that bear a strong resemblance to their corresponding pixels on the bounding box due to the presence of some road pixels on the bounding box itself. Consequently, these background pixels within the bounding box and their projections onto the bounding box share very similar characteristics. To quantify this background similarity, we compute it based on the pixel's four corresponding projections on the bounding box edges. This similarity is defined by the following formulas:

$$S_{\text{bottom}} = \text{sim}(Pixel_{ij}, Boundary_{bottom}) \tag{12}$$

$$S_{\text{top}} = \text{sim}(Pixel_{ij}, Boundary_{top}) \tag{13}$$

$$S_{\text{left}} = \text{sim}(Pixel_{ij}, Boundary_{left}) \tag{14}$$

$$S_{\text{right}} = \text{sim}(Pixel_{ij}, Boundary_{right}) \tag{15}$$

Out of the four boundary similarity values S_{bottom}, S_{top}, S_{left}, and S_{right} we choose the maximum one and denote it as max_sim. max_sim represents the

(a) Computational Methodology   (b) Image with box   (c) Background Similarity

Fig. 4. (a) The illustration depicts the process for computing background similarity by evaluating the similarity between each pixel inside the bounding box and its four projections onto the bounding box edges. The maximum value from these four is selected. Subsequently, a threshold is applied to the similarity map; values falling below this threshold are assigned a zero. (b) A input image with box annotations. (c) The background similarity map from (b)

strongest similarity to any of the four bounding box borders for a given pixel. Selecting the maximum value allows us to determine if at least one of the edges is a good match for classifying the pixel as potential background (Fig. 4).

$$maxsim = max(S_{bottom}, S_{top}, S_{left}, S_{right}) \qquad (16)$$

We establish a threshold criteria for the maximum similarity value, maxsim. If maxsim for a given pixel exceeds this set threshold, we categorize that pixel as belonging to the background. Conversely, if maxsim falls below the threshold, we refrain from assigning a definitive label to that pixel, leaving it ambiguous between foreground and background. In essence, the threshold of maxsim allows us to selectively classify pixels with strong enough background edge similarity as background, while pixels that do not exhibit such pronounced similarity remain without a committed designation.

$$bgsim = \begin{cases} maxsim & \text{if } maxsim \geq \text{threshold} \\ 0 & \text{if } maxsim < \text{threshold} \end{cases} \qquad (17)$$

In calculating the similarity between a pixel inside the bounding box and its corresponding projection on the bounding box edge, we adopted the same strategy in calculating neighboring similarity in Eq. 8.

3.2   Background Loss

The background loss function is designed to promote pixels with high background similarity values to be classified as background. Specifically, it is constructed using the background similarity map, with the goal of making pixels that are

Image with box

Background similarity

Fig. 5. illustrates the visualization of background similarity maps, where the background loss promotes the classification of pixels exhibiting a high degree of similarity in the background similarity map as belonging to the background.

very similar to the background more likely to be labeled as such. We formulate the background loss according to the following equation:

$$L_{bg} = \frac{\sum_{ij \in mask} bgsim_{ij} y_{ij}}{\sum_{ij \in mask} bgsim_{ij}} \in (0, 1) \tag{18}$$

$bgsim_{ij}$ represents the background similarity map value at position(i, j) that we mentioned in Sect. 3.1, ranging between 0 and 1. y_{ij} denotes the predicted mask value at position (i, j), which can be interpreted as the predicted probability of the pixel being the foreground; a value of 1 indicates the pixel is foreground, while 0 signifies it belongs to the background (Fig. 5).

3.3 Foreground Loss

As previously discussed, the purpose of the foreground loss is to mitigate the impact of the background loss on pixels in the foreground (e.g., Fig. 6). For pixels exhibiting high similarity with their adjacent counterparts, there are two possible scenarios: they could either be part of the foreground or the background. Thus, for pixels with a high neighboring similarity, the foreground loss is designed to promote their classification as foreground. This is because background pixels with high similarity to their neighbors are regulated by the background loss. Ultimately, this ensures that only the truly foreground pixels are encouraged to be identified as such.

$$L_{fg} = -1_{\{s_e \geq t\}} \frac{\sum_{i,j \in mask} \sum_{e \in G} S_e y_{ij}}{\sum_{i,j \in mask} \sum_{e \in G} S_e} \in (0, 1) \tag{19}$$

(a) $L_{projection} + L_{pairwise} + \lambda L_{background}$ (b) $L_{projection} + L_{pairwise} + \lambda L_{background} + \beta L_{foreground}$

Fig. 6. (a) The model trained without foreground loss. (b) The model after incorporating foreground loss. The impact of background loss on foreground pixels is mitigated by the inclusion of foreground loss.

The same as in Sect. 2.4, the graph G denotes a central pixel surrounded by its eight adjacent pixels, where each pixel is represented as a vertex and the connecting edges reflect the similarity between the central pixel and its neighbors. The term S_e corresponds to the weights of the graph edges represent adjacent similarity, which are utilized when computing the pairwise loss described in Eq. 8. y_{ij} represents the predict mask value, within the interval of 0 to 1, at the grid position (i, j). Imagine we possess a batch of downscaled input images formatted as (B, 3, W, H) with corresponding predict masks formatted as (B, C, W, H). In this case, adjacency similarity map S_e will take the form of a five-dimensional tensor with dimensions (B, C, 8, W, H), where the third dimension represents the similarity between a pixel and its eight surrounding neighbors.

4   Experiment

We select Boxinst [10] with the MS_R_50_1x.yaml configuration as our baseline, utilizing a ResNet50 [12] backbone pre-trained on the ImageNet [13] dataset. Our implementation follows the practice of Boxinst [10], we trained our network on a single RTX 3090 GPU. Faced with memory constraints, we consulted the official GitHub Issues page [11] for strategies on training models with limited memory. This led us to decrease the batch size from 16 to 4. To maintain training effectiveness, we proportionally scaled down the learning rate from 0.01 to 0.0025 and increased the training iterations from 90,000 to 360,000. We also increased the multi-step scheduler from (60,000, 80,000) to (240,000, 320,000). All other hyperparameters remained unchanged and matched those of the official Boxinst [10] configuration. For the experimentation of our proposed loss function, we explored a range of weight combinations between background and foreground losses. We also experimented with varying the background similarity thresholds to identify the most optimal setting. We trained and evaluated our model on

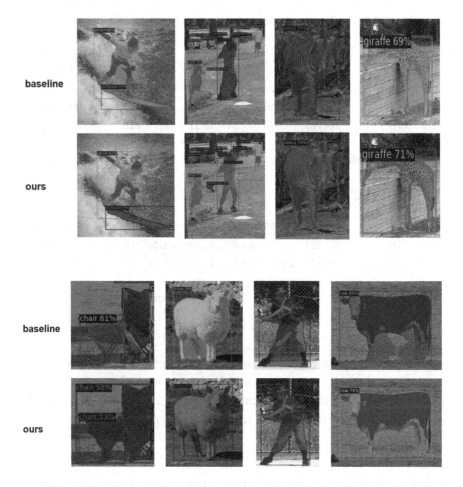

Fig. 7. A comparison between our proposed method and the baseline

the MS COCO [5] train2017 and val2017 dataset. It includes a grand total of 2.5 million instances that have been labeled across 328,000 images. During the training stage, only bounding box annotations were utilized (Fig. 7).

5   Result

Both our model and the baseline BoxInst [10] were trained from scratch under the same conditions for comparative analysis. In Table 1 and 2, experiments are conducted to determine the optimal weighting λ and β for the two proposed loss functions. Table 3 and 4 are dedicated to assessing the performance of our model against different background thresholds.

Table 1. Box AP with varying foreground and background loss weights.

model	threshold	λ	β	AP	AP50	AP75	APs	APm	APl
baseline	-	-	-	39.10	57.79	42.21	23.75	42.73	50.03
ours	0.3	0.0125	0.0125	39.22	57.93	42.30	23.51	**43.09**	**50.08**
ours	0.3	0.0125	0.0250	**39.40**	**58.10**	**42.71**	**23.84**	42.99	50.00
ours	0.3	0.0125	0.0375	36.95	55.21	39.89	21.58	40.52	47.39

Table 2. Mask AP with varying foreground and background loss weights.

model	threshold	λ	β	AP	AP50	AP75	APs	APm	APl
baseline	-	-	-	29.89	51.97	29.74	13.50	32.57	44.91
ours	0.3	0.0125	0.0125	30.06	52.25	29.82	13.76	32.80	44.62
ours	0.3	0.0125	0.0250	**30.98**	**52.36**	**31.54**	**13.94**	**33.34**	**45.76**
ours	0.3	0.0125	0.0375	29.19	50.01	29.54	12.76	31.41	43.14

Table 3. Box AP with varying background similarity threshold.

model	threshold	λ	β	AP	AP50	AP75	APs	APm	APl
baseline	-	-	-	39.10	57.79	42.21	23.75	42.73	50.03
ours	0.2	0.0125	0.0250	39.15	57.83	**42.73**	22.74	**43.03**	49.95
ours	0.25	0.0125	0.0250	39.18	57.85	42.40	23.41	42.93	**50.23**
ours	0.3	0.0125	0.0250	**39.40**	**58.10**	42.71	**23.84**	42.99	50.00
ours	0.35	0.0125	0.0250	39.04	57.75	42.17	22.72	42.95	49.66

Table 4. Mask AP with varying background similarity threshold.

model	threshold	λ	β	AP	AP50	AP75	APs	APm	APl
baseline	-	-	-	29.89	51.97	29.74	13.50	32.57	44.91
ours	0.2	0.0125	0.0250	30.76	**52.44**	**31.55**	13.46	**33.41**	45.50
ours	0.25	0.0125	0.0250	30.71	52.35	31.35	13.69	33.16	**45.91**
ours	0.3	0.0125	0.0250	**30.98**	52.36	31.54	**13.94**	33.34	45.76
ours	0.35	0.0125	0.0250	30.53	52.10	31.05	13.15	33.22	45.08

6   Conclusion

Our study introduced an innovative approach to address the issue of background misclassification in Box-supervised Supervised Segmentation. We developed a technique for assessing background similarity and introduced a specialized background loss function to mitigate errors in background pixel classification. Furthermore, we incorporated a foreground loss function specifically intend to reduce the negative impact that background loss adjustments have on the accuracy of foreground pixel classification. Our approach yielded a 1.09% improvement in Average Precision (AP) on the MS COCO [5] val2017 dataset.

References

1. Khoreva, A., Benenson, R., Hosang, J., Hein, M., Schiele, B.: Simple does it: weakly supervised instance and semantic segmentation. In: Proceedings of the IEEE Conference on Computer Vision and Pattern Recognition, pp. 876–885 (2017)
2. Huang, Z., Wang, X., Wang, J., Liu, W., Wang, J.: Weakly-supervised semantic segmentation network with deep seeded region growing. In: Proceedings of the IEEE Conference on Computer Vision and Pattern Recognition, pp. 7014–7023 (2018)
3. Hsu, C.-C., Hsu, K.-J., Tsai, C.-C., Lin, Y.-Y., Chuang, Y.-Y.: Weakly supervised instance segmentation using the bounding box tightness prior. In: Advances in Neural Information Processing Systems, vol. 32 (2019)
4. Everingham, M., Van Gool, L., Williams, C.K.I., Winn, J., Zisserman, A.: The pascal visual object classes (VOC) challenge. Int. J. Comput. Vis. **88**, 303–338 (2010)
5. Lin, T.-Y., et al.: Microsoft COCO: common objects in context. In: Fleet, D., Pajdla, T., Schiele, B., Tuytelaars, T. (eds.) ECCV 2014. LNCS, vol. 8693, pp. 740–755. Springer, Cham (2014). https://doi.org/10.1007/978-3-319-10602-1_48
6. Tian, Z., Shen, C., Chen, H., He, T.: FCOS: fully convolutional one-stage object detection. In: Proceedings of the IEEE/CVF International Conference on Computer Vision, pp. 9627–9636 (2019)
7. He, K., Gkioxari, G., Dollár, P., Girshick, R.: Mask R-CNN. In: Proceedings of the IEEE International Conference on Computer Vision, pp. 2961–2969 (2017)
8. Lin, T.-Y., Dollár, P., Girshick, R., He, K., Hariharan, B., Belongie, S.: Feature pyramid networks for object detection. In: Proceedings of the IEEE Conference on Computer Vision and Pattern Recognition, pp. 2117–2125 (2017)
9. Tian, Z., Shen, C., Chen, H.: Conditional convolutions for instance segmentation. In: Vedaldi, A., Bischof, H., Brox, T., Frahm, J.-M. (eds.) ECCV 2020. LNCS, vol. 12346, pp. 282–298. Springer, Cham (2020). https://doi.org/10.1007/978-3-030-58452-8_17
10. Tian, Z., Shen, C., Wang, X., Chen, H.: Boxinst: high-performance instance segmentation with box annotations. In: Proceedings of the IEEE/CVF Conference on Computer Vision and Pattern Recognition, pp. 5443–5452 (2021)
11. AdelaiDet. https://github.com/aim-uofa/AdelaiDet/issues/325. Accessed 28 Nov 2023
12. He, K., Zhang, X., Ren, S., Sun, J.: Deep residual learning for image recognition. In: Proceedings of the IEEE Conference on Computer Vision and Pattern Recognition, pp. 770–778 (2016)
13. Deng, J., Dong, W., Socher, R., Li, L.-J., Li, K., Fei-Fei, L.: Imagenet: a large-scale hierarchical image database. In: 2009 IEEE Conference on Computer Vision and Pattern Recognition, pp. 248–255. IEEE (2009)

Clustering of Face Images in Video by Using Deep Learning

Eito Tada and Takio Kurita[✉]

Graduate School of Advanced Science and Engineering, Hiroshima University, Hiroshima, Japan
{m225553,tkurita}@hiroshima-u.ac.jp

Abstract. In deep learning research, self-supervised learning is one of the recent hot topics, and it is not necessary to prepare labels for the training sample. In this study, we would like to consider how to train the model parameters without explicit training labels from video. As an example task, we consider the problem of understanding the person's identity in the video based on the face images captured from the video by using face detection and face tracking. The face images are not annotated with the person's identity, but we can notice that the face images in the tracked sequence are the same person. Also, the face images in the different sequences in the same frame must be different persons. In this paper, we develop an automatic clustering method of face images in the video using these clues. The paper introduces two techniques: the incorporation of Center loss into the loss function and the addition of Auto Encoder structure to the network. Including Center loss ensures that tracked groups of face images (Track) have features closer to the average features of their respective Track, resulting in features invariant to facial variations and noise. Additionally, the addition of AutoEncoder structure aids in dimensionality reduction, enabling the extraction of high-quality features. The combination of these methods yields improved clustering accuracy compared to prior research. Furthermore, this paper explores approaches related to Online Clustering, which relaxes the constraints on determining the number of clusters. This alternative approach achieves comparable accuracy without the need for precise determination of the cluster count.

Keywords: deep learning · self-supervised learning · video clustering

1 Introduction

In recent years, the spread of distribution services such as "TikTok" and "YouTube" has made it easier for people to post videos, and the absolute number of videos has increased. As a result, we spend more time immersed in these videos. To watch the desired video from a large number of videos, research is actively being conducted to classify video sound and behavior using deep learning [1], as well as to summarize video content in an easy-to-understand [2]. Deep

© The Author(s), under exclusive license to Springer Nature Singapore Pte Ltd. 2024
G. Irie et al. (Eds.): IW-FCV 2024, CCIS 2143, pp. 14–26, 2024.
https://doi.org/10.1007/978-981-97-4249-3_2

Fig. 1. An example of a Track

learning requires a large number of labels for analysis. Furthermore, it is impossible for humans to manually label and use such a huge amount of data. There is also a growing interest in research dealing with unlabeled data. In the field of images, in particular, there have been many studies using methods such as contrastive learning, which exploits similarities between images [3,4]. However, unsupervised learning specific to videos has not been studied in its current state, and the usual explanation task in videos does not identify the characters and intercepts information about the characters [5,6]. To truly understand a video, the "who" part of "who is doing what" is essential. In other words, understanding the characters is essential (Fig. 1).

Based on the above, this paper attempts to improve the clustering accuracy of face images in unannotated videos to facilitate understanding of videos. In this study, face detection and face tracking are performed on a certain video, face images are cropped, features are extracted using deep learning, and clustering is performed for each character. Because this paper clusters face images extracted from videos as well as images, it is possible to take advantage of information specific to videos that is not available in the case of images. That information is that the "set of face images obtained by face tracking (**Track**)" is the same person, which is obtained when face tracking is performed on videos. In this paper, we attempt two methods using video-specific information.

- We introduce a loss function called "Center loss" to exploit the video-specific information that the images in Track are the same person. Compared to the previous studies, the features for each Track are collected at a single point to avoid clustering errors within the Track.
- We introduced the AutoEncoder architecture. By using AutoEncoder in the MLP layer of the training layer, we expected to improve the accuracy of dimensionality reduction. In previous studies, most clustering methods were based on the number of characters. However, to truly understand a video, clustering must be performed without knowing the number of characters in the video, and the number of characters must be estimated. In this paper, we attempted an online clustering method using a softmax function in the middle layer of the AutoEncoder architecture. This enables clustering without specifying the number of clusters and automatically setting the number of clusters.

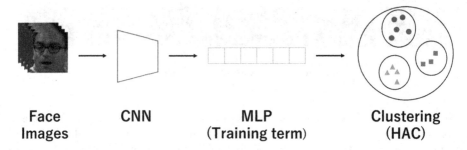

Face   **CNN**   **MLP**   **Clustering**
Images   **(Training term)**   **(HAC)**

Fig. 2. Structure of this model. CNN part is used pre-trained models and MLP layer part is trained using our method. The clustering part is labelled with HAC.

2   Related Work

In the field of face recognition, face recognition models such as Deepface [7] and FaceNet [8] have been proposed to extract high-quality latent spaces from face images without various limitations. These models have been used for various tasks because of their high generalization performance and ability to extract representative features independent of various external factors.

V. Sharma et al. proposed a method to utilize these face recognition models by inputting face images extracted from videos into a face recognition model, calculating the average features for each Track from the high-quality features obtained, and performing clustering for each Track [9]. This method did not take into account the relationship between face images extracted from videos and demonstrated high accuracy by simply inputting the images to the face recognition model. Subsequently, a method was developed to further learn using video features.

2.1   Contrastive Learning

In recent years, metric learning has become a powerful tool in unsupervised expression learning. The simplest method is to use a loss function called contrastive loss [10]. For a given image, this function sets the positive samples to be images of different views of the same image obtained from data expansion, etc., and the negative samples to be images of different views of the same image. Then, by setting a loss function that increases the similarity for the positive samples and decreases the similarity for the negative samples, higher-quality features can be extracted.

However, this learning requires comparing a large number of negative samples with positive samples to improve discrimination accuracy. Furthermore, in this method, positive samples can be explicitly determined by data expansion, while the selection of negative samples requires various arguments. For example, SimCLR [11] and InfoNCE [12] set the image with data augmentation as the positive sample and the other images in the batch as the negative sample to set different views of the same image as positive samples. Since these methods set the samples in the batch as negative samples, they are highly sensitive to the batch size; BYOL [13] and Simsiam [14] do not set negative samples and only compute the similarity to the positive sample obtained from the data reinforcement.

However, metric learning in video clustering, which is our objective task in this study, can explicitly select negative samples by using video features.

2.2 Tsiam

Vistam et al. proposed metric learning to correctly cluster images in the same track [15]. They used Contrastive loss as the loss function. As mentioned above, Contrastive learning requires a positive or negative sample for a given image. First, they used the assumption that the images in the Track are the same person since the Track is a set of face images that can be tracked, and each face image in the Track is of course the same person. Positive samples were constructed by randomly selecting images from the Tracks. The next step was to select negative samples. Setting up a negative sample in an image was very difficult, but here we used the characteristics in the video, allowing us to set up an explicit negative sample. We present their two methods for setting negative samples.

- Case is when the face images co-occur in the same frame. In this case, the co-occurring face images are naturally different persons, and the Tracks to which the face images belong are different persons. This is information that does not exist in the case of a simple image and is unique to video. Using this information, it is possible to randomly select a negative sample from the tracks of co-occurring face images for a given face image.
- The second case is when there are no co-occurring face images. In this case, the similarity of each Track is measured and the face image from the Track with the lowest similarity is selected and used as the negative sample.

Compared to previous methods that relied on little information between Tracks, this method was able to achieve higher accuracy by setting positive and negative samples based on the video characteristics.

3 Our Approach

Our approach is designed based on the previous work Tsiam [15]. A trained convolutional neural network for face image is used to extract high-quality facial features $x_i \in \mathbb{R}^H$. The feature vector x_i obtained from the trained Convolutional Neural Network is input to two fully connected layers $g1(\cdot)$ and $g2(\cdot)$ for metric learning. The M-dimensional output vector z_i is calculated as

$$z_i = g_2(g_1(x_i))$$

where $H > M$.

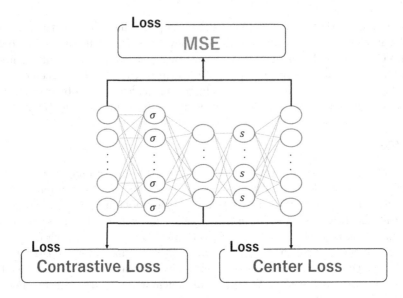

Fig. 3. Overview of training at MLP layer. The features of input and output layer were used in MSE and the features of intermediate layer were used in Contrastive Loss and Center Loss.

Metric learning is performed on the feature z_i. Contrastive loss is used for metric learning as the loss function with reference to Tsiam [15]

$$l_{contra} = y_i * d(z_i, z_j) +$$
$$(1 - y_i) * max(\alpha - d(z_i, z_j), 0) \qquad (1)$$

where $y_i \in [0, 1]$ is 1 when the sample is positive, and 0 when it is negative. The function $d(z_i, z_j)$ is the Euclidean distance between the vectors z_i and z_j. Positive and negative samples were set up like Tsiam [15].

3.1   Center Loss

The Set of face images as Track obtained from face tracking in the video is always the same person. This is the only information in the video that is not present in the image. We considered exploiting this information further. Tsiam [15] used metric learning to randomly select face images from the same Track for positive samples to bring the features in the Track closer together. However, this is not a very strong constraint since the face images are taken at random. Therefore, we considered applying a stronger constraint on the information that the characters in a track are the same person. Therefore, we used center loss [16].

Center loss is a method to minimize the variation among classes in a classification problem by calculating the average amount of features within each class and then bringing the amount of features closer to the average amount of features.

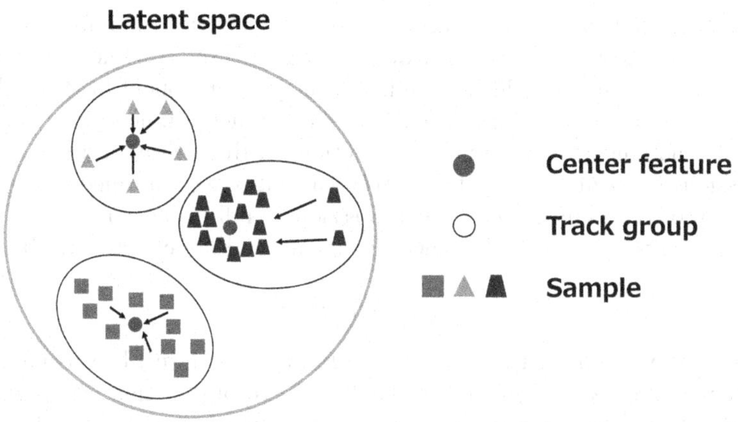

Latent space

Fig. 4. Bring each sample closer to the average feature of the corresponding Track so that the features in the Track come together at a single point.

Since the feature values within the same Track are always the feature values extracted from the same person, they should be close to each other. Therefore, the center loss is used to ensure that all samples in a Track are close to the average feature values (Fig. 4). This is expected to minimize the variation within each Track, where there are various face images with different facial orientations and expressions.

The feature vector z_i should be close to the average feature of the Track containing z_i. Let c_m be the average feature of Track m. Then, the center loss is defined as

$$l_{center} = \frac{1}{N} \sum_{i=1}^{N} \|\mathbf{z}_i - \mathbf{c}_m\|_2^2 \qquad (2)$$

where N is the number of samples, c_m is updated at each iteration using the following update formula. The center (the average) feature is defined as

$$c_m^{(n)} \leftarrow c_m^{(n-1)} - \epsilon \Delta c_m^{(n-1)} \qquad (3)$$

For initialization, we have to calculate the average features of each Track before the training. The relationship between the features to be extracted and the loss function is shown in Fig. 3.

3.2 AutoEncoder

AutoEncoder is a neural network [17]. It consists of multiple intermediate layers, compresses high-dimensional input data into low-dimensional data, and reconstructs the low-dimensional compressed data into the dimensions of the input data. In doing so, it compares the input data with the reconstructed output data using least-squares error, etc. in the loss function to bring the output data closer to the input data. This makes it possible to extract the information necessary to reproduce the input data in the intermediate layer, i.e., high-quality low-dimensional data. In addition, unlike principal component analysis (PCA), which is widely used as a dimensionality reduction method, neural networks can be used for nonlinear dimensionality reduction. In this research, dimensionality compression of feature vectors for metric learning was performed. To improve the quality of this dimensionality compression, a full-connect layer was added immediately after the two full-connect layers and a decoder was introduced as

$$\hat{x}_i = g_3(z_i)) \tag{4}$$

where $\hat{x}_i$ is the output of feature,$g_3(\cdot)$ is a full connect layer. In this paper, the least squares error is used as the loss function for reconstruction. By minimizing the error between the input data and the reconstructed output data, the output data can be made closer to the input data. The least squares error is defined as

$$l_{mse} = \frac{1}{N} \sum_{i=1}^{N} (x_i - \hat{x}_i)^2 \tag{5}$$

From the above, the finally loss function is

$$L = l_{contra} * \lambda_1 + l_{center} * \lambda_2 + l_{mse} * \lambda_3 \tag{6}$$

where λ_1 and λ_2 and λ_3 are hyperparameters.

3.3 Online Clustering

Online clustering is a clustering method in which sample features and clustering are trained by providing pseudo-labels. In online clustering, the number of clusters can be set automatically to accommodate changing feature values. In this study, to promote understanding of the videos, it is desirable to be able to estimate the number of characters in the videos. However, most of the previous studies assume that the number of characters is known and perform clustering by specifying the number of clusters. To promote understanding of videos, online clustering should be used, which can handle the case where the number of characters is unknown. In this method, a softmax function is used as an activation function in the middle layer of AutoEncoder to enable online clustering. The softmax function is an activation function that transforms the network output into a probability distribution. We attempted to introduce online clustering that does not rely on hierarchical clustering by obtaining the class of the maximum output value as a pseudo-label, namely,

$$y_i = max(softmax(z_i)) \tag{7}$$

where y_i is a pseudo-label. Pseudo-label is assigned from the dimensionality of the intermediate layer. In this study, a pseudo-label is generated from the M-class, which is the number of dimensions of the intermediate layer.

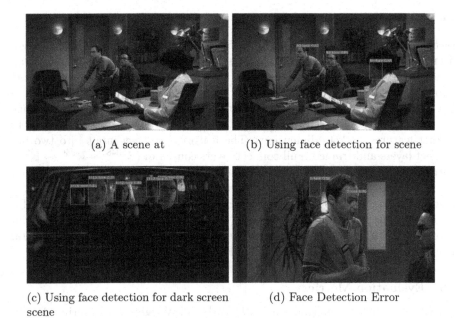

(a) A scene at   (b) Using face detection for scene

(c) Using face detection for dark screen   (d) Face Detection Error
scene

Fig. 5. Results of face detection in BBT dataset

4   Experiments

4.1   Dataset

We used season 1 of "The Big Bang Theory" (BBT) and season 5 of "Buffy the Vampire Slayer" (Buffy) [18,19]. For BBT, We performed face detection and face tracking on BBT ourselves and removed noisy face images. A Scene with the BBT video display in Fig. 5 (a). Furthermore, face detection is performed on that scene in Fig. 5 (b). There are also various scenes in the video, such as those with low brightness, as shown in Fig. 5 (c). In addition, noisy face images were generated due to the failure of the face-tracking as in Fig. 5 (c). Such noisy face images were manually eliminated in the following experiments. The face-tracking experiment focused on six main characters. The total number of tracks was 568 and the total number of frames was 50547 in BBT dataset. The number of tracks and frames corresponding to each person is shown in Table 1. As can be seen from the table, there is a large variation in the number of tracks and frames for each person. For Buffy, we also used the dataset of Visharm et al[1] For these as well, there is a large bias in the number of data for each character. There are six characters, 568 total tracks, and 39263 total frames.

---

[1] https://vivoutlaw.github.io/data_bbt_bf.txt.

4.2   Implementation Details

Face detection and face tracking YOLOv5 [20] and Deepsort mixed tracking algorithms were used to obtain the BBT dataset. Faces were detected by YOLOv5, an object detection architecture pre-trained on the COCO dataset, and a Deepsort algorithm was run to track the detected faces and acquire face images for each Track. We adopt a pre-trained CNN (Resnet50) with VGGface2. The input image is resized to 224*224 RGB size and input to the pre-trained CNN (Resnet50) to extract features of 2048 dimensions. The features are then input into two full connect layers and trained. Full connect layers consist of ($\mathbb{R}^{2048} \rightarrow \mathbb{R}^{256} \rightarrow \mathbb{R}^{32}$). Batch Normalization and ReLu as activation functions were used after the linear layer. For clustering, features of $\mathbb{R}^{32}$ extracted from the linear layer were used. Hierarchical Agglomerative Clustering (HAC) with Ward's method was used for clustering. One more full connect layer ($\mathbb{R}^{256}$) was added to make the AutoEncoder structure possible. This allows the restoration of high-dimensional data. The structure of the model is shown in Fig. 2.

4.3   Evaluation Metric

Normalized Mutual Information(NMI) [21] and Weighted Clustering Purity (WCP) [22] were used as the clustering evaluation measures. NMI is a means of preparing correct data and evaluating it in an information-theoretic manner using the amount of mutual information with the clustering results. NMI is defined as

$$\text{NMI} = \frac{2 \cdot I(\hat{T}; T)}{H(\hat{T}) + H(T)} \tag{8}$$

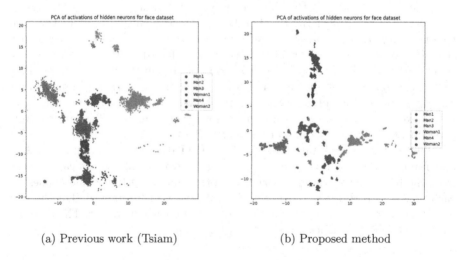

(a) Previous work (Tsiam)   (b) Proposed method

Fig. 6. PCA visualization of the output values of all combined layers of Tsiam and Proposed method, showing clustering at the Frame level. Each color represents a character.

Table 1. Number of Track and facial images (Frame) per character in BBT dataset

People	Track (%)	Frame (%)
Man1	25 (4.4%)	1832 (3.6%)
Man2	218 (38.4%)	19990 (39.5%)
Man3	185 (32.6%)	17741 (35.1%)
Man4	32 (16.7%)	3009 (13.9%)
Woman1	95 (5.6%)	17741 (6.0%)
Woman2	13 (2.3%)	931 (1.8%)
Total	568	50547

where $\hat{T}$ is the probability variable of the predictive cluster, T is the probability variable for the correct cluster, $H()$ is the average information content (entropy), $I()$ is mutual information content.

WCP is a measure of how many correct labels are included in each cluster. WCP is defined as

$$\text{WCP} = \frac{1}{N} \sum_{c \in C} n_c \cdot \text{purity}_c \tag{9}$$

where n_c is the number of data points in the cluster, C is the set of clusters, and *purity* is the most frequently assigned class in the cluster.

4.4 Main Experiment

We compared the proposed method with Tsiam, which achieves the highest accuracy in previous studies using quantitative learning, and experimented with two different methods: Track level, which computes the average features of the samples in a track and obtains labels for each track by HAC from the average features of each track; and Frame level, which obtains labels from each sample by HAC and clusters them by frames.

Our1 is a conventional method with the addition of a loss function called center loss. As a result, as shown in Table 2, the accuracy of Our1 is higher than that of the conventional method. This is thought to be because the addition of the Center loss brings each sample closer to the average feature values of each Track, and the feature values of the samples within the same Track are almost equal. We took the 32-dimensional features of the middle layer and used Principal Component Analysis (PCA) to perform dimensionality reduction and visualization (Fig. 6). Comparison with previous studies shows that our method is divided into several chunks for each sample. By introducing center loss, we were able to collect the features of each sample per track.

Our2 with the addition of the AutoEncoder structure achieved the highest accuracy in many cases. This may be due to the AutoEncoder structure's success in improving the quality of low-dimensional data. These results indicate that the coexistence of the three loss functions and the addition of our constraints contributed to the improved accuracy.

Table 2. Comparison of Methods using NMI and WCP on the BBT s0101 and Buffy s05e02 Dataset. Our1 employs center loss, while Our2 utilizes center loss and AutoEncoder.

Dataset	BBT s01e01				Buffy s05e02			
Method	Track		Frame		Track		Frame	
	NMI	WCP	NMI	WCP	NMI	WCP	NMI	WCP
Tsiam	95.03	97.01	96.66	97.92	82.51	90.14	84.91	92.73
Our1	96.28	98.94	98.64	99.70	82.67	90.85	**87.35**	**93.64**
Our2	**96.93**	**99.12**	**98.91**	**99.76**	**84.07**	**91.55**	86.50	93.30

4.5   Online Clustering

We used softmax for the middle layer of the AutoEnocder structure and measured accuracy using the class of maximum output values as a pseudo-label. As a result, we were able to achieve the same or higher accuracy than the previous work with Tsiam using hierarchical clustering. The advantage of online clustering is that, unlike hierarchical clustering, it is not necessary to specify the number of clusters when assigning labels, and the optimal number of clusters can be automatically estimated by setting the axis of the middle layer to n dimensions. In other words, it is easy to estimate the number of characters.

We applied the proposed method to predict the number of clusters. Results from the BBT dataset are shown in Table 4. One or more pseudo-labels were generated in 12 classes. However, the number of classes that produced 500 or more pseudo-labels, which closely matched the number of true labels, was 6. This coincided with the number of individuals in the dataset. From this, it can be inferred that estimating the number of individuals using online clustering is possible under certain conditions (Table 3).

Table 3. Comparison of online clustering (OC) and Hierarchical Agglomerative Clustering (HAC) in BBT

Method	Frame	
	NMI (%)	WCP (%)
Tsiam (HAC)	96.66	97.92
Ours (OC)	95.20	98.40

Table 4. The total number of classes that generated pseudo-labels for n or more instances in BBT. The total number of output classes corresponds to the expected number of characters.

Number of pseudo labels	The total number of classes
1 or more	12
100 or more	7
500 or more	6

5   Conclusion

In this paper, we propose a method to incorporate the center loss into the loss function and an autoencoder structure into the network to improve the accuracy of face image clustering in videos. By adding the center loss to the loss function, it is possible to extract features that are robust to changes in face images in the track by making the feature values of the face images in the track closer to the average feature values. In addition, the AutoEncoder structure enabled high-quality dimensionality reduction without losing important information during dimensionality reduction. As a result, the clustering accuracy was improved over conventional methods.

We also introduced a softmax function in the intermediate layer and an online clustering method. As a result, we achieved the same or better accuracy than the conventional hierarchical clustering method, which sets the number of clusters for the learned pseudo-labels without setting the number of clusters for clustering. Currently, no constraints are used in this online clustering method. It is expected that adding constraints to this online clustering method in the future will further improve the accuracy. For example, similar to the motivation for adopting Center loss as the loss function, constraints could be set so that samples in the same Track are given the same pseudo-label. We need clustering without setting the number of clusters to truly facilitate our understanding of the videos. Based on the above, this online clustering method should require further research.

References

1. Thoker, F.M., Doughty, H., Snoek, C.G.M.: Tubelet-contrastive self-supervision for video-efficient generalization (2023)
2. Otani, M., Song, Y., Wang, Y.: Video summarization overview (2022)
3. Zhan, X., Xie, J., Liu, Z., Ong, Y.S., Loy, C.C.: Online deep clustering for unsupervised representation learning (2020)
4. Li, Y., Yang, M., Peng, D., Li, T., Huang, J., Peng, X.: Twin contrastive learning for online clustering. Int. J. Comput. Vision **130**(9), 2205–2221 (2022)
5. Rohrbach, A., Rohrbach, M., Tang, S., Joon Oh, S., Schiele, B.: Generating descriptions with grounded and co-referenced people (2017)
6. Liu, D., Keller, F.: Detecting and grounding important characters in visual stories (2023)

7. Taigman, Y., Yang, M., Ranzato, M., Wolf, L.: Deepface: closing the gap to human-level performance in face verification (2014)
8. Schroff, F., Kalenichenko, D., Philbin, J.: A unified embedding for face recognition and clustering (2015)
9. Sharma, V., Sarfraz, M., Stiefelhagen, R.: A simple and effective technique for face clustering in TV series (2017)
10. Koch, G., Zemel, R., Salakhutdinov, R.: Siamese neural networks for one-shot image recognition (2015)
11. Chen, T., Kornblith, S., Norouzi, M., Hinton, G.: A simple framework for contrastive learning of visual representations (2020)
12. van den Oord, A., Li, Y., Vinyals, O.: Representation learning with contrastive predictive coding (2018)
13. Grill, J.-B., et al.: Bootstrap your own latent: a new approach to self-supervised learning (2020)
14. Chen, X., He, K.: Exploring simple siamese representation learning (2020)
15. Sharma, V., Sarfraz, M., Stiefelhagen, R.: Selfsupervised learning of face representations for video face clustering (2019)
16. Wen, Y., Zhang, K., Li, Z., Qiao, Yu.: A discriminative feature learning approach for deep face recognition. In: Leibe, B., Matas, J., Sebe, N., Welling, M. (eds.) ECCV 2016. LNCS, vol. 9911, pp. 499–515. Springer, Cham (2016). https://doi.org/10.1007/978-3-319-46478-7_31
17. Hinton, G.E., Salakhutdinov, R.R.: Reducing the dimensionality of data with neural networks (2006)
18. Bauml, M., Tapaswi, M., Stiefelhagen, R.: Semi-supervised learning with constraints for person identification in multimedia data (2013)
19. Tapaswi, M., Bauml, M., Stiefelhagen, R.: Knock! knock! who is "it?" probabilistic person identification in TV-series (2012)
20. Brostrom, M.: Real-time multi-object tracker using yolov5 and deep sort (2020)
21. Strehl, A., Ghosh, J.: Cluster ensembles - a knowledge reuse framework for combining multiple partitions. J. Mach. Learn. Res. **3**, 583–617 (2002)
22. Tapaswi, M., Parkhi, O.M., Rahtu, E., Sommerlade, E., Stiefelhagen, R., Zisserman, A.: Total cluster: a person agnostic clustering method for broadcast videos (2014)

Exploring the Impact of Various Contrastive Learning Loss Functions on Unsupervised Domain Adaptation in Person Re-identification

Ge Cao⬦ and Kanghyun Jo$^{(\boxtimes)}$⬦

Department of Electrical, Electronic and Computer Engineering,
University of Ulsan, Ulsan 44610, Republic of Korea
{caoge,acejo}@ulsan.ac.kr

Abstract. Person Re-identification has drawn great attention in the industrial surveillance system. This paper focuses on the unsupervised domain adaptive case using different contrastive learning loss functions at the source domain and target domain training. Although there are substantial disparities in the data distributions between the source dataset and the target dataset, distinct training strategies on the source dataset continue to exert a significant influence on the ultimate efficacy of Unsupervised Domain Adaptation results, which could be observed in the data distribution of the target dataset before undergoing unsupervised training. This paper systematically conducts the visualization and analysis of the distinct effectiveness of different loss functions on the pre-trained backbone models, especially the clustering quality. Extensive experiments on three large-scale person re-identification datasets achieve commendable results and substantiates the assertions posited in this paper.

Keywords: Contrastive learning · Unsupervised domain adaptive · Clustering visualization

1 Introduction

With the universal application of the monitoring systems, further analysis of the obtained data has been put on the agenda. Person re-identification (reID) is the common research field in intelligent surveillance systems. In the past decade, thanks to the development of deep learning and large-scale open-source datasets [1–3], the performance in the person reID field has improved gradually, especially in the unsupervised person reID field [4–6]. In practical industrial applications, it is easy to obtain the raw data without manual annotation at a lower cost. The unsupervised domain adaptive person reID aims at supervised pretraining on the massive source dataset, transfer to the target dataset and then training with an unsupervised strategy. In this paper, we demonstrate all the training processes under the UDA case.

© The Author(s), under exclusive license to Springer Nature Singapore Pte Ltd. 2024
G. Irie et al. (Eds.): IW-FCV 2024, CCIS 2143, pp. 27–38, 2024.
https://doi.org/10.1007/978-981-97-4249-3_3

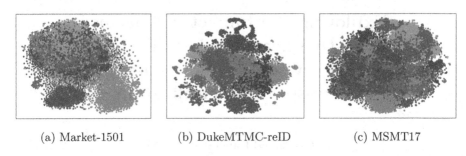

(a) Market-1501   (b) DukeMTMC-reID   (c) MSMT17

Fig. 1. T-SNE [14] visualizations for three commonly applied person reID datasets. Each solid circle represents the feature of one image in the training set, where different colors denote the captured camera ID.

With the popularity of contrastive learning [7,8], a promising unsupervised training pipeline for person reID has evolved and achieved state-of-the-art in this field [5,9], we called clustering-based methods in this paper. Wang *et al.* [10] found evidence supporting that the images of one identity have a strong possibility to be clustered into multiple sub-clusters due to the different capturing cameras. Subsequently, various pieces of research [11,12] applied camera ID to thoroughly address the unsupervised person reID case.

In this paper, the baseline for the source pretraining and target unsupervised training for the UDA person reID is introduced. [10] and [12] demonstrate that the clustering results of the training data would tend to assemble with the capturing camera ID with the ImageNet [13] pre-trained backbone. As shown in Fig. 1, the data distribution of features extracted by ImageNet pre-trained backbone from three large-scale datasets demonstrates that images captured from the same camera are gathered. The mentioned observed phenomenon consists of two major factors: 1) High similarity of the background due to unchanged camera position; 2) Pedestrians have similar poses in the same camera, in other words, high similarity of the foreground information. However, it is not meant to be in the same condition as the UDA case. Based on the supervised training on the source dataset, the backbone has obtained a certain level of ability to focus on the foreground information instead of the background interference.

In this paper, we exploit the influence caused by different source training strategies for the cross-domain transfer learning part. For the target dataset training, we also implement various contrastive learning loss functions for detailed analysis.

2 Related Work

The related works of this paper are mainly from the unsupervised person reID field and also the contrastive learning field.

2.1   Unsupervised Person Re-identification

As mentioned in the introduction, due to the high cost of manual annotation, person reID under the unsupervised training case has been more fit for the practical application. The unsupervised training works could be divided into two kinds, purely unsupervised case and domain adaptive case. The main difference lies in whether the source dataset is used for pre-training. This paper focuses on the unsupervised domain adaptive person reID case.

The UDA person reID has attracted industry attention for quite some time. Zhong *et al.* [4] applied exemplar memory [15] in the UDA field, which significantly memorized and updated the representations of the instance feature. Subsequently, Wang *et al.* [16] adopted the main architecture of the memory bank and designed multi-label class loss to boost the training efficiency. With cluster-based methods becoming mainstream in the unsupervised person reID field, Fu *et al.* [17] proposed to use part of the training image to enhance the cluster results only using the full image. Ge *et al.* [6] utilized the method of teacher-student mutual learning for better learning the features with online and offline refined pseudo labels. Afterward, Zhao *et al.* [18] and Zheng *et al.* [19] continuously adopted the approach and focused on enhancing the clustering quality with different processing strategies.

2.2   Contrastive Learning in Person Re-identification

The contrastive learning achieved great success in the unsupervised or semi-supervised representation learning field [7,8]. The loss proposed in contrastive learning cases commonly works by pulling positive samples together while pushing negative samples apart.

For the person reID task, Ge *et al.* [5] leveraged the contrastive learning consideration into an unsupervised training process, and analyzed the cluster reliability. Dai *et al.* [9] summarized various of contrastive losses at the cluster level and instance level. Wang *et al.* [10] introduced proxy-level contrastive learning into the unsupervised person reID, which improved the performance by learning the domain descrepancy intra- or inter-camera domain. In this paper, we train the UDA person reID backbone with cluster-level and camera proxy-level to analyze the performance.

3   Methodology

3.1   UDA Person Re-identification Pipeline

Assume we have the source dataset and a target dataset, denoted as $X_S = \{x_1^S, x_2^S, ..., x_{N_S}^S\}$ and $X_T = \{x_1^T, x_2^T, ..., x_{N_T}^T\}$, respectively. Firstly, supervised training would be processed on the X_S using the identity ground truth ID. There are various supervised training strategies [20,21] that could be used, and each of them gives a different final data distribution to the source dataset due to the different loss functions.

After the training on the X_S, the pre-trained weight should be loaded, and the unsupervised training on the target domain X_T starts. Without annotation data, we need to apply mathematical algorithms to generate a pseudo label for each training instance to complete the training. DBSCAN [22] is the most commonly applied method in the cluster-based unsupervised person reID case, which could divide the enormous training instances into multiple clusters and find out the outliers. After the clustering part, the pseudo label $y_i \in \mathbb{N}^Y$ for x_i^T is generated, where Y denotes the number of clusters. The detailed architecture and loss function are introduced in the subsequent subsections.

3.2   Unsupervised Training on the Target Domain Dataset

The unsupervised training strategy applies cluster-level contrastive learning and camera proxy-level learning following [9,10].

For the cluster-level contrastive learning, the loss function is set by,

$$L_{cluster} = -\sum_{i=1}^{B} \frac{S(y_i, x_i)}{\sum_{j=1}^{Y} S(j, x_i)}, \tag{1}$$

where B denotes the batch size, $S(y_i, x_i) = exp(M[y_i]^T \cdot f_\theta(x_i)/\tau)$ and $f_\theta(\cdot)$ denotes the backbone network function. M denotes the memory bank [15] for storing the centroid feature of each cluster. The updating scheme for the memory bank is defined by,

$$M[y_i] \leftarrow \mu M[y_i] + (1 - \mu)f_\theta(x_i), \tag{2}$$

As proposed in [10], the camera proxy-level contrastive learning utilizes different memory banks and loss functions. After obtaining the cluster-level pseudo label $y_i \in \mathbb{N}^Y$, we divide each cluster c_j into n_j proxies, where $j = 1, 2, ..., Y$ denotes the index of cluster and n_j denotes the j-th cluster contain images captured from the number of n_j cameras. So the proxy-level memory bank is defined by $M'[p_i]$, where $p_i \in \mathbb{N}^P$ and P denotes the number of proxies. The updating scheme is not changed from the cluster-level memory bank. The contrastive learning loss function for this case is defined by,

$$L_{proxy} = -\sum_{i=1}^{B} (\frac{1}{|Pos|} \sum_{p \in Pos} log \frac{S(u, x_i)}{\sum_{p \in Pos} S(p, x_i) + \sum_{n \in Neg} S(n, x_i)}), \tag{3}$$

in which Pos and Neg denote the positive set and hard negative set for the target x_i, respectively. The positive set includes the index of the proxies belonging to the same cluster, and the hard negative set contains the numbers of the nearest negative proxies' index.

3.3   Supervised Training on the Source Domain Dataset

As the supervised training case on the source dataset X_S, we no longer elaborate on the specific process. Although there are many works [20, 23] proposed various backbone or loss functions, this paper only applies the cluster-level and proxy-level contrastive learning loss functions for fair comparison and analysis.

Due to the supervised learning on the source dataset, we can easily obtain labels for each identity. In other words, before each training session, we have 100% accurate clustering results. Then the supervised training would still follow the strategy we mentioned in the unsupervised case.

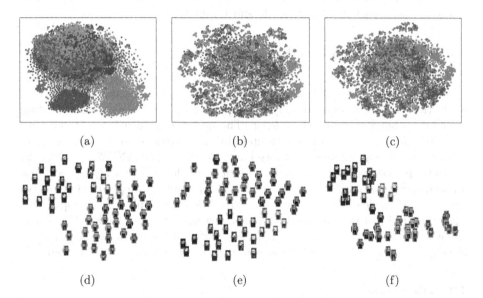

(a)   (b)   (c)

(d)   (e)   (f)

Fig. 2. T-SNE [14] visualizations for different directly transfer case from DukeMTMC-reID dataset to Market-1501 dataset. (Subfigure (a) and (d): Directly transfer without pretraining on X_S; Subfigure (b) and (c): Directly transfer with cluster-level training scheme on X_S; Subfigure (c) and (f): Directly transfer with proxy-level training scheme on X_S.) In the subfigures (a), (b), and (c), different color represents different camera ID. In the subfigures (d), (e), and (f), the color of the bounding box denotes the identity ID, and the color of instance circles denotes the camera ID of the corresponding instance.

4   Experiments

4.1   Dataset and Evaluation Metrics

Three large-scale datasets are applied in this paper: Market-1501 [1], DukeMTMC-reID [2] and MSMT17 [3].

Market-1501 contains 12,936 images captured from 6 cameras in the training set. The training set and test set include images from 751 and 750 identities, respectively. The domain descrepancy among different cameras mainly lies in resolution and background interference.

DukeMTMC-reID contains images from 8 cameras and 16,522 images from 702 identities are captured for the training set.

MSMT17 is a relatively larger dataset for person reID, which contains 32,621 images captured from 15 cameras and 1,041 identities for the training set. Performance is evaluated by the Cumulative Matching Characteristic (CMC) and mean Average Precision (mAP), as the common practice. For the CMC measurement, we report Rank-1, Rank-5, and Rank-10.

4.2   Implementation Details

The ResNet-50 [24] pre-trained on the ImageNet [13] dataset is applied in the supervised source domain training. Compared with the original backbone network, the final fully connected layer is replaced with a global average pooling layer and a batch normalization layer. The updating rate μ is set to 0.2, and there is a $L2$ normalization before updating the memory bank whether using a cluster-level or proxy-level memory bank. For the DBSCAN [22], a threshold of 0.5 is applied for whether cluster-level or proxy-level clustering process. The temperature hyperparameter τ is set to 0.10 for whether cluster-level or proxy-level contrastive learning loss function. The ADAM is applied as the optimizer with an initial learning rate of 0.00035 and a weight decay of 0.0005. The batch size is 32 for both two levels of training, especially for the proxy-level contrastive learning, we follow [10] to define randomly collect 4 images per proxy (Table 1).

4.3   Discussions

As mentioned above, we adopt cluster-level and proxy-level contrastive learning loss functions for supervised source domain training. Even though the ground truth is used in this case for perfect "clustering quality", the backbone would perform different effectiveness when directly transferred to the target domain.

Figure 2 shows the T-SNE visualization when we load the pre-trained weight to the target domain with different source training strategies. Figure 2 has 6 subfigures, subfigures (a), (b), and (c) denote the data distribution of all the images in the Market-1501 training set with the ImageNet pre-trained transfer directly, DukeMTMC-reID dataset pre-training with cluster-level loss, DukeMTMC-reID dataset pre-training with proxy-level loss, respectively. Compared with subfigure (a), subfigures (b) and (c) obviously no longer exhibit data distribution features that are gathered with the camera ID. However, we cannot determine where there would be a clustering phenomenon with the same camera ID among a few visually similar identity instances. Hence, we find some instances of two attire similar identities from the Market-1501 dataset and show the T-SNE visualization in subfigures (d), (e), and (f), which correspond one-to-one with the training

Table 1. The final UDA results for the experiment case mentioned in this paper and the comparison with state-of-the-art algorithms. The results on three target person Re-ID datasets, Market-1501 [1], DukeMTMC-Re-ID [2], and MSMT17 [3].

Methods	DukeMTMC → Market1501				Market1501 → DukeMTMC			
	mAP/%	R-1/%	R-5/%	R-10/%	mAP/%	R-1/%	R-5/%	R-10/%
ECN [4]	43.0	75.1	87.6	91.6	40.4	63.3	75.8	80.4
SSG [17]	58.3	80.0	90.0	92.4	53.4	73.0	80.6	83.2
MMCL [16]	60.4	84.4	92.8	95.0	51.4	72.4	82.9	85.0
MMT [6]	71.2	87.7	94.9	96.9	65.1	78.0	88.8	92.5
NRMT [18]	71.7	87.8	94.6	96.5	62.2	77.8	86.9	89.5
MEB-Net [25]	76.0	89.9	96.0	97.5	66.1	79.6	88.3	92.2
HGA [26]	70.3	89.5	93.6	95.5	67.1	80.4	88.7	90.3
UNRN [19]	78.1	91.9	96.1	97.8	69.1	82.0	90.7	93.5
GLT [27]	79.5	92.2	96.5	97.8	**69.2**	**82.0**	**90.2**	**92.8**
Directly Transfer^c	22.2	44.7	64.1	71.8	20.8	35.5	51.1	58.2
cluster-level	60.7	77.5	86.5	89.7	61.3	76.6	84.9	97.1
proxy-level	**83.8**	**93.4**	**97.1**	98.0	66.9	81.6	89.5	91.7
Directly Transfer^p	24.3	49.9	66.9	73.1	22.4	39.1	54.8	62.2
cluster-level	72.4	85.6	93.0	95.2	61.9	76.8	85.5	88.2
proxy-level	83.1	92.8	97.0	**98.1**	68.1	81.8	89.7	91.9
Methods	DukeMTMC → MSMT17				Market1501 → MSMT17			
	mAP/%	R-1/%	R-5/%	R-10/%	mAP/%	R-1/%	R-5/%	R-10/%
ECN [4]	10.2	30.2	41.5	46.8	8.5	25.3	36.3	42.1
SSG [17]	13.3	32.3	-	50.1	13.2	31.6	-	49.6
MMCL [16]	16.2	43.6	54.3	58.9	15.1	40.8	51.8	56.7
MMT [6]	23.2	50.1	63.9	69.8	22.9	49.2	63.1	68.8
HGA [26]	26.8	58.6	64.7	69.2	25.5	55.1	61.2	65.5
UNRN [19]	26.2	54.9	67.3	70.6	25.3	52.4	64.7	69.7
GLT [27]	27.7	59.5	70.1	74.2	26.5	56.6	67.5	72.0
Directly Transfer^c	4.8	14.3	23.4	28.8	3.3	9.6	17.8	21.9
cluster-level	12.6	29.1	40.0	45.3	17.6	40.4	53.0	58.9
proxy-level	38.4	67.8	78.4	82.0	37.5	66.9	77.4	80.8
Directly Transfer^p	6.1	18.1	29.1	34.6	4.1	11.7	20.7	25.8
cluster-level	22.7	48.5	60.9	66.1	23.0	47.9	60.1	65.2
proxy-level	**41.2**	**71.0**	**80.9**	**84.1**	**40.6**	**69.7**	**79.7**	**83.1**

case depicted in subfigures (a), (b), and (c) mentioned above. Compared with subfigure (d), subfigure (e) shows the visualization results with a direct transfer from DukeMTMC-reID to Market-1501, which demonstrates better initial clustering quality than ImageNet pre-trained (subfigure (d)). Then the subfigure (f) shows the closer intra-class correlation.

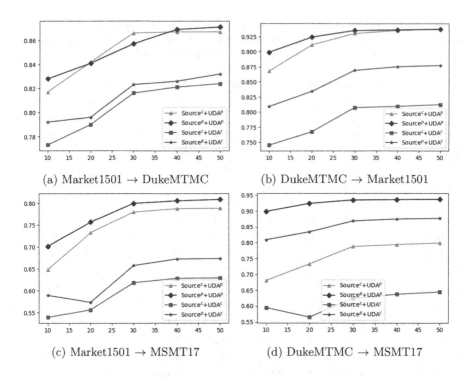

Fig. 3. Clustering quality over different epochs from different source pre-training strategies and different target unsupervised training strategies, where ^{c} and ^{p} denote training with cluster-level and proxy-level loss function, respectively.

Also, the direct transfer results for the UDA case in Table. I also demonstrates that the source pre-training with camera ID information is better. To further analyze the effectiveness of the clustering quality in the target domain of unsupervised training, Fig. 3 depicts the clustering performance evaluation results using "adjusted mutual information score"[1] for four UDA cases with two kinds of source pre-training strategy. The UDA model pre-trained with the proxy-level loss function obtains better clustering quality in almost all UDA cases.

4.4   Comparison with State-of-the-art Methods

This paper provides a comparison with other research in the Table. I. This paper shows the performance and comparisons for four UDA cases: "DukeMTMC-reID → Market1501", "Market1501 → DukeMTMC-reID", "DukeMTMC-reID → MSMT17", and "Market1501 → MSMT17". The performance for "Directly Transfer" and "UDA" cases are also demonstrated in the table, where "Directly Transfer^c" and "Directly Transfer^p" denote source dataset training with cluster-level and proxy-level loss functions, respectively. "Directly transfer" means

---

[1] Clustering performance evaluation.

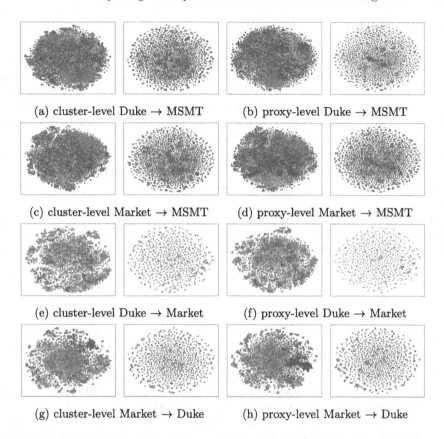

(a) cluster-level Duke → MSMT   (b) proxy-level Duke → MSMT

(c) cluster-level Market → MSMT   (d) proxy-level Market → MSMT

(e) cluster-level Duke → Market   (f) proxy-level Duke → Market

(g) cluster-level Market → Duke   (h) proxy-level Market → Duke

Fig. 4. T-SNE [14] visualizations for four UDA cases. The left and right images in each subfigure show the T-SNE results for direct transfer case and UDA training case, respectively. The "X→Y" denotes the process of pretraining on the domain X and unsupervised training on the domain Y.

directly evaluating by the pre-trained model (pre-trained on the source dataset) without training on the target dataset. Compared with other research, the performance achieved by this paper shows great improvement in most UDA cases. By observing the results of direct transfer, it can be noted that the source pre-training with proxy-level loss function is better than using cluster-level, a trend that extends to the UDA case as well. For analyzing this phenomenon, T-SNE visualizations for the direct transfer and UDA case are depicted in Fig. 4. In the T-SNE visualization, every point denotes the 2D projection position of a training sample. For trained network models, we expect the sample features extracted by the model to aggregate with each other based on their similarity. In the direct transfer case, the feature of one identity ID is mixed and gathered with the camera ID, no matter the cluster-level or the proxy-level loss function. After the UDA training, the data distribution exhibits the gathering condition with identity ID.

5   Conclusion

The study of unsupervised person re-identification has been an enduring focus for an extended duration. Results of this paper obtained from extensive testing on three large datasets and four UDA cases are progressively converging towards those achieved through supervised learning paradigms. This paper predominantly employs two unsupervised contrastive learning loss functions to adapt the source dataset and the target dataset. The abundance of visual representations substantiates the efficacy of the experimental outcomes, contributing to a thorough comprehension of the influence exerted by distinct loss functions on the performance of transfer learning models.

Acknowledgement. This results was supported by "vanishing Regional Innovation Strategy (RIS)" through the National Research Foundation of Korea(NRF) funded by the Ministry of Education(MOE)(2021RIS-003)

References

1. Zheng, L., Shen, L., Tian, L., Wang, S., Wang, J., Tian, Q.: Scalable person re-identification: a benchmark. In: Proceedings of the IEEE International Conference on Computer Vision, pp. 1116–1124 (2015)
2. Zheng, Z., Zheng, L., Yang, Y.: Unlabeled samples generated by gan improve the person re-identification baseline in vitro. In: Proceedings of the IEEE International Conference on Computer Vision, pp. 3754–3762 (2017)
3. Wei, L., Zhang, S., Gao, W., Tian, Q.: Person transfer gan to bridge domain gap for person re-identification. In: Proceedings of the IEEE Conference on Computer Vision and Pattern Recognition, pp. 79–88 (2018)
4. Zhong, Z., Zheng, L., Luo, Z., Li, S., Yang, Y.: Invariance matters: exemplar memory for domain adaptive person re-identification. In: Proceedings of the IEEE/CVF Conference on Computer Vision and Pattern Recognition, pp. 598–607 (2019)
5. Ge, Y., Zhu, F., Chen, D., Zhao, R., et al.: Self-paced contrastive learning with hybrid memory for domain adaptive object re-id. Adv. Neural. Inf. Process. Syst. **33**, 11309–11321 (2020)
6. Ge, Y., Chen, D., Li, H.: Mutual mean-teaching: pseudo label refinery for unsupervised domain adaptation on person re-identification. arXiv preprint arXiv:2001.01526 (2020)
7. Chen, T., Kornblith, S., Norouzi, M., Hinton, G.: A simple framework for contrastive learning of visual representations. ICML. arXiv preprint arXiv:2002.05709 (2020)
8. He, K., Fan, H., Wu, Y., Xie, S., Girshick, R.: Momentum contrast for unsupervised visual representation learning. In: Proceedings of the IEEE/CVF Conference on Computer Vision and Pattern Recognition, pp. 9729–9738 (2020)
9. Dai, Z., Wang, G., Yuan, W., Zhu, S., Tan, P.: Cluster contrast for unsupervised person re-identification. In: Proceedings of the Asian Conference on Computer Vision, pp. 1142–1160 (2022)

10. Wang, M., Lai, B., Huang, J., Gong, X., Hua, X.-S.: Camera-aware proxies for unsupervised person re-identification. In: Proceedings of the AAAI Conference on Artificial Intelligence, vol. 35, pp. 2764–2772 (2021)
11. Chen, H., Lagadec, B., Bremond, F.: ICE: inter-instance contrastive encoding for unsupervised person re-identification. In: Proceedings of the IEEE/CVF International Conference on Computer Vision, pp. 14960–14969 (2021)
12. Xuan, S., Zhang, S.: Intra-inter camera similarity for unsupervised person re-identification. In: Proceedings of the IEEE/CVF Conference on Computer Vision and Pattern Recognition, pp. 11926–11935 (2021)
13. Deng, J., Dong, W., Socher, R., Li, L.J., Li, K., Fei-Fei, L.: Imagenet: a large-scale hierarchical image database. In: 2009 IEEE Conference on Computer Vision and Pattern Recognition, pp. 248–255. IEEE (2009)
14. Van der Maaten, L., Hinton, G.: Visualizing data using t-sne. J. Mach. Learn. Res. 9(11) (2008)
15. Wu, Z., Xiong, Y., Yu, S.X., Lin, D.: Unsupervised feature learning via non-parametric instance discrimination. In: Proceedings of the IEEE Conference on Computer Vision and Pattern Recognition, pp. 3733–3742 (2018)
16. Wang, D., Zhang, S.: Unsupervised person re-identification via multi-label classification. In: Proceedings of the IEEE/CVF Conference on Computer Vision and Pattern Recognition, pp. 10981–10990 (2020)
17. Fu, Y., Wei, Y., Wang, G., Zhou, Y., Shi, H., Huang, T.S.: Self-similarity grouping: a simple unsupervised cross domain adaptation approach for person re-identification. In: Proceedings of the IEEE/CVF International Conference on Computer Vision, pp. 6112–6121 (2019)
18. Zhao, F., Liao, S., Xie, G.-S., Zhao, J., Zhang, K., Shao, L.: Unsupervised domain adaptation with noise resistible mutual-training for person re-identification. In: Vedaldi, A., Bischof, H., Brox, T., Frahm, J.-M. (eds.) ECCV 2020. LNCS, vol. 12356, pp. 526–544. Springer, Cham (2020). https://doi.org/10.1007/978-3-030-58621-8_31
19. Zheng, K., Lan, C., Zeng, W., Zhang, Z., Zha, Z.-J.: Exploiting sample uncertainty for domain adaptive person re-identification. In: Proceedings of the AAAI Conference on Artificial Intelligence, vol. 35, pp. 3538–3546 (2021)
20. Zhou, K., Yang, Y., Cavallaro, A., Xiang, T.: Omni-scale feature learning for person re-identification. In: Proceedings of the IEEE/CVF International Conference on Computer Vision, pp. 3702–3712 (2019)
21. Wang, P., Zhao, Z., Fei, S., Xingyu, Z., Boulgouris, N.V.: Horeid: deep high-order mapping enhances pose alignment for person re-identification. IEEE Trans. Image Process. 30, 2908–2922 (2021)
22. Ram, A., Jalal, S., Jalal, A.S., Kumar, M.: A density based algorithm for discovering density varied clusters in large spatial databases. Int. J. Comput. Appl. 3(6), 1–4 (2010)
23. Chen, W., Chen, X., Zhang, J., Huang, K.: Beyond triplet loss: a deep quadruplet network for person re-identification. In: Proceedings of the IEEE Conference on Computer Vision and Pattern Recognition, pp. 403–412 (2017)
24. He, K, Zhang, X., Ren, S., Sun, J.: Deep residual learning for image recognition. In: Proceedings of the IEEE Conference on Computer Vision and Pattern Recognition, pp. 770–778 (2016)
25. Zhai, Y., Ye, Q., Lu, S., Jia, M., Ji, R., Tian, Y.: Multiple expert brainstorming for domain adaptive person re-identification. In: Vedaldi, A., Bischof, H., Brox, T., Frahm, J.-M. (eds.) ECCV 2020. LNCS, vol. 12352, pp. 594–611. Springer, Cham (2020). https://doi.org/10.1007/978-3-030-58571-6_35

26. Zhang, M., et al.: Unsupervised domain adaptation for person re-identification via heterogeneous graph alignment. In: Proceedings of the AAAI Conference on Artificial Intelligence, vol. 35, pp. 3360–3368 (2021)
27. Zheng, K., Liu, W., He, L., Mei, T., Luo, J., Zha, Z.J.: Group-aware label transfer for domain adaptive person re-identification. In: Proceedings of the IEEE/CVF Conference on Computer Vision and Pattern Recognition, pp. 5310–5319 (2021)

Automatic Measured Drawing Generation for *Mokkan* Using Deep Learning

Wataru Ohyama[1]($\boxtimes$), Yoshinori Hatano[2], and Hajime Baba[3]

[1] Tokyo Denki University, Tokyo, Japan
`w.ohyama@mail.dendai.ac.jp`
[2] Ritsumeikan University, Kyoto, Japan
[3] Nara National Research Institute for Cultural Properties, Nara, Japan

Abstract. This research proposes a method that automatically generates measured drawings for *mokkan* (wooden strips) using deep-learning technology. The proposed method inputs an image containing one strip of *mokkan* captured by smartphone or tablet cameras and outputs a measured drawing for the input image. This report details the proposed deep-learning-based method and the dataset collected for training and evaluation of the proposed method. The performance of the proposed method has been empirically confirmed using 337 images of real *mokkan*. The proposed method has several contributions that promote historical research of *mokkan*.

Keywords: *mokkan* · image conversion · deep learning · U-Net

1 Introduction

To manage and promote the reuse of *mokkan* (historical wooden strips) research outcomes, organization and accumulation of digital archives are important. In order to include the digital photographic data of *mokkan* (Fig. 1(a)) in various databases, tasks such as interpretation and tagging of the data based on textual information on *mokkan* are necessary. The recording notebooks created during the interpretation process (schematic diagrams, Fig. 1(b)), including information about shape of a strip of *mokkan* and brush strokes on the *mokkan*, are necessary to read the characters and understand the *mokkan* as textual material. However, researchers carry out much of this work manually, they are not always accurate regarding shape and brush strokes. There is a desire to develop support tools that can reduce labor, improve efficiency, and enhance accuracy.

Mokkanshop, a support tool for the interpretation of *mokkan* scripts, is a software equipped with image processing to enhance the visibility of ink traces that are difficult to observe due to decay or wood grain effects, and it also features a candidate character reference function based on glyph shapes. This software requires to manually set the image processing parameters within the method to maintain the tool's versatility for application to *mokkan* in various conditions.

This research was supported by JSPS KAKENHI Grant Number JP18H05221.

© The Author(s), under exclusive license to Springer Nature Singapore Pte Ltd. 2024
G. Irie et al. (Eds.): IW-FCV 2024, CCIS 2143, pp. 39–50, 2024.
https://doi.org/10.1007/978-981-97-4249-3_4

On the other hand, deep-learning technology is rapidly improving performance and is utilized for classification and recognition, image generation, and transformation. There is hope for the high-precision and automation of image processing for *mokkans* using this technology. Although deep-learning is gradually utilized in studying historical documents, it has not been sufficiently exploited in *mokkan* research.

In this study, the authors propose a method that leverages deep-learning technology to automatically create accurate measured drawings of *mokkan* from digitally photographed images, capturing both the shape of the *mokkan* strip and the ink traces of brush strokes. An example of a *mokkan*-measured drawing automatically created by the proposed method is shown in Fig. 1(c). This report explains the details of the proposed method and introduces a web application tool that has been implemented to use the proposed method on smartphones and other devices conveniently.

The automatic generation of measured *mokkan* drawings realized in this study contributes to *mokkan* research in the following ways:

1. It contributes to labor savings for researchers, enabling the collection of high-quality historical information from diverse perspectives.
2. It improves the visibility of the characters written on *mokkan*, allowing for studying characters as "images".
3. It can be used as a preprocessing step for automatically recognizing *mokkan* characters.

2 Related Work

The observation and research of *mokkan* mainly consist of three aspects:

- the observation of processing and usage traces on the wood part,
- the assessment of the residual condition of the *mokkan*,
- the observation and interpretation of characters through the identification of ink traces.

In particular, the observation of ink traces is a critical difference between the usual observation of wooden products and that of *mokkan*, making it an essential point in the observation of *mokkans*. The visibility of the ink traces on mokkans is often reduced due to

1. the fading of the ink traces themselves,
2. discoloration of the wood due to the adherence of metal ions,
3. decay of the wood,
4. wood grain and other noises from the wood material.

In response to these conditions, there are methods to clarify the traces through chemical treatment. While chemical treatment is highly effective against the obscurity of ink traces caused by metal ions, there is a risk of damage to the

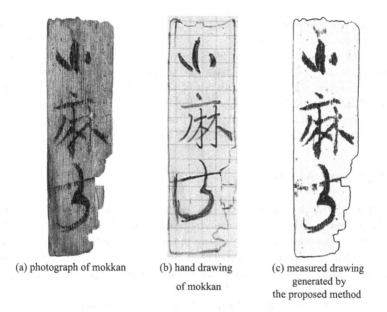

(a) photograph of mokkan   (b) hand drawing
of mokkan

(c) measured drawing
generated by
the proposed method

Fig. 1. Examples of (a) *mokkan*, (b) handwritten sketch of *mokkan*, (c) measured drawing generated by the proposed method.

wood of *mokkan*, and it is not expected to be effective against the obscurity caused by the wood itself.

Infrared, introduced in the 1980s, to clarify ink traces is highly effective and remains a potent technique for enhancing ink trace visibility. However, in terms of simplicity and convenience, there are many challenges compared to acquiring visible light images.

Computer processing, including automatic character recognition, has become widespread with the spread of digital images. There have been many cases where the human eye, which can easily distinguish wood grain and ink traces or unconsciously correct blurring, has inadvertently emphasized these as ink traces. These issues have also occurred frequently when using infrared images. Furthermore, the records of ink trace observation must be linked and correspond to the observation records of the wood part. In other words, the position within the outline of the *mokkan* should be accurately reflected at a minimum.

Against this backdrop, there is a strong demand in *mokkan* research for a system that can easily extract and record ink traces and the shape of *mokkans* while primarily using visible light photographs. In *mokkan* research, work is being done to clarify ink traces on *mokkans* through digital image processing. Various software dedicated to *mokkan* research has been developed, such as Mokkanshop, an annotation tool for *mokkan* images, and Mojizokin [1], an image processing software for character images to be input into the glyph search system Mojizo. However, these software applications do not automate image processing and require user operation, necessitating manual setting of image editing parameters for each image.

In recent years, numerous studies have used significantly improved deep-learning technology to analyze historical document images. In the technology related to *mokkan*, which is the subject of this research, examples include binarization of ancient document images [2,3,6] and recognition of cursive script [4]. However, no research examples related to image processing realize the generation of measured drawings of an entire *mokkan*, as in this study.

3 Proposed Method

The outline of the proposed method is shown in Fig. 2. The proposed method takes an image of single mokkan taken by a smartphone or tablet camera as input and outputs a measured drawing of the *mokkan* that includes its shape and ink traces. The image transformation neural network of the proposed method has a structure inspired by U-Net [5], which is originally proposed for image region segmentation.

The processing steps of the proposed method are as follows:

(1) In the preprocessing section, the input *mokkan* image is enlarged or reduced to maintain the aspect ratio so that the horizontal size becomes W [pixels], and then it is divided into small blocks of $W \times W$ [pixels] in size. This process allows the neural network to perform image transformation on a small block basis in the subsequent stage.
(2) The neural network transform each small block. The neural network outputs a small block of measured drawings, of which size is same as the input block.
(3) As a post-processing step, the output small blocks from the neural network are rearranged and resized to restore the original size of *mokkan* image.

3.1 Preprocessing

The proposed method takes an image of a single tablet of *mokkan* placed vertically on a white cloth (for cushioning). The preprocessing section consists of the following image processing:

(1) The white cloth region, which is regarded as the outside region of mokkan, is removed using Otsu's binarization method so that the *mokkan* region in the image is extracted.
(2) The horizontal size of the mokkan region is enlarged or reduced while keeping the aspect ratio fixed so that it becomes equal to the preset small block size (W [pixels]).
(3) The entire *mokkan* region is divided into groups of small blocks of $W \times W$ [pixels]. The small blocks are cut out such that they overlap by $W/2$ [pixels] in the vertical direction of the *mokkan*. If a small block extends beyond the *mokkan* region, it is complemented by the image of the opposite side region.

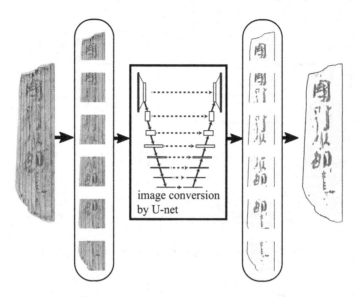

Fig. 2. Outline of the proposed method

The size of small block is a parameter that affects the overall performance, computation time, and memory size required by the subsequent image transformation neural network. This study conducted preliminary experiments using part of the experimental dataset, and $W = 192$ was set by considering the balance between performance and memory usage.

3.2 Image Conversion

The configuration of the image transformation neural network, which is central part of the proposed method, is shown in Fig. 3. The network mainly comprises two parts: an encoder and a decoder.

In the encoder, convolution layers with kernel sizes of 3×3 and 2×2, respectively, are applied repeatedly to the input image, along with max-pooling layers. The number of feature maps doubles with each application of the convolution module.

In the decoder, feature maps are up-sampled, and deconvolution layers with a kernel size of 2×2 is applied repeatedly. Contrary to the encoder, the number of feature maps is halved with each processing application. Skip connections are established between the corresponding layers of the encoder and decoder. In the final layer, a 1×1 convolution is applied to align the feature maps with the output image.

The internal configuration of the image transformation neural network was determined by conducting preliminary experiments using a part of the experimental dataset, in the same way as the decision of the small block size in the previous section, considering the balance between performance and memory usage.

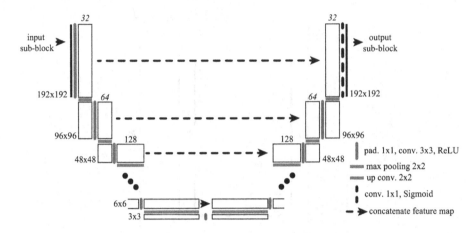

Fig. 3. Neural network configuration in the proposed method

3.3 Postprocessing

The small blocks output by the image transformation neural network are placed in the exact location as the input small blocks to reconstruct the entire image of the *mokkan*. In the areas where small blocks overlap, the values of the corresponding pixels are averaged. The reconstructed mokkan image is then enlarged or reduced to its original size.

3.4 Dataset

A dataset of *mokkan* images was prepared to train the image transformation neural network and evaluate the performance of the proposed method. The dataset consists of 200 images of preserved *mokkans* and annotations for the ink traces on each. The images included in the dataset were created using the following procedure.

First, a single preserved *mokkan* was photographed on a white cloth with a smartphone camera (Android SO-02K). No exceptional management was conducted for the lighting environment during the shooting.

Subsequently, annotations were manually added to the areas with ink traces in the color *mokkan* images. *Mokkan* researchers did this annotation work. At the same time, the area of the white cloth on which the *mokkan* was placed was removed as a background area. Examples of the color images of the *mokkan* and the annotations provided are shown in Fig. 4(a) and (b). The color images and annotations were placed on separate layers and saved as multi-layer TIFF files. Furthermore, from the images of *mokkan* shavings taken under controlled lighting conditions, 137 examples of larger *mokkan* images were selected, and annotations were similarly added to the ink traces. The total number of *mokkan* images used in the experiments in this report is 337.

Based on the images with annotations, the outlines of the *mokkan* regions were drawn in black, and the ink trace regions were copied from the *mokkan* images to create teacher images for training the image transformation neural network. An example of a teacher image is shown in Fig. 4(c).

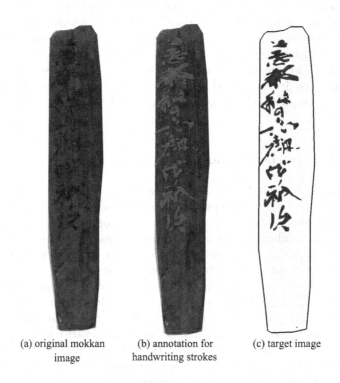

(a) original mokkan image   (b) annotation for handwriting strokes   (c) target image

Fig. 4. Example of *mokkan* image for neural network training

3.5   Training of Neural Network

The image transformation neural network is trained to transform the small blocks from the *mokkan* images into the small blocks of the target images (measured drawings) using the small blocks cut out from both the *mokkan* images and the target images. The loss function used for training is the mean absolute error between the target and the output images, and Adam is used as the optimization algorithm. To ensure a sufficient number of images for training, images flipped horizontally and vertically from the *mokkan* images were added to the training data.

4   Evaluation

We evaluated the effectiveness of the proposed method by evaluation experiments using actual *mokkan* images. For the evaluation experiments, the image dataset mentioned in the previous section (337 *mokkan* images) was randomly divided into five groups, and experiments were conducted using a 5-fold cross-validation method.

Multiple researchers visually confirmed measured drawings created by the proposed method, and their accuracy and effectiveness were verified.

Furthermore, to facilitate the automatic creation of mokkan measured drawings by the proposed method, a neural network trained using all 337 mokkan images was implemented in Javascript and released as a web application tool. This tool allows for creating measured drawings on a web browser, processing the creation of mokkan measured drawings, and creating measured drawings for uploaded mokkan photos or mokkans photographed with a smartphone or tablet camera.[1]

5   Results and Discussion

An example of measured drawings automatically created by the proposed method is shown in Fig. 5. The figure displays the *mokkan* image and the measured drawing created by the proposed method for the *mokkan*. From these results, it can be confirmed that it is possible to create measured drawings that accurately capture the shape and ink traces of the *mokkan*, regardless of the color tone of the wood or the state of the wood grain.

Figure 5(a) to (e) are the results of measured drawings for preserved *mokkan*. The method consistently extracts ink traces and reflects them in the measured drawings regardless of the color of the *mokkan* base, the intensity, or the fineness of the grain. Particularly in (b), characters and symbols are correctly recognized and reflected in the measured drawing at the red marker part.

Figure 5(f) to (i) are examples of processing results for shaved *mokkan*. Especially in cases like (h) and (i), where the base color of the *mokkan* is dark and ink traces are difficult to observe, the ink traces are correctly recognized and reflected in the measured drawings. Visual confirmation by multiple *mokkan* researchers revealed that satisfactory quality measured drawings could be created for about 80% of the 327 *mokkan* images used in the experiments.

However, it was also found that the measured drawings generated by the proposed method include characteristic error examples. Figure 6 shows error examples of measured drawings generated by the proposed method. In (a), the arrows and (d) at arrow B mistakenly detect indentations in the *mokkan* as ink traces. In (b), the ink traces in the measured drawing are generally blurry. The cause of this example is thought to be that the base of the *mokkan* differs from other ones, and the horizontal size of the *mokkan* image is more extensive compared to others, making the ink traces (characters) relatively small and blurry during post-processing enlargement. In (c) at the arrow and (d) at arrow A, the

---

[1] The image and annotation dataset of 200 processed *mokkan* is available at the following address: https://repository.nabunken.go.jp/dspace/handle/11177/7944. Also, the web application of the proposed method is published at the following address: https://ohym.org/MokumeDemo/index_e.html.

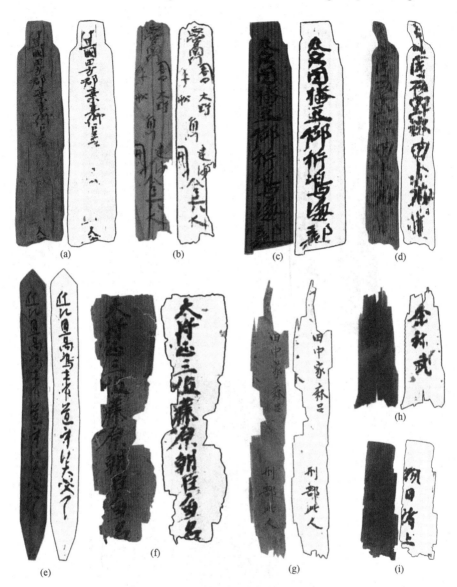

Fig. 5. Examples of generated measured drawing

ink traces became faint and were not reflected in the measured drawing. These errors seem improvable by expanding the training data and enriching the types of *mokkan* images included in the data.

When multiple *mokkan* researchers used the web application implemented in this study, the app's success rate of automatic measured drawing creation by the app was about 80% for the file upload version and about 40–50% for the camera

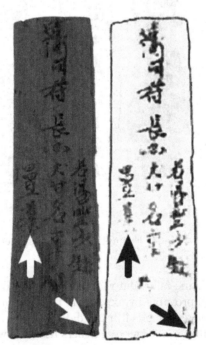

Fig. 6. Examples of error in generated measured drawings

shooting version. In the camera shooting version, the results varied due to the influence of shooting conditions, such as the camera performance of the device and the lighting environment.

The progress of this research is considered to bring the following five significant contributions to mokkan research:

1. By easily obtaining the underlying drawings of *mokkan* measured drawings, researchers can focus on detailed observations of *mokkans* and characters, enabling the collection of higher-quality historical information from diverse perspectives.
2. The collection of many obvious character samples allows for studying characters as "images" and research beyond the meaning of "text."
3. Characters and images that are currently unreadable and thus have not been assigned character codes can be considered as subjects of research.
4. By applying this research, the possibility of application expands to other materials with low-visibility characters, such as ink-inscribed pottery, engraved tiles, and stone inscriptions.
5. Acceleration of machine learning and the expected progress in studying automatic recognition of *mokkan* characters.

6   Conclusion

In this study, the authors proposed a method for automatically creating virtual schematic drawings from digitally photographed *mokkan* images, including the shape of the *mokkan* and ink traces. Experiments using actual image data suggested that the proposed method can automatically create virtual schematic drawings. This method is expected to make it convenient and quick to create accurate records of the shape of *mokkan*.

In the future, the plan is to expand the training data and introduce adversarial learning to not only apply the method to preserved *mokkan* but also *mokkan* stored in waterlogged conditions, incorporate it into ancient document glyph search systems, and integrate and supplement it with researchers' visual judgments and revisions through additional learning.

References

1. Mojizokin. https://apps.apple.com/us/app/mojizokin/id1211838518?l=ja&ls=1. Accessed 8 Nov 2020
2. Ayyalasomayajula, K.R., Malmberg, F., Brun, A.: PDNet: semantic segmentation integrated with a primal-dual network for document binarization. Pattern Recogn. Lett. **121**, 52–60 (2019)
3. He, S., Schomaker, L.: DeepOtsu: document enhancement and binarization using iterative deep learning. Pattern Recogn. **91**, 379–390 (2019)
4. Lamb, A., Clanuwat, T., Kitamoto, A.: KuroNet: regularized residual u-nets for end-to-end Kuzushiji character recognition. SN Comput. Sci. **1**(177) (2020)

5. Ronneberger, O., Fischer, P., Brox, T.: U-Net: convolutional networks for biomedical image segmentation. In: Navab, N., Hornegger, J., Wells, W.M., Frangi, A.F. (eds.) MICCAI 2015. LNCS, vol. 9351, pp. 234–241. Springer, Cham (2015). https://doi.org/10.1007/978-3-319-24574-4_28
6. Sulaiman, A., Omar, K., Nasrudin, M.F.: Degraded historical document binarization: a review on issues, challenges, techniques, and future directions. J. Imaging 5(48) (2019)

Monocular Absolute 3D Human Pose Estimation with an Uncalibrated Fixed Camera

Atsunori Moteki[1,2]([envelope]) [ID], Yukio Hirai[2], Genta Suzuki[2], and Hideo Saito[1] [ID]

[1] Graduate School of Science and Technology, Keio University, Yokohama, Japan
hs@keio.jp
[2] Artificial Intelligence Laboratory, Fujitsu Limited, Kawasaki, Japan
{moteki.atsunori,yhirai,suzuki.genta}@fujitsu.com

Abstract. In this paper, we propose a method for absolute 3D human pose estimation (HPE) with an uncalibrated monocular camera. In the case of analyzing workers' movement with an existing uncalibrated camera, the previous method cannot estimate absolute human pose due to the lack of information on camera parameters. Our proposed method overcomes this limitation by determining the position and scale of humans based on the pose of surrounding objects. Specifically, we predict the intrinsic and extrinsic parameters of the camera through user-guided manual manipulation. Subsequently, the estimated human pose is transformed from local coordinates to global coordinates for each frame. This absolute coordinate representation allows for real-time prediction of human movements relative to objects. To assess the efficacy of our method, we conducted three kinds of experiments. A user study revealed that the proposed user-guided method archives accurate estimation of camera parameters. Quantitative evaluation using a public dataset demonstrated that our method can predict human pose with practical accuracy, providing a benchmark for future enhancements. Qualitative evaluation with a unique dataset showed that our method could easily generate digital twin representations across diverse environments and camera positions.

Keywords: Absolute Human Pose Estimation · Camera Calibration

1 Introduction

There is a growing demand for the metaverse or digital twin in manufacturing sectors, aiming to enhance productivity [1,13]. To achieve this objective, it is crucial to recognize and visualize the interaction between humans and objects. For instance, estimating a worker's operation time can be facilitated by observing their interaction with devices or the act of grasping objects. In recent manufacturing facilities, surveillance cameras have been strategically deployed for the detection of hazardous work conditions or suspicious behavior. Due to the total decrease in implementation costs, the recognition of the interactions using existing surveillance cameras is desired.

© The Author(s), under exclusive license to Springer Nature Singapore Pte Ltd. 2024
G. Irie et al. (Eds.): IW-FCV 2024, CCIS 2143, pp. 51–66, 2024.
https://doi.org/10.1007/978-981-97-4249-3_5

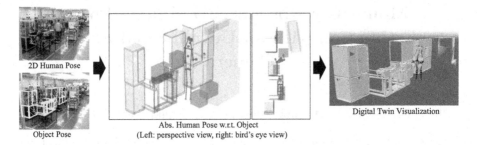

2D Human Pose

Object Pose

Abs. Human Pose w.r.t. Object
(Left: perspective view, right: bird's eye view)

Digital Twin Visualization

Fig. 1. Output example of the proposed method. The estimated absolute human pose concerning the object can be displayed from various viewpoints, such as perspective or bird's-eye view. In addition, action recognition of the human is achieved by detecting the entry of each joint into 3D Region of Interest (ROI) regions, depicted as orange boxes. Estimated absolute human poses are used for digital twin visualization. (Color figure online)

However, a critical challenge arises from the inherent limitations of these surveillance cameras, which are typically unmovable and uncalibrated. Moreover, a considerable number of these surveillance cameras are of the PTZ (Pan-Tilt-Zoom) type, resulting in frequent variations in focal length and camera pose. Consequently, simultaneous estimation of intrinsic and extrinsic camera parameters and absolute human pose becomes imperative for detecting interactions between humans and objects in a world coordinate system.

This paper introduces a novel approach for monocular absolute human pose estimation utilizing uncalibrated cameras. The central output of our method is illustrated in Fig. 1. Initially, we employ a vanishing point-based method to automatically calculate the camera's focal length. However, this parameter estimation approach is susceptible to noise and variations in scene structure. Additionally, since the ground truth parameters are unknown to the users, they cannot judge the output values as reliable output. To mitigate these challenges, our proposed method integrates the CAD model of the object, modifying the focal length while concurrently estimating the object's pose through manual operation. This verification process enhances estimation accuracy and ensures the reliability of estimates. Subsequently, we estimate the 3D human pose relative to the world coordinate system, accounting for real scale and position. This coordinate transformation is based on anchor joint positions, which are estimated using a multilayer homography derived from the camera parameters. This approach can deal with the situation of partially occluded scenes of the body. Finally, our method facilitates the estimation of interactions between human actions and specific regions of interest (ROIs) on the object. The resulting poses can be seamlessly integrated into digital twin representations using CG renderers such as Unity.

To validate our method, we conducted three types of experiments. A user study on camera parameter estimation illustrates the effectiveness of our information presentation method during mouse manipulation (Sect. 4.1). Through quantitative experiments on a public dataset, our method demonstrates comparable results against state-of-the-art absolute Human Pose Estimation (HPE) methods (Sect. 4.2). Furthermore, we successfully generated digital twin representations using data captured in real-world factory settings (Sect. 4.3).

In summary, our proposed method makes three significant contributions. First, we introduce a method for estimating intrinsic and extrinsic camera parameters through user-guided manual operation, ensuring the reliability of estimated values. Second, we present an absolute HPE method leveraging multi-layered homography, enabling straightforward joint position estimation even in occluded scenes. Third, we provide a means of visualizing real-world scenarios, incorporating humans and objects by retargeting avatar movements.

2   Related Work

2.1   Object Pose Estimation

According to the survey conducted by Marullo et al. [19], there are three primary types of methods for estimating the 6 degrees-of-freedom (DoF) object pose from a monocular image: feature-based, template-based, and learning-based approaches.

The feature-based method [24,26] matches correspondences between 2D images and 3D models using local features. While the feature-based method is robust against partial occlusion or cluttered backgrounds, it requires objects with distinctive textures to generate meaningful local features.

The template-based method [12,31] generates 2D object images from various viewpoints and compares them with the input image to estimate the object's pose. While the template-based method offers high accuracy, there is typically a trade-off between accuracy and execution speed.

The learning-based methods have become mainstream in this field with the rise of deep learning, which can be further categorized into three types: 1) The bounding box (BB) prediction and Perspective-n-Points (PnP) algorithm-based approach [30,37] train models to establish mappings between image points and their corresponding 3D positions. 2) The classification-based approach [11,22] and 3) the regression-based approach [34,35] leverage convolutional neural networks (CNNs) to address classification or regression problems. While learning-based methods often outperform other approaches in terms of accuracy, they require significant costs for data collection and training.

In the proposed method, we adopt a feature-based approach that leverages edge information. In real factory or store environments, where monocular fixed cameras are installed, it is challenging to gather sufficient training data from multiple viewpoints. However, artificially constructed objects typically contain abundant edges, making them suitable reference objects in such scenarios.

Regarding the edge-based method, Han and Zhao [8] predicted the pose of aircraft structural parts by integrating inertial sensor data and a voting scheme. In contrast, in our method, we manually select edges, taking into consideration the specific use cases in real-world settings. We do so for the following reasons: 1)

Objects often experience partial occlusion due to various obstacles present in the environment. 2) Camera intrinsic parameters are either unknown or inaccurate, causing estimation failure of object pose. The algorithm for edge-based pose estimation is introduced in Sect. 3.1.

2.2 Human Pose Estimation

The literature on 3D human pose estimation from monocular RGB images is extensive, as indicated by survey papers [40]. It can be broadly classified into two approaches: skeleton-based and model-based methods. Skeleton-based methods [2,3,18,20,25,27,33,38,41] aim to predict the 3D positions of the joints of a human skeleton. Model-based methods, on the other hand, aim to reconstruct a complete human mesh using a predefined human body model such as SMPL [15]. Given our focus on inferring the absolute 3D joint positions of humans, we will primarily discuss the skeleton-based approach in the remainder of this paper.

Previous skeleton-based approaches have addressed two main situations: single-person pose estimation and multi-person pose estimation.

For **single-person pose estimation**, there are two main types: direct estimation and 2D to 3D lifting. Direct estimation methods [25,29] predict the 3D human pose directly from 2D images without relying on intermediate 2D skeleton results. On the other hand, 2D to 3D lifting methods [3,18] predict the 3D human pose using an intermediate estimation of the 2D human pose. Chen and Ramanan [3] proposed a 2D-3D lifting method based on pose matching, where a database of 2D projected poses from various viewpoints and corresponding 3D poses is used for query matching. The 3d-baseline method [18] employs a fully connected residual network to regress 3D joint locations from 2D joint locations.

For **multi-person pose estimation**, two paradigms are commonly employed: bottom-up and top-down. Bottom-up methods [2,33] first detect individual joint keypoints and then group them to form the 3D pose of each person. In contrast, top-down methods [27,41] first detect the individuals in the image and then estimate the 3D pose of each person separately.

In many previous methods for multi-person pose estimation, the output 3D human pose coordinates are typically based on the root joint, such as the hip joint. However, for recognition of interaction between objects and humans, it is crucial to have absolute coordinate outputs and appropriate scale settings. Methods like 3DMPPE [20] infer the 3D absolute root localization and root-relative pose estimation, while Zhan et al. [38] propose Ray3D, an end-to-end network that achieves absolute human pose estimation by training a camera embedding using extrinsic camera parameters. As the Ray3D network includes both intrinsic and extrinsic camera parameters within its model, the process of acquiring training data and conducting fine-tuning becomes necessary, particularly when accounting for changes in camera position or focus. However, the proposed method eliminates the need for acquiring a large amount of training data, as it estimates camera parameters using geometric methods.

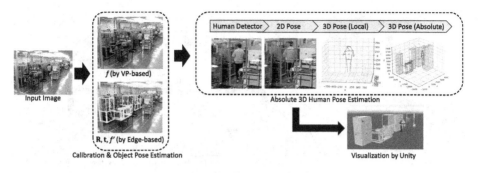

Fig. 2. The system flow of the system.

3 Method

In this paper, we regard the object coordinate fixed at the real site as the world coordinate of the system. Using this assumption, the extrinsic camera parameters can be acquired as the inverse matrix of the object pose from a camera. Figure 2 represents the overall system flow of the proposed method. By using an input image, the focal length of the camera is estimated by the vanishing point-based method. The pose of the object is predicted and the focal length is modified via adjustment through the user's manipulation. Based on these parameters, the absolute 3D human pose is estimated by a top-down approach. Then visualizing the avatar by retargeting the absolute human pose is processed at every frame.

3.1 Camera Calibration and Object Pose Estimation

When the camera image is initially input, the focal length of the camera f and the object pose (rotation from camera to object $\mathbf{R}_c^o$, translation from camera to object $\mathbf{t}_c^o$) are calculated in the proposed method. f is estimated using vanishing lines, which are extracted from the captured image using the Line Segment Detector (LSD) algorithm [7]. These extracted edges are classified into three directions, representing the x, y, and z-axes. The vanishing point-based method [23] is then used to predict the focal length of the camera. However, the predicted value can be influenced by environmental conditions. In real factory scenes, where numerous objects are present, some irrelevant edges may be classified in the main three directions, leading to estimation errors in the focal length and object pose.

To address this issue, we propose a method that can estimate the object pose while simultaneously modifying the predicted focal length shown in Fig. 3. Initially, 2D edges extracted by LSD are collected and integrated into 2D lines. Similarly, 3D fragmented lines are reconstructed from the provided obj-format CAD model, and these lines are integrated into 3D ridgelines using the method proposed by Moteki and Saito [21]. The 3D ridgelines are projected onto an image using the estimated focal length and default pose values. Subsequently, the 3D ridgelines corresponding to each 2D line are manually selected.

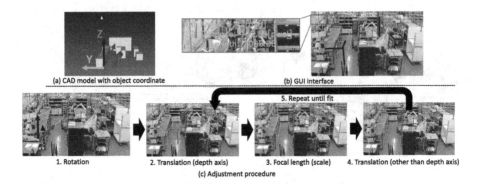

(a) CAD model with object coordinate   (b) GUI interface

5. Repeat until fit

1. Rotation   2. Translation (depth axis)   3. Focal length (scale)   4. Translation (other than depth axis)

(c) Adjustment procedure

Fig. 3. Object pose estimation while modifying the focal length. (a): The example of the CAD model and its object coordinates. (b): GUI interface example. Corresponding lines are shown in red (2D lines) and blue (3D ridgelines). θ_d, D_d, f are shown on upper left. (c): Adjustment procedure. (Color figure online)

Next, the user adjusts the 7 DoF $(f, \mathbf{R}_c^o, \mathbf{t}_c^o)$ so that the projected CAD model has a similar appearance to the object in the image. Since adjusting all 7 degrees of freedom simultaneously can be challenging for a general user, the GUI (Graphical User Interface) provides step-by-step instructions on how to adjust them (shown in Fig. 3(c)). The sequences for adjustment are as follows:

1. **Rotation** To match the direction of the object coordinate system (solid line) with the projected world coordinate system (dotted line)
2. **Translation along depth axis** To make θ_d reach a local minimum
3. **Focal length** To fit the scale of the CAD model to the actual object
4. **Translation along vertical and horizontal axes** To align the origin of the object coordinate system with the appropriate position in the image
5. **Iteration** Repeat 2–4 until complete fit of actual object and CAD model

The challenge of manipulating the 7 DoF is primarily rooted in the similar motion patterns exhibited by the projected CAD model when undergoing changes in translation along the depth axis and adjustment in focal length. To deal with it, GUI shows the information about the differential angle θ_d, differential distance D_d, and focal length f. The differential angle/distance means the averaged angle/distance computed between each corresponding 2D and 3D line on the image coordinate system. After rotation adjustment, the user applies translation along the depth axis to make θ_d reach a local minimum. Then the user fits the position of the coordinate system on the image to make D_d reach a local minimum. These two types of adjustment are repeated multiple times, facilitating the convergence of the focal length to an optimal value. Finally, making use of the information of line pairs and the modified focal length, the Accurate Subset-based Perspective-n-Lines (ASPnL) algorithm [36] deduces the 6 DoF object pose $\mathbf{R}_c^o, \mathbf{t}_c^o$.

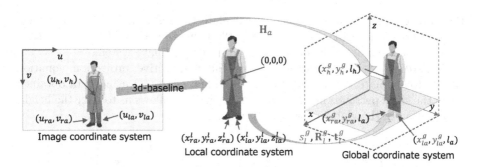

Fig. 4. The concept of absolute 3D human pose estimation. The absolute z hip position l_h is calculated by predicted objected pose $\mathbf{R}_c^o, \mathbf{t}_c^o$, and image coordinate values. Absolute (x, y) positions are calculated by the homography $\mathbf{H}$ predicted by object pose $\mathbf{R}_c^o, \mathbf{t}_c^o$ and l_a. By using the pair of the local and the global coordinate value, the transformation parameters $s_l^g, \mathbf{R}_l^g, \mathbf{t}_l^g$ are updated at every frame. Although three anchor points (left ankle, right ankle, hip) are used for transformation in this figure, other joints such as both shoulders can be utilized as anchor points.

3.2 Absolute 3D Human Pose Estimation

Our method utilizes a top-down approach for 3D HPE. Initially, humans are detected using YOLOX-X [6], and a 2D human pose is estimated for each individual using CPN [4]. The estimated 2D pose is then lifted to a 3D pose using 3d-baseline [18]. During the training of 3d-baseline, we employ a combination of datasets including the CMU motion capture database [5], MakeHuman [16], Unity Mocap Data from the Asset Store [32], and an original dataset acquired by our laboratory to enhance the generalization performance.

In this paper, we refer to this lifted 3D pose as the local 3D pose. The coordinate system of the local 3D pose is hip-centered, and its scale is estimated by 3d-baseline. To adjust the local pose to an absolute coordinate system, which we refer to as the global coordinate, our method employs a similarity transformation with anchor points. The concept of this transformation is illustrated in Fig. 4.

In this approach, we define two sets of three anchor points to estimate the similarity transformation parameters for converting from the local to the global coordinate system: (hip, left ankle, right ankle) or (hip, left shoulder, right shoulder). Although the following section describes the case of both ankles, the same principles can be applied to both shoulders as well. Let $(x_{la}^l, y_{la}^l, z_{la}^l)$ and $(x_{ra}^l, y_{ra}^l, z_{ra}^l)$ represent the local coordinates of the left and right ankles, respectively. Similarly, $(x_{la}^g, y_{la}^g, z_{la}^g)$, $(x_{ra}^g, y_{ra}^g, z_{ra}^g)$, and (x_h^g, y_h^g, z_h^g) denote the global coordinates of the left ankle, right ankle, and the center of the hip.

For estimating x^g and y^g, we perform a homography-based estimation using a planar surface assumption: $(x_{la}^g, y_{la}^g, 1)^{\mathrm{T}} = \mathbf{H}_a(u_{la}, v_{la}, 1)^{\mathrm{T}}$. (u_{la}, v_{la}) represents the predicted 2D coordinate of the left ankle, and $\mathbf{H}_a$ denotes the homography matrix between the camera image plane and the horizontal plane, where the z coordinate corresponds to the height of the ankle. It is important to note that the same equation can be applied to calculate the right ankle. The matrix $\mathbf{H}_a$ can be derived from the object pose $\mathbf{R}_c^o, \mathbf{t}_c^o$. Thus, the origin of the coordinates (x^g, y^g) corresponds to the origin of the object coordinate system.

Regarding z^g, the algorithm solves the perspective projection equation (Eq. 1) to estimate the height of each individual's hip (l_h) using data obtained when the same person is in a standing position. This allows us to infer the height information in the global coordinate system.

$$\begin{pmatrix} u_h \\ v_h \\ 1 \end{pmatrix} = \mathbf{A}(\mathbf{R}_w^c | \mathbf{t}_w^c) \begin{pmatrix} x_h^g \\ y_h^g \\ l_h \\ 1 \end{pmatrix} = \mathbf{A}(\mathbf{R}_w^c | \mathbf{t}_w^c) \begin{pmatrix} \frac{x_{ra}^g + x_{la}^g}{2} \\ \frac{y_{ra}^g + y_{la}^g}{2} \\ l_h \\ 1 \end{pmatrix} \quad (1)$$

where $\mathbf{A}$, $\mathbf{R}_w^c$, and $\mathbf{t}_w^c$ represent the intrinsic and extrinsic camera parameters respectively, which are estimated by $\mathbf{R}_w^c = (\mathbf{R}_c^o)^{-1}, \mathbf{t}_w^c = (\mathbf{t}_c^o)^{-1}$. (u_h, v_h) represents the predicted 2D coordinate of the center of the hip. Since there are two possible solutions for solving Eq. 1 to estimate l_h, we calculate the average of l_h and select the appropriate solution with a lower variance. This ensures a more reliable estimation of the height in the global coordinate system.

Using the predicted global anchor points, our method estimates the parameters of the similarity transformation: s_l^g (scale), $\mathbf{R}_l^g$ (rotation), and $\mathbf{t}_l^g$ (translation). To accomplish this, we employ Procrustes Analysis [17], which minimizes the least squares difference between the transformed coordinates and the optimal values. Finally, all local 3D joint coordinates are transformed to global 3D joint coordinates by $X^g = s_l^g \mathbf{R}_l^g X^l + \mathbf{t}_l^g$. The calculation of $(s_l^g, \mathbf{R}_l^g, \mathbf{t}_l^g)$ and $X^g = (x^g, y^g, z^g)$ is performed for each frame in real-time. One advantage of this algorithm is its fast computation, and it does not require a GPU for processing. However, a limitation of this algorithm is that it can only globalize the human pose when the person is in a standing position. Despite this limitation, it is worth noting that in many manufacturing scenarios, humans are often in a standing posture while working or making purchases. In our experiments, we will evaluate the accuracy difference between the proposed method with standing and without standing poses.

3.3   Visualization

At object pose or absolute HPE, the coordinate system is right-handed and Z-up direction, which is the same as OpenCV. By contrast, the coordinate system of Unity is left-handed and Y-up direction. Therefore, it is necessary to convert the coordinate system with respect to: 1) camera extrinsic parameter, 2) CAD model, 3) absolute 3D human pose.

We utilize JustWithJoints assets [10] to retarget a converted absolute 3D human pose to an avatar. Since the absolute 3D pose is estimated with respect to an object-centered coordinate system, users don't have to set the position of a camera, CAD models, and avatars manually.

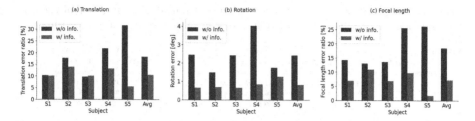

Fig. 5. The result of the user study. (a), (b) and (c) show the error ratio of translation, the angular distance of rotation, and the error ratio of focal length.

4   Evaluation

4.1   User Study for Object Pose Estimation

For the evaluation of partial manual manipulation of the object pose estimation, we measured the accuracy of parameter estimation with and without the proposed method.

Experimental Condition. In this experiment, five colleagues of the author, aged between their twenties and fifties were collected as participants. The participants first adjusted the parameters without knowing the information such as differential angle or how to adjust effectively mentioned in Sect. 3.1. Then, they adjusted the parameters with adjusting information. For image data, we utilized GX-line data, as illustrated in Fig. 3, along with a corresponding CAD model. We set the initial value of the intrinsic parameter as calculated by vanishing point-based method [23] and the extrinsic parameter as an intentionally incorrect value. To ensure consistent results and minimize the impact of pair selection on accuracy, a predefined set of seven 2D-3D pairs, distributed across the entire image, was used. As the evaluation criteria, we utilized the error ratio of translation e_t [%], error of rotation e_r [deg] (from Xu et al. [36]), error ratio of focal length e_f [%]. The ground truth values were calibrated by the method of Zhang [39] in advance.

Result. Figure 5 illustrates the experimental results. The conditions with adjusting information and without adjusting information are hereinafter referred to as *w/ info* and *w/o info*. Regarding the accuracy of the translation, it is noteworthy that for some participants (S1, S3), there is minimal disparity between the *w/ info* and *w/o info* conditions. However, for other participants, the *w/ info* condition outperforms the *w/o info* condition. Conversely, concerning the accuracy of rotation and focal length, all participants consistently achieved superior performance under the *w/ info* condition compared to the *w/o info* condition. In summary, our findings indicate an overall enhancement in the accuracy of adjustments when adjusting information is presented.

Table 1. The result of quantitative evaluation on Human3.6M dataset. f of the previous method means the f consecutive frames are utilized for human pose estimation.

Abs-MPJPE	Dir.	Disc.	Eat.	Greet.	Phone	Photo	Pose	Purch.	Sit	SitD.	Smoke	Wait	WalkD.	Walk	WalkT.	Average
PoseFormer ($f=9$) [41]	112.6	137.1	117.6	145.8	113.0	166.0	125.5	113.8	128.8	245.7	122.7	144.8	125.0	118.9	129.3	136.5
RIE ($f=9$) [28]	143.2	133.2	143.9	142.7	110.9	151.4	125.9	98.4	136.4	273.4	127.5	138.9	126.8	107.3	116.0	138.4
Ray3D ($f=1$) [38]	80.1	100.8	123.8	125.5	110.7	111.8	96.1	99.3	129.4	176.3	106.8	129.2	120.4	109.1	106.6	115.1
Ray3D ($f=9$) [38]	92.9	97.4	139.8	118.6	113.8	105.9	84.5	74.9	148.6	165.7	116.6	113.9	98.2	83.6	87.9	109.5
Ours	142.7	172.8	450.7	221.5	481.1	209.7	164.1	162.3	889.4	850.5	487.5	244.4	199.3	213.3	208.8	339.9

4.2 Quantitative Evaluation by Public Dataset

For quantitative evaluation, we utilized a public dataset to measure the accuracy of absolute human pose estimation.

Dataset and Experimental Condition. According to the author's investigation, no public dataset was found to meet the following criteria: 1) presence of both humans and objects on the floor in the video, 2) interactions between them, and 3) availability of ground-truth poses for both humans and objects. Therefore, we evaluated the accuracy of absolute human pose estimation using the Human3.6M (H36M) dataset [9]. H36M consists of 3.6 million video frames recorded with four synchronized cameras, with ground truth joint positions captured by a motion capture system. Since the intrinsic and extrinsic parameters of all cameras were obtained in advance, we calculated the homography for the ankle/shoulder height and used it for human pose estimation. Note that the height of hip l_h of each subject is estimated in advance using the *Walking* motion. (S9: $l_h = 931.05 \pm 22.63$ mm, S11: $l_h = 912.1 \pm 22.63$ mm) We adopted the evaluation protocol used in the previous works [38,41]: we used two subjects (S9 and S11) and performed testing on every 64th frame. As an evaluation metric, we calculated the average Abs-MPJPE (Absolute Mean Per Joint Position Error) across all four cameras at every sampled frame. Abs-MPJPE proposed by Ray3D [38] measures the distance between the predicted and ground truth poses for 14 joints in the world coordinate system.

Result. The results are presented in Table 1, which includes the results of previous methods [28,38,41] for reference. Our method realized an accuracy of less than 200mm in the *Standing* action group. However, the accuracy of our method was generally worse than that of the previous methods. One reason for this is that our 2D-3D lifting method (3d-baseline) is trained using diverse datasets beyond H36M to improve generalization performance, as mentioned in Sect. 3.2. The required accuracy may vary depending on the specific application. Therefore, if higher accuracy is needed, additional domain-specific training can be applied. Additionally, our method allows for the replacement of the local 3D pose estimation algorithm with other state-of-the-art methods, if desired.

In terms of performance for different actions, there are larger errors observed in actions such as *Eating, Phoning, Sitting, SittingDown, and Smoking* compared

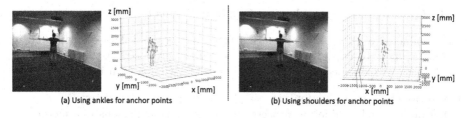

(a) Using ankles for anchor points   (b) Using shoulders for anchor points

Fig. 6. The difference of selecting anchor points between ankle and shoulder. The charts above show the homography planes calculated by the method. The charts below represent absolute 3D human poses at frame 256 of *Walking*, S11. The dashed line denotes ground-truth poses and the solid line denotes estimated poses by the proposed method.

Table 2. Average processing time of each module.

Module	Reader	Human Detector	2D Pose	3D Pose (Local)	3D Pose (Absolute)	All
Time [ms]	2.6	41.7	41.6	3.0	0.7	89.6

to the *Standing* action group. This is because the global height values (l_h) change during these actions. Since the current algorithm relies on pre-defined height values, it would be preferable to have a framework that allows for the flexible determination of height values depending on the specific action.

We also investigated the impact of anchor point selection on the estimation results. In this case, we used the shoulder joints as anchor points and calculated the height of the shoulders in advance (S9: $l_s = 1420.58 \pm 19.92$ mm, S11: $l_s = 1412.10 \pm 19.26$ mm). The homography with the height of the shoulders was then calculated, and absolute 3D human poses were estimated using these anchor points. As shown in Fig. 6, when using the shoulders as anchor points, there is a significant error in both position and scale estimation. This is because the height of the camera is similar to the height of the shoulders, and even a slight prediction error in the 2D pose can result in a large error in the global coordinates (x^g, y^g). To mitigate this issue, it would be necessary to adopt a framework that automatically selects anchor points based on the uncertainty of each joint. This would allow for a more robust estimation by considering the confidence levels of the estimated values.

We also measured the average processing time for each frame using a PC equipped with an Intel Core i7-6700K CPU and NVIDIA Titan X GPU. The processing time breakdown, excluding visualization, is shown in Table 2. We were able to achieve real-time estimation, with the prediction of an absolute 3D pose taking less than 1 ms per frame.

4.3   Qualitative Evaluation by Original Dataset

We conducted a qualitative evaluation using our original datasets captured in various scenes. To validate the performance of the proposed method using real-world data, we collected three different datasets with a conventional IP camera.

QM-line The cell production process of a single person in a factory
GX-line The cell production process involving multiple persons in a factory
Mini-car The assembly task performed by a worker in a laboratory

In these datasets, both ankles were used as anchor points for pose estimation, except for *Mini-car* dataset where both shoulders were utilized due to limited visibility of the lower body. The lengths l_h and l_s were estimated or measured in advance for the respective datasets.

Result. Figure 7 provides examples of the output generated by our method, showcasing the visualization capabilities using Unity. The camera viewpoints in Unity closely match the actual camera viewpoints, offering a realistic representation. Additionally, users have the freedom to manipulate the camera position and orientation, enabling viewing from any desired perspective. This flexibility is a key advantage of our visualization approach. Another potential use case for our method is 3D action recognition. The orange and red boxes in *3D Absolute HPE* column indicate specific 3D ROIs. When a certain joint (specifically, the right ankle) enters the ROI, the color of the ROI turns red. By defining actions within each ROI, it becomes possible to perform 3D action recognition. Similarly, our method can be used to recognize interactions with the surrounding environment or other individuals by leveraging the absolute pose representation.

In the case of *Mini-car* dataset, where the lower body is not visible in the image, only the estimation results for the upper body are shown. The proposed method exhibits robustness against occlusion, making it suitable for scenarios where partial visibility of the human pose is present. By knowing the height of three joints in advance, a transformation from local to global coordinates can be achieved.

4.4   Discussion

One limitation of our method is the assumption that z^g remains fixed. In scenarios such as manufacturing or retail scenes, where workers or customers may transition between standing and sitting positions, our method cannot handle the dynamic changes in z^g. To address this limitation, an adaptive setting for z^g should be implemented. One possible solution is to utilize action recognition results. By training each action with local 3D joint coordinates, z^g can be adjusted dynamically based on the recognized action.

Another limitation is the requirement of OBJ format CAD data to set the world coordinate. If the CAD data of the object cannot be acquired in advance, camera parameter estimation described in Sect. 3.1 cannot be adopted. However,

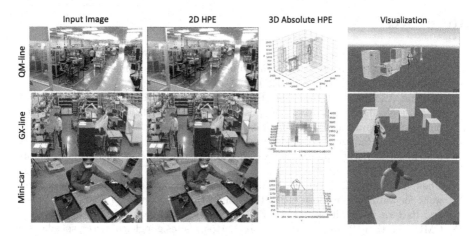

Fig. 7. The results of the visualization with three kinds of dataset. Each column from left to right shows input images, 2D HPE results, absolute 3D HPE results, and visualization by Unity. Note that the scale of the three axes at *3D Absolute HPE* differs due to the visibility. (Color figure online)

if there are some objects whose size is known, such as a standardized desk or pallet, it is possible to predict $\mathbf{R}_c^o$ and $\mathbf{t}_c^o$ of the object using PnP algorithms [14]. Subsequently, our method can calculate the homography value $\mathbf{H}_a$ for absolute pose estimation based on the predicted object pose, enabling the estimation of absolute human poses even without pre-acquired CAD data for the objects involved. We should expand the scope of the application situation.

5 Conclusion

We proposed the monocular absolute 3D HPE method by using the objects surrounding the humans. This method allows for real-time visualization in on-site environments where an uncalibrated monocular camera is used and acquiring a large amount of training dataset is challenging. The user study revealed the proposed information presentation method realizes accurate intrinsic and extrinsic parameter estimation. The quantitative evaluation using a public dataset demonstrated that our method achieves an accuracy of less than 200mm in estimating absolute human joint positions in standing. Furthermore, the qualitative evaluation showed the versatility of our method in handling various real-world scenarios, such as distant or close camera placement, limited visibility of the upper body, and multiple people. Future work will focus on implementing adaptive height settings to handle poses other than standing and developing methods for pose estimation without relying on CAD data.

References

1. Alpala, L.O., Quiroga-Parra, D.J., Torres, J.C., Peluffo-Ordóñez, D.H.: Smart factory using virtual reality and online multi-user: towards a metaverse for experimental frameworks. Appl. Sci. **12**(12) (2022)
2. Benzine, A., Chabot, F., Luvison, B., Pham, Q.C., Achard, C.: PandaNet: anchor-based single-shot multi-person 3D pose estimation. In: IEEE Conference on Computer Vision and Pattern Recognition, pp. 6855–6864 (2020)
3. Chen, C.H., Ramanan, D.: 3D human pose estimation = 2D pose estimation + matching. In: IEEE Conference on Computer Vision and Pattern Recognition, pp. 5759–5767 (2017)
4. Chen, Y., Wang, Z., Peng, Y., Zhang, Z., Yu, G., Sun, J.: Cascaded pyramid network for multi-person pose estimation. In: IEEE Conference on Computer Vision and Pattern Recognition, pp. 7103–7112 (2018)
5. CMU Motion Capture Database. https://sites.google.com/a/cgspeed.com/cgspeed/motion-capture. Accessed 1 Jan 2024
6. Ge, Z., Liu, S., Wang, F., Li, Z., Sun, J.: YOLOX: exceeding YOLO series in 2021. arXiv:2107.08430 (2021)
7. von Gioi, R.G., Jakubowicz, J., Morel, J.M., Randall, G.: LSD: a fast line segment detector with a false detection control. IEEE Trans. Pattern Anal. Mach. Intell. **32**, 722–732 (2010)
8. Han, P., Zhao, G.: Line-based initialization method for mobile augmented reality in aircraft assembly. Vis. Comput. **33**, 1185–1196 (2017)
9. Ionescu, C., Papava, D., Olaru, V., Sminchisescu, C.: Human3.6M: large scale datasets and predictive methods for 3D human sensing in natural environments. IEEE Trans. Pattern Anal. Mach. Intell. **36**(7), 1325–1339 (2014)
10. JustWithJoints: Body controller with joint locations (2022). https://assetstore.unity.com/packages/3d/animations/justwithjoints-body-controller-with-joint-locations-127172. Accessed 1 Jan 2024
11. Kehl, W., Manhardt, F., Tombari, F., Ilic, S., Navab, N.: SSD-6D: making RGB-based 3D detection and 6D pose estimation great again. In: IEEE Conference on Computer Vision and Pattern Recognition, pp. 1530–1538 (2017)
12. Konishi, Y., Hanzawa, Y., Kawade, M., Hashimoto, M.: Fast 6D pose estimation from a monocular image using hierarchical pose trees. In: Leibe, B., Matas, J., Sebe, N., Welling, M. (eds.) ECCV 2016. LNCS, vol. 9905, pp. 398–413. Springer, Cham (2016). https://doi.org/10.1007/978-3-319-46448-0_24
13. Kritzinger, W., Karner, M., Traar, G., Henjes, J., Sihn, W.: Digital twin in manufacturing: a categorical literature review and classification. IFAC-PapersOnLine **51**(11), 1016–1022 (2018)
14. Lepetit, V., Moreno-Noguer, F., Fua, P.: EPnP: an accurate O(n) solution to the PnP problem. Int. J. Comput. Vis. **81**, 155–166 (2009)
15. Loper, M., Mahmood, N., Romero, J., Pons-Moll, G., Black, M.J.: SMPL: a skinned multi-person linear model. ACM Trans. Graph. **34**(6) (2015)
16. MakeHuman. http://www.makehumancommunity.org. Accessed 1 Jan 2024
17. Mardia, K., Kent, J.T., Bibby, J.M.: Multivariate Analysis. Academic Press, Cambridge (1979)
18. Martinez, J., Hossain, R., Romero, J., Little, J.J.: A simple yet effective baseline for 3D human pose estimation. In: IEEE Conference on Computer Vision and Pattern Recognition, pp. 2659–2668 (2017)

19. Marullo, G., Tanzi, L., Piazzolla, P., Vezzetti, E.: 6D object position estimation from 2D images: a literature review. Multimedia Tools Appl. **82**(16), 24605–24643 (2022)
20. Moon, G., Chang, J.Y., Lee, K.M.: Camera distance-aware top-down approach for 3D multi-person pose estimation from a single RGB image. In: International Conference on Computer Vision, pp. 10132–10141 (2019)
21. Moteki, A., Saito, H.: Object pose estimation using edge images synthesized from shape information. Sensors **22**(24), 9610 (2022)
22. Mousavian, A., Anguelov, D., Flynn, J., Košecká, J.: 3D bounding box estimation using deep learning and geometry. In: IEEE Conference on Computer Vision and Pattern Recognition, pp. 5632–5640 (2017)
23. Orghidan, R., Salvi, J., Gordan, M., Orza, B.: Camera calibration using two or three vanishing points. In: 2012 Federated Conference on Computer Science and Information Systems (FedCSIS), pp. 123–130 (2012)
24. Pavlakos, G., Zhou, X., Chan, A., Derpanis, K.G., Daniilidis, K.: 6-DoF object pose from semantic keypoints. In: IEEE International Conference on Robotics and Automation (ICRA), pp. 2011–2018 (2017)
25. Pavlakos, G., Zhou, X., Derpanis, K.G., Daniilidis, K.: Coarse-to-fine volumetric prediction for single-image 3D human pose. In: IEEE Conference on Computer Vision and Pattern Recognition, pp. 1263–1272 (2017)
26. Peng, S., Zhou, X., Liu, Y., Lin, H., Huang, Q., Bao, H.: PVNet: pixel-wise voting network for 6DoF object pose estimation. IEEE Trans. Pattern Anal. Mach. Intell. **44**(06), 3212–3223 (2022)
27. Rogez, G., Weinzaepfel, P., Schmid, C.: LCR-Net++: multi-person 2D and 3D pose detection in natural images. IEEE Trans. Pattern Anal. Mach. Intell. **42**(05), 1146–1161 (2020)
28. Shan, W., Lu, H., Wang, S., Zhang, X., Gao, W.: Improving robustness and accuracy via relative information encoding in 3D human pose estimation. In: ACM International Conference on Multimedia, pp. 3446–3454 (2021)
29. Sun, X., Shang, J., Liang, S., Wei, Y.: Compositional human pose regression. In: International Conference on Computer Vision, pp. 2621–2630 (2017)
30. Tekin, B., Sinha, S.N., Fua, P.: Real-time seamless single shot 6D object pose prediction. In: IEEE Conference on Computer Vision and Pattern Recognition, pp. 292–301 (2018)
31. Ulrich, M., Wiedemann, C., Steger, C.: Combining scale-space and similarity-based aspect graphs for fast 3D object recognition. IEEE Trans. Pattern Anal. Mach. Intell. **34**(10), 1902–1914 (2012)
32. Unity Asset Store. https://assetstore.unity.com. Accessed 1 Jan 2024
33. Wang, C., Li, J., Liu, W., Qian, C., Lu, C.: HMOR: hierarchical multi-person ordinal relations for monocular multi-person 3D pose estimation. In: Vedaldi, A., Bischof, H., Brox, T., Frahm, J.-M. (eds.) ECCV 2020. LNCS, vol. 12348, pp. 242–259. Springer, Cham (2020). https://doi.org/10.1007/978-3-030-58580-8_15
34. Wang, G., Manhardt, F., Tombari, F., Ji, X.: GDR-Net: geometry-guided direct regression network for monocular 6D object pose estimation. In: IEEE Conference on Computer Vision and Pattern Recognition, pp. 16611–16621 (2021)
35. Wu, J., et al.: Real-time object pose estimation with pose interpreter networks. In: IEEE/RSJ International Conference on Intelligent Robots and Systems (IROS), pp. 6798–6805 (2018)
36. Xu, C., Zhang, L., Cheng, L., Koch, R.: Pose estimation from line correspondences: a complete analysis and a series of solutions. IEEE Trans. Pattern Anal. Mach. Intell. **39**(6), 1209–1222 (2017)

37. Yang, Z., Yu, X., Yang, Y.: DSC-PoseNet: learning 6DoF object pose estimation via dual-scale consistency. In: IEEE Conference on Computer Vision and Pattern Recognition, pp. 3906–3915 (2021)
38. Zhan, Y., Li, F., Weng, R., Choi, W.: Ray3D: ray-based 3D human pose estimation for monocular absolute 3D localization. In: IEEE Conference on Computer Vision and Pattern Recognition, pp. 13106–13115 (2022)
39. Zhang, Z.: A flexible new technique for camera calibration. IEEE Trans. Pattern Anal. Mach. Intell. **22**(11), 1330–1334 (2000)
40. Zheng, C., et al.: Deep learning-based human pose estimation: a survey. ACM Comput. Surv. **56**(1), 1–37 (2023)
41. Zheng, C., Zhu, S., Mendieta, M., Yang, T., Chen, C., Ding, Z.: 3D human pose estimation with spatial and temporal transformers. In: International Conference on Computer Vision, pp. 11656–11665 (2021)

Technical Skill Evaluation and Training Using Motion Curved Surface in Considered Velocity and Acceleration

Kaoru Mitsuhashi(✉) 🆔

Teikyo University, Utsunomiya, Tochigi 320-8551, Japan
mitsuhashi.kaoru.gz@teikyo-u.ac.jp

Abstract. Sports skill differences between beginners and experts are visualized and quantified by curvature and area of motion curved surfaces using Microsoft Kinect. However, the technical skills of the engineer are not clarified. The technical skills need expert motion trajectory, rhythm, and well-timing. In this paper, we visualize and quantify technical skills, such as engineering and job training. In addition, we suggest the velocity curved surface and acceleration curved surface in motion curved surfaces, and the beginner exercises the skill training using the motion curved surfaces. In this result, the beginner skill improves using the motion curved surface training.

Keywords: technical skill · motion curved surface · velocity/acceleration visualization

1 Introduction

In the traditional skill transmissions and successions of athletes and technicians in sports and engineering, it is often the case that they acquire skills through actual practice after imitating the skills of an expert or receiving verbal explanations. Then, the beginner's skill acquisitions from experts are often influenced by the expert's skill level, the beginner's understanding of the explanation, and the beginner's judgment. The way beginner's feel and think are different from that of experts. Therefore, in the absence of an expert, the behavior of skill transfer can change significantly, making it difficult to acquire skills and requiring a great deal of time to acquire them. Experts often judge the skill level of beginners qualitatively, and it is difficult to judge the skill level quantitatively [1, 2].

To quantitatively evaluate skills, a method is currently used that measures the movements of experts and beginners using motion capture, extracts the differences in their movements, and judges them. This method involves attaching spherical markers to the body and analyzing the movements by taking pictures from multiple directions. However, this method has several limitations, such as the need for large equipment, the requirement that subjects wear markers, and the difficulty of evaluating the behavior of normal work. In addition, it is not possible to evaluate the skill level when an expert is not available to evaluate. Then, it is necessary to have an environment that can quantitatively evaluate the behavior of beginners using predetermined standard.

© The Author(s), under exclusive license to Springer Nature Singapore Pte Ltd. 2024
G. Irie et al. (Eds.): IW-FCV 2024, CCIS 2143, pp. 67–80, 2024.
https://doi.org/10.1007/978-981-97-4249-3_6

In previous research, we capture the movements of experts and beginners using the Microsoft Kinect (Kinect). Kinect can measure the three-dimensional (3D) positions, as it can recognize images and depth positions [3, 4]. In addition to extracting only the human outline, it can also measure the coordinates of the skeleton and joints. The coordinates of multiple skeletons and joints are connected in a time series and between joints, and multiple movement trajectories are smoothed using approximation methods. By representing the motion of experts as curves, we can visually and quantitatively display the area and curvature of the curves, which visualizes the skills of experts and extracts the differences between the movements of experts and beginners. This has made it possible to analyze the magnitude of the position, velocity, and acceleration of joints at each time in the movement as velocity curves and acceleration curves.

The previous research has accumulated a large amount of data on the motion curves of sports movements and has been able to identify the differences between the movements of experts and beginners from the shape, curvature, and timing of the curves [3, 4]. On the other hand, the technical skill movements of workman have not yet been fully clarified. Technical skill movements are expected to be more precise and repetitive than sports movements. This is because workman in manufacturing industries, for example, need to consistently produce high-precision products. Skill visualization and quantification are expected to be a method for improving the rate of improvement in the understanding of skill training learners. This allows skill learners to engage in self-training at their discretion and acquire knowledge, theory, and skills tailored to their understanding and proficiency. However, the correlation and effectiveness of skill visualization and acquisition speeds (velocity) are not clarified.

In this research, we visualize the behavior of technical skill training movements as curves to reveal quantitative characteristics of expert's skills in the same way to sports movements. We track the trajectories of each joint for technical skill training movements, such as hammering and hand finishing work using Kinect. After that, we compare the motion curves of curvature, velocity, and acceleration between beginners and experts. We extract quantitative and clear differences between beginners and experts, clarify the quantitative characteristics of experts, and investigate whether motion curves can contribute to the improvement of skill acquisition.

2   Motion Curved Surface Evaluation

2.1   Creation and Display

In this research, we use Microsoft Kinect v2 (Kinect) to track the joints of humans. Kinect displays the movements of each joint using depth and image recognition. Figure 1(a) shows the tracking situation using Kinect. Kinect is mounted at a height of 1.5 m, and the distance between Kinect and the user (human) is 2.0 m. The measurement joint points are both hands, elbows, shoulders, neck, head, knees, and ankles. Figure 1(b) shows the movement of a subject sitting with their arms open. Joint positions are measured using Kinect SDK 2.0 and OpenCV libraries, and lines of motion are displayed [5, 6].

We display the motion of a subject measured by Kinect as a surface. To display the surface, we save the data of the measured point cloud of the subject based on the time series and fit the point cloud to a surface. Parametric curves are created in 3D CAD

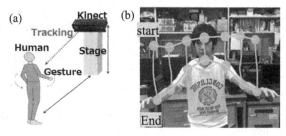

Fig. 1. Kinect tracking situation and movie view. Left is situation (a), right is joint and trajectories in Kinect movie view (b).

software such as Rhinoceros ™ [7]. A parametric curve is determined by a parameter. We can find the coordinates x, y, and z for a given time t, if we set time as the parameter t. If we consider this as a single coordinate in three dimensions, we can draw a curve by plotting the coordinates with small intervals of t (It is called a parametric curve). We use a loft surface when making a surface. A loft surface is created by connecting the selected parametric curves in sequence. The motion surface is defined as the u-direction between joints and the v-direction as the temporal trajectory of the subject. The motion surfaces are approximations of the joint trajectory in the joint and time directions. The curvature of the surface is displayed using RGB color gradients or zebra mapping. Figure 2(a) shows all the joint trajectories. Figure 2(b) shows the visualized motion curved surface. The dimensions, normal, tangents, and curvatures of the surface can be calculated from the generated surface. Here, we omit the calculation methods for curvature because there are various references available, but the changes in the motion trajectory can be confirmed by the curvature of the surface [7, 8].

Next, we use RGB color gradient distribution to display the curvature. When the curvature $\rho_{u,v}$ is $\rho_{min} < \rho_{u,v} < \rho_{max}$, the RGB color gradient distribution is represented as follows in Eq. (1), (2), with the maximum curvature as ρ_{max} and the minimum curvature as ρ_{min}.

$$(r, g, b) = \begin{cases} (255, 0, 0) & \left(\because \rho_{u,v} = \rho_{max}\right) \\ (255, \text{temp}, 0) & \left(\because \rho_{u,v} - \rho_{min} \geq 0.75(\rho_{max} - \rho_{min})\right) \\ (\text{temp}, 255, 0) & \left(\because \rho_{u,v} - \rho_{min} \geq 0.50(\rho_{max} - \rho_{min})\right) \\ (0, 255, \text{temp}) & \left(\because \rho_{u,v} - \rho_{min} \geq 0.25(\rho_{max} - \rho_{min})\right) \\ (0, \text{temp}, 255) & \left(\because \rho_{u,v} \geq \rho_{min}\right) \\ (0, 0, 255) & \left(\because \rho_{u,v} = \rho_{min}\right) \end{cases} \quad (1)$$

$$\text{temp} = 0.5 \times \left[1.0 - \cos\left\{4\pi\left(\frac{\rho_{u,v} - \rho_{min}}{\rho_{max} - \rho_{min}}\right)\right\}\right] \times 255 \quad (2)$$

Here, r, g, and b represent the intensity of the color. ρ_{max} is represented by red, ρ_{min} is represented by blue, and $0.5 \times (\rho_{max} + \rho_{min})$ is represented by green. This allows for the representation of sudden changes in the trajectory and gradual changes in the trajectory with color and shape.

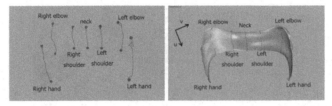

Fig. 2. Motion curved surface using Rhinoceros ™. Left is 7 joints and trajectories (a), right is parametric curved surface (b).

2.2 Calculation Method of Velocity and Acceleration Surface

Conventional motion surfaces are approximations of the joint trajectories in the joint and time directions, and the surface curvature is displayed using RGB color gradients. However, the trajectory and curvature display alone cannot represent the strength and timing of forces and velocities, or the rhythm. Therefore, we propose a new motion surface (velocity motion surface and acceleration motion surface) using differential geometry. Kinect captures the position of joints and time (timestamp). Therefore, it is possible to represent velocity and acceleration by differentiating each joint coordinate. When the coordinates $\mathbf{P}_{u,v}$ representing the trajectories of each joint and the time (timestamp) t are stored, the velocity $\mathbf{S}_{u,v}$ at the coordinate $\mathbf{P}_{u,v}$ can be expressed as Eq. (3), (4).

$$\mathbf{S}_{u,v} = \frac{\left|\mathbf{P}_{u,v} - \mathbf{P}_{u,v-1}\right|}{t_{u,v} - t_{u,v-1}} \tag{3}$$

$$\mathbf{S}_{u,0} = 0 \tag{4}$$

Here, the direction of $\mathbf{S}_{u,v}$ is already determined, so it is represented by its absolute value. The direction is in the joint direction, so the direction difference is not taken. Additionally, the acceleration $\mathbf{a}_{u,v}$ can be expressed as Eq. (5), (6).

$$\mathbf{a}_{u,v} = \frac{\mathbf{S}_{u,v} - \mathbf{S}_{u,v-1}}{t_{u,v} - t_{u,v-1}} \tag{5}$$

$$\mathbf{a}_{u,0} = 0 \tag{6}$$

Here, $\mathbf{a}_{u,v}$ will have positive and negative values. Additionally, it is also possible to express the propulsive force of the body as a propulsive force surface by accumulating mass to each coordinate of the acceleration surface.

Next, we use RGB color gradient distribution to display the velocity and acceleration. When the velocity $\mathbf{S}_{u,v}$ is at $\mathbf{S}_{min} < \mathbf{S}_{u,v} < \mathbf{S}_{max}$, the RGB color gradient distribution is represented as follows in like Eq. (1), with the maximum velocity as $\mathbf{S}_{max}$ and the minimum velocity as $\mathbf{S}_{min}$. $\mathbf{S}_{max}$ is represented by red, $\mathbf{S}_{min}$ is represented by blue, and $0.5 \times (\mathbf{S}_{max} + \mathbf{S}_{min})$ is represented by green. This allows for the representation of sudden changes in the trajectory and gradual changes in the trajectory with color and shape. The acceleration surface $\mathbf{a}_{u,v}$ can also be calculated in the same way.

The development environment is Visual Studio Community 2019, the programming language is C++, and the libraries are OpenGL. The animation of the user's skeleton model can be displayed and can be displayed simultaneously with the surface, as shown in Fig. 3. The joints are represented by blue spheres, and the skeleton is represented by gray. The visualized motion curved surface method is the same as using approximation. Therefore, the motion surface with curvature representation can be used to evaluate the abrupt changes, smoothness of trajectory, and magnitude of motion based on its shape, trajectory, and curvature. The velocity surface can be used to evaluate the rhythm of motion, the interval between movement and stop, based on the changes of fast and slow. The acceleration surface can be used to evaluate the timing of acceleration or deceleration and the degree of acceleration and deceleration. By using these three types of motion surfaces, it is possible to evaluate the details of motion more quantitatively and visually than in previous research [7].

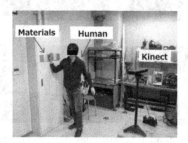 

Fig. 3. Motion curved surface using Visual Studio. Left is motion tracking situation (a), right is skeleton animation with motion curved surface (b).

2.3 Velocity and Acceleration Surface Display

Using this calculation method, the motion of throwing darts is expressed using motion velocity surfaces and motion acceleration surfaces. The investigated motions are darts throwing, crawl swimming, and karate receiving actions, which are investigated in previous research [3, 4].

Figure 4 shows the motion surfaces of the right hand, right elbow, and right shoulder of experts and beginners in the dart-throwing motion. Table 1 shows the maximum velocity, minimum velocity, maximum acceleration, minimum acceleration, and acceleration timing position (maximum acceleration position or velocity position). From Fig. 4, the velocity or acceleration range is indicated next to the surface. As a result, differences in shape, curvature, and area are observed in previous studies [3, 4], but the velocity and acceleration/deceleration timing positions can be seen. As shown in Fig. 4, the experts are fastest just before the dart is released, and their velocity is faster than that of beginners. The acceleration is also similar. We find that they are only applying force at the time of release. On the other hand, beginners are fastest at the beginning of the throw. This is because the dart is already at a constant velocity at the time of release, and the timing of release is ambiguous. According to the expert opinions, it is necessary to impart a snap to the wrist at the moment of release. In other words, it is necessary to apply force at the moment of release. To verify the difference in these movements, we performed a numerical analysis. We find that experts have the fastest velocity and acceleration at the time of dart release, while beginners have the fastest velocity and acceleration at the beginning of the arm swing.

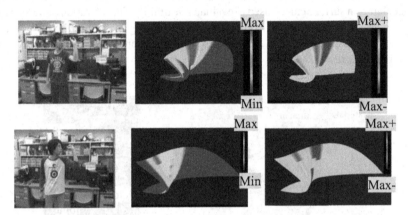

Fig. 4. Motion curved surface in darts-throwing. Top left is expert motion movie (a), top center is expert velocity surface (b), top right is expert acceleration surface (c), bottom left is beginner motion movie (d), bottom center is beginner velocity surface (e), and bottom right is beginner acceleration surface (f).

Table 1. Darts-throwing maximum/minimum velocity/acceleration, timing position (velocity: m/s, acceleration: m/s^2).

	S_{max}	S_{min}	a_{max}	a_{min}	Position
Expert	3.30	0.0	27.98	−19.13	Release
Beginner	2.43	0.0	29.60	−9.84	Start

Figure 5 shows the motion surfaces of the right hand, right elbow, and right shoulder of experts and beginners in the crawl swimming motion. The crawl motion is only the upper body. Table 2 shows the maximum velocity, minimum velocity, maximum acceleration, minimum acceleration, and acceleration timing position (maximum acceleration position or velocity position). As shown in Fig. 5, the maximum velocity and maximum acceleration of the arm are faster in experts than in beginners. Furthermore, experts are fastest at the time of the downstroke (entry), while beginners are fastest at the time of the upstroke (exit). We find that the timing of applying force to the arm is different. According to the expert opinions, it is necessary to enter the hand in a way that pushes the water. In other words, it is necessary to apply the most force or be the quickest at the time of entry.

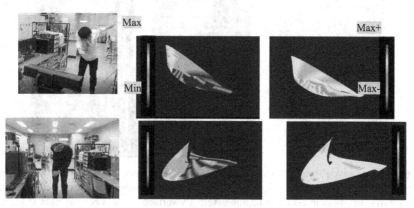

Fig. 5. Motion curved surface in crawl swimming. Top left is expert motion movie (a), top center is expert velocity surface (b), top right is expert acceleration surface (c), bottom left is beginner motion movie (d), bottom center is beginner velocity surface (e), and bottom right is beginner acceleration surface (f).

Table 2. Swimming crawl maximum/minimum velocity/acceleration, timing position (velocity: m/s, acceleration: m/s^2).

	S_{max}	S_{min}	a_{max}	a_{min}	Position
Expert	6.02	0.0	64.96	−68.40	Down
Beginner	5.73	0.0	47.85	−85.52	Upper

Figure 6 shows the motion surfaces of the right hand, right elbow, and right shoulder of experts and beginners in the karate defense motion. Table 3 shows the maximum velocity, minimum velocity, maximum acceleration, minimum acceleration, and acceleration timing position (maximum acceleration position or maximum velocity position). The maximum velocity and maximum acceleration of the arm are faster in beginners than in experts. Furthermore, experts are fastest at the time of the upstroke (defense), while beginners are fastest at the time of the downstroke (release). This also revealed that the timing of applying force to the arm is different. According to the expert opinions, the arm trajectory should be short, and force should be applied at the moment the arm stops. In other words, it is necessary to accelerate at the time of the upstroke.

Fig. 6. Motion curved surface in karate defense. Top left is expert motion movie (a), top center is expert velocity surface (b), top right is expert acceleration surface (c), bottom left is beginner motion movie (d), bottom center is beginner velocity surface (e), and bottom right is beginner acceleration surface (f).

Table 3. Karate defense maximum/minimum velocity/acceleration, timing position (velocity: m/s, acceleration: m/s^2).

	S_{max}	S_{min}	a_{max}	a_{min}	Position
Expert	1.42	0.0	4.12	−3.30	Upper
Beginner	4.02	0.0	22.06	−24.45	Down

3 Analyzation and Effectiveness Using Motion Curved Surface of Technical Skill

3.1 Measurement of Technical Skill Motion

In the previous chapter, we prove that the evaluation of sports movements using our motion curved surfaces is effective. Therefore, we also evaluate technical skill motion in the same way. Technical skill motions are hammering and hand sanding. Hammering includes the tasks of tapping the workpiece to secure it in the vice on a milling machine and engraving the metal. Hand sanding is the task of smoothing or removing the workpiece by hand using sandpaper, and it is a task to reduce surface roughness and size error (dimensional error). The subjects are three males, one of them is an expert and two of them are beginners.

Figure 7 shows the hammering motion of an expert. The hammering motion is divided into two phases: the upward swing and the downward swing. It shows a photograph in the upper left corner, a human silhouette and bone image in the upper right corner, and a 3D image in the lower part. Both the silhouette and the bone are tracked in three dimensions. Figure 7(a) shows the motion before hitting, and Fig. 7(b) shows the motion immediately after hitting. We can display the motion from the animation of the skeleton alone, but we cannot extract the differences between the motions of experts and beginners.

Fig. 7. Hammer punch skill motion. Top is before punch (a), bottom is in punching (b).

Figure 8 shows the hand sanding motion of an expert. It is divided into two phases: before pressing the sandpaper and immediately after pressing. It shows a photograph in the upper left corner, a human silhouette and bone image in the upper right corner, and a 3D image in the lower part. Both the silhouette and the bone are tracked in three dimensions. Figure 8(a) shows before pressing, and Fig. 8(b) shows immediately after pressing. Like Fig. 7, we can know the motion from the animation of the skeleton alone, but we cannot extract and see the differences between the motions of experts and beginners. Therefore, it is necessary to evaluate by expressing it as a motion surface.

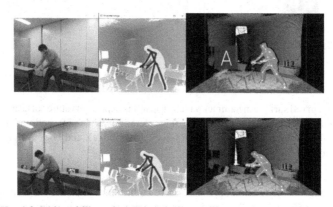

Fig. 8. Hand finishing skill motion. Top is before pulling (a), bottom is after pulling (b).

3.2 Analyzation Using Motion Curved Surface

Since we find that technical skill cannot be evaluated from only skeleton animation, technical skill movements are expressed using motion curved surfaces. Figure 9 shows the motion curved surfaces of the right hand, right elbow, and right shoulder of experts and beginners in hammering movements. Table 4 shows the maximum velocity, maximum acceleration, maximum deceleration, maximum curvature, and surface area. From Fig. 9, the velocity or acceleration range is indicated on the side of the surface. In previous paper, differences in shape, curvature, and area are shown [3, 4]. In this result, they are added velocity and acceleration/deceleration timing. From Fig. 9 and Table 4, the velocity is similar for both experts and beginners, but the experts have the largest deceleration immediately before hitting. Beginners have a larger acceleration. Experts have the fastest initial movement. This suggests that experts are applying force immediately before hitting. According to the expert opinions, they apply force to their wrists at the moment of hitting. Therefore, it is necessary to apply force at the moment of hitting.

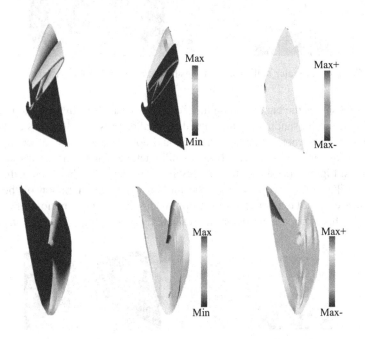

Fig. 9. Motion curved surface in hammer punch. Top left is expert curvature surface (a), top center is expert velocity surface (b), top right is expert acceleration surface (c), bottom left is beginner motion movie (d), bottom center is beginner velocity surface (e), and bottom right is beginner acceleration surface (f).

Figure 10 shows the motion surfaces of the right hand, right elbow, and right shoulder of experts and beginners in sandpaper hand finishing movements. Table 5 shows the maximum velocity, maximum acceleration, maximum deceleration, maximum curvature, and area. From Fig. 10, the velocity or acceleration range is indicated on the side of the surface. From Fig. 10 and Table 5, the velocity and acceleration are similar for both experts and beginners. However, the trajectory of the experts is curved. This is because the experts are curved when they rub and push the sandpaper. On the other hand, beginners are pushing it flat. According to the expert opinions, they apply force to

Table 4. Hammer punch maximum curvature/velocity/acceleration, area (velocity: m/s, acceleration: m/s^2, curvature: 1/m, area: m^2).

	S_{max}	a_{max}	a_{min}	ρ_{max}	Area
Expert	3.84	28.27	−59.16	2.62	0.95
Beginner	3.95	51.41	−37.00	2.20	0.84

their entire body at the moment of rubbing. Therefore, it is necessary to put the weight of the entire body on the body at the moment of rubbing. However, the difference between experts and beginners in terms of velocity and acceleration is small. Therefore, by using 3 types of motion curved surfaces, we can derive the differences between experts and beginners in technical skill movements.

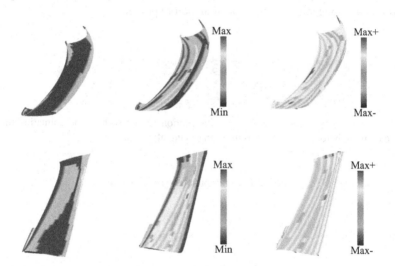

Fig. 10. Motion curved surface in hand finishing. Top left is expert curvature surface (a), top center is expert velocity surface (b), top right is expert acceleration surface (c), bottom left is beginner motion movie (d), bottom center is beginner velocity surface (e), and bottom right is beginner acceleration surface (f).

Table 5. Hand finishing maximum curvature/velocity/acceleration, area (velocity: m/s, acceleration: m/s^2, curvature: 1/m, area: m^2).

	S_{max}	a_{max}	a_{min}	ρ_{max}	Area
Expert	1.56	22.54	−22.67	1.73	0.063
Beginner	1.11	14.23	−11.64	0.52	0.09

3.3 Effectiveness of Technical Skill Training

To establish a skill transfer method, beginner learners train in hammering and hand finishing movements using motion curved surfaces. Learners are trained using the skeleton animation display and motion curved surface display. Motion curved surfaces are created before and after both movie viewing training and motion curved surface training, and the degree to which the beginner's movements approached the expert's movements is verified from the motion curved surfaces and finished products.

First, we investigate the training effect of hammering by using the punching operation of an engraving. Figure 11 shows the shapes of the punching operation of an engraving before and after training. The engraving is the number character "0". From Fig. 11, the number of the engraving is easier to see clearly after training. It is desirable to measure the depth of the engraving as a numerical evaluation, but it is impossible to measure. Therefore, we measure the length of the visible engraving. Table 6 shows the average length of the engraving. From Table 6, we find that the average length of the engraving after training is longer and more stable than before practice.

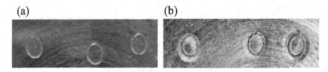

Fig. 11. Engraving by hammer punching using motion curved surface and animation training. Left is engraving before training (a), right is engraving after training (b).

Table 6. Hammer punching training effect

Before	After
6.9 mm average	8.8 mm average

Next, we investigate the training effect of hand finishing work. In the case of flat materials, it is extremely difficult to evaluate the polishing condition of sandpaper. Therefore, in this study, we evaluate the polishing condition by chamfering the corners of the material. Figure 12 shows the shapes of the chamfering of the corners of the material by hand finishing work before and after training. The sandpaper is rubbed in the direction from bottom to top. From Fig. 12, the area before the start of finishing is over-polished before training, while the area after training is evenly polished. Table 7 shows the polishing range of the chamfering. From Table 6, we find that the polishing range after training is narrower and more stable than before practice. As a result of measuring the variation in the width of the polishing, the variation is 0 to 5.5 mm before training, while it is 2.2 to 4.5 mm after training. Therefore, we find that the finishing skills after training can be polished with a stable force.

(a) 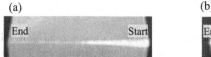   (b)

Fig. 12. Chamfering by hand finishing using motion curved surface and animation training. Left is chamfering before training (a), right is chamfering after training (b).

Table 7. Hand finishing training effect

Before	After
0–5.5 mm (±2.25 mm)	2.2–4.5 mm (±1.15 mm)

4 Conclusion

We clarify the differences between the movements of experts and beginners from the shape of the surface, curvature, and timing of speed and acceleration by accumulating a large amount of data on the motion surfaces of sports movements. In addition, we clarify the technical skills character by visualizing the technical skill motion as the motion curved surface in a quantitative character (parameter) using Microsoft Kinect like sports movements.

First, we define the curvature surface, velocity surface, and acceleration surface of the motion curved surface, and explain the differences in the color gradation of each. After that, we investigate the differences between the movements of experts and beginners in sports and technical skill motion in terms of the shape of the surface, curvature, and timing of speed and acceleration. As a result, we find that there are differences in the trajectory, velocity (speed), and acceleration timing between experts and beginners.

After that, we track the trajectories of each joint in hammer tapping and finishing operations, which are part of technical skill motion using Kinect, and connect the tracked trajectories of each joint in both time series and between joints and approximated the shape as a motion curved surface. We display the curvature, velocity, and acceleration from the motion curved surface in color gradation to visualize the trajectory, timing, and other factors of the movement. As a result, we can extract the quantitative and clear differences between beginners and experts by comparing the motion curved surfaces of curvature, velocity, and acceleration of beginners and experts quantitatively. Furthermore, we can confirm the improvement of skills in both hammer tapping and finishing operations by conducting training using motion curved surfaces for beginners. In the future, we will investigate whether it can contribute to the improvement of skill acquisition for beginners.

Acknowledgments. This work is supported by JSPS KAKENHI Grant-in-Aid for Scientific Research (C) KAKENHI Grant Number 22K02881.

References

1. Takeo, Y., Natsu, W.: Development of valuation method for measurement skill training. In: Proceedings of International Symposium on Standardization Education and Research 2011, Tokyo, Japan, pp. 130–145 (2011)
2. Murao, T., Hirao, Y., Hashimoto, H.: Skill level evaluation for Taijiquan based on curve fitting and logarithmic distribution diagram of curvature. SICE J. Control Meas. Syst. Integr. **4**(1), 001–005 (2011)
3. Mitsuhashi, K., Hashimoto, H., Ohyama, Y.: The curved surface visualization of the expert behavior for skill transfer using Microsoft Kinect. In: 11th International Conference on Informatics in Control, Automation and Robotics (ICINCO 2014), 1–3 September, Wien, Austria, pp. 550–555 (2014)
4. Mitsuhashi, K., Hashimoto, H., Ohyama, Y.: Motion curved surface analysis and composite for skill succession using RGBD camera. In: 12th International Conference on Informatics in Control, Automation and Robotics (ICINCO 2015), 21–23 July, Colmar, France (2015)
5. Falahati, S.: OpenNI cookbook. Packt Publishing Ltd. (2013)
6. Zhang, Z.: Microsoft kinect sensor and its effect. IEEE Multimedia **19**(2), 4–10 (2012)
7. Li, Y., Gu, P.: Free-form surface inspection techniques state of the art review. Comput. Aided Des. **36**(13), 1395–1417 (2004)
8. Najman, L., Romon, P. (eds.): Modern Approaches to Discrete Curvature, vol. 2184. Springer, Berlin (2017). https://doi.org/10.1007/978-3-319-58002-9

A Benchmark for 3D Reconstruction with Semantic Completion in Dynamic Environments

Qin-yuan Zhou[1]([⊠]), Seiya Ito[1,2], and Kazuhiko Sumi[1]

[1] Aoyama Gakuin University, Sagamihar, Kanagawa 252-5258, Japan
zhouqinyuanrunner@gmail.com
[2] National Institute of Information and Communications Technology (NICT),
Tokyo 184-8795, Japan

Abstract. Reconstructing the complete geometry of a 3D scene is essential for real-world applications involving service robotics or autonomous vehicles. A promising approach to achieve this is a combination of 3D reconstruction and semantic completion. However, the dataset for evaluating this is limited to static environments, even though real-world environments are dynamic, such as those containing moving objects. Building a dataset of real-world dynamic environments to reveal the impact of dynamic objects on 3D reconstruction is an important factor in moving the field forward. To this end, we propose a method to synthesize a dynamic 3D scene with moving objects. The key consideration is to composite naturally moving objects into the 3D scene. We adopt humans as moving objects and utilize a method to generate natural human motion. The generated human motion is composited into a static 3D scene and rendered with the specified camera path. We use the data acquired from this process to evaluate 3D reconstruction with semantic completion. In addition, we analyze the relationship between the percentage of frames occupied by dynamic objects and accuracy to reveal the impact of dynamic objects. The code is available at https://github.com/zhouqinyuanrunner/Dyna3DBench.

Keywords: Semantic Scene Completion · Dynamic Scene · 3D Reconstruction · Human Motion

1 Introduction

Understanding both the geometry and semantics of 3D scenes is essential for a variety of applications, such as robot navigation and augmented reality. While humans have the ability to comprehend 3D environments and effortlessly infer both geometry and context, even if they are barely visible from their field of

---

This work was supported by JSPS KAKENHI Grant Number 22K17978.

© The Author(s), under exclusive license to Springer Nature Singapore Pte Ltd. 2024
G. Irie et al. (Eds.): IW-FCV 2024, CCIS 2143, pp. 81–92, 2024.
https://doi.org/10.1007/978-981-97-4249-3_7

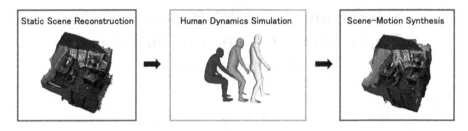

Fig. 1. Workflow of our dynamic scene generation. Left: A 3D reconstruction of the scene based on RGB-D and camera pose data. Mid: Human dynamics generation based on scene context. Right: Synthesizing dynamic objects into a static 3D scene.

view, this task is still quite challenging for computers [14]. This is because the data captured by visual sensors is limited, providing only fragmentary glimpses of the environment due to the restricted observation range and noise inherent in the measurements. Consequently, without prior knowledge, the representation of the scene is partial and incomplete.

To address this, semantic scene completion (SSC), which seeks to reconstruct the complete geometry of an entire scene with semantic labels by combining geometric and semantic understanding, has been studied [27]. Typical SSC methods [5] take data from a single viewpoint as input and predict geometry and semantic labels, including regions invisible to the sensor. However, in the single viewpoint setting, the scale of the target scene is limited. In contrast, SSC approaches that handle multiple viewpoints have been proposed to cover a wider area and work on fusing information across various viewpoints [32]. However, the datasets typically used for these frameworks are derived from static contexts [8]. This limits their application to dynamic real-world scenarios, such as those involving moving objects, and the analysis of the impact of dynamic objects on SSC models in real-world scenes has been overlooked.

In this paper, we propose a method to synthesize dynamic 3D scenes that integrate moving objects, specifically humans, to mirror real-world variability (Fig. 1). This method achieves generating natural human motion and compositing it into static 3D scenes, creating datasets that enable the evaluation of 3D reconstruction techniques in the presence of dynamic objects. Additionally, we present an analytical approach utilizing the synthesized datasets to investigate the influence of dynamic entities on the performance of the SSC model.

The contributions of our work are summarized as follows:

- We propose a novel method for composing datasets of indoor 3D scenes, including dynamic objects.
- We propose a method for measuring the impact of dynamic objects on the performance of SSC models, highlighting the significance of addressing dynamic objects in the practical application of the SSC model.
- We analyze the relationship between the percentage of frames occupied by dynamic objects and the performance of SSC model results to reveal the impact of dynamic objects.

2   Related Work

This study aims to analyze methods for reconstructing the complete 3D geometry of a scene in a dynamic environment. This section primarily introduces the development trends of the SSC models and the evolution of the related datasets. Note that although some studies have been conducted on 3D reconstruction in dynamic environments [2,3,15], these are out of scope because they reconstruct sensor-observed regions. In addition, since this study treats humans as dynamic objects, we also review the trends in 3D human motion generation.

2.1   Semantic Scene Completion

SSC methods can be divided into single-view and multi-view approaches. Single-view approaches focus on using learned patterns and prior knowledge for filling unseen areas [29,31,35], whereas multi-view approaches concentrate on integrating visual data from multiple views [23,39]. Additionally, SSC methods can also be classified by inputs as follows.

3D Grid-Based. The predominant method is the 3D occupancy grid, where each cell is marked as either occupied or vacant [12,26,32,34]. An alternative approach is the Truncated Signed Distance Field (TSDF), which calculates the signed distance to the nearest surface at specific 3D points [4,7,9,11]. TSDF provides more comprehensive signals than occupancy grids or point clouds, but it has drawbacks [29]. TSDF requires extensive computational resources, posing challenges for real-time applications.

3D Point Cloud. Despite the advantages of this method, only a few recent SSC studies have adopted point clouds for input encoding [24,25,33,37]. Among them, Zhong et al.'s study [37] enhances point data with RGB features by combining them. In contrast, Rish et al. [24,25] focus on reprojecting point features into a top-view format.

2D Representations Depth maps or 2D polar-encoded LiDAR data, known as range images, are frequently used 2D formats in SSC due to their capacity to store geometric information. Many researchers [1,6,13,17–21,31] have either used these formats alone or combined them with other types of data.

In this work, we employ SCFusion [32], a framework that combines an incremental 3D reconstruction and semantic scene completion. SCFusion utilizes occupancy maps and fuses semantically completed models of multiple views with high accuracy.

Benchmark Datasets. Benchmark datasets commonly employed in SSC, such as NYUv2 [28] and ScanNet [8], predominantly feature static environments and omit dynamic elements. The 3D models reconstructed from these original datasets are incomplete in terms of being able to reconstruct only the observed scene. In order to build datasets with complete geometry that can be leveraged for SSC, approaches such as NYUCAD [36] and CompleteScanNet [32], which use local matching approaches have been proposed that use local matching to incorporate CAD models. However, such approaches implicitly assume a static environment and overlook the complex challenges posed by dynamic entities, including moving humans. In this work, we synthesizes the dataset containing dynamic human motion that mimics real-world randomness in a static scene to provide a realistic context for SSC.

2.2   3D Human Motion Generation

In the field of motion generation, various methods have been proposed to generate motion based on specific conditions, such as text, audio, or 3D scenes [38]. Within this line of research, Conditional Variational Autoencoder (CVAE) [22,38] is a promising method that can produce motion in complex conditions. However, CVAE often suffers from Posterior Collapse [30], where latent variables are ignored due to the use of strong decoders. This is particularly likely to occur in motion generation with complex input conditions such as 3D scan data [8].

To avoid Posterior Collapse, SceneDiffuser [16] has been proposed using a diffusion model. Diffusion models are a new paradigm in the field of generation, and SceneDiffuser takes advantage of them to realize generation, optimization, and planning in a coherent framework. The framework improves robustness and versatility in generating 3D motion under diverse and complex conditions and shows overall effective results.

3   Dynamic 3D Scene Synthesis

We propose a framework for generating dynamic scene datasets as illustrated in Fig. 1. Our framework is primarily divided into three parts: static scene reconstruction, human dynamics simulation, and scene-motion synthesis. Our framework reconstructs a static 3D scene and integrates dynamic objects afterward. In this work, we focus on human figures as dynamic elements, considering scenarios where individuals move within a scene. To simulate human motion, we employ a diffusion-based method [16] that creates realistic movements adapted to 3D scenes. In the subsequent sections, we describe our framework in detail.

3.1   Static Scene Reconstruction with Complete Geometry

Initially, we construct 3D scenes using 3D reconstruction techniques such as SLAM. We assume that this process yields a 3D model of the scene, the posed frames used for reconstruction, and the camera information. Since the 3D model that can be obtained with typical 3D reconstruction is only the scene observed by the sensor, local matching [32,36] is applied to reconstruct the complete geometry. Note that the models obtained in this process do not have semantic labels. If semantic labels are needed, off-the-shelf semantic segmentation is used. We exemplify with the ScanNet dataset [8], simulating the act of a moving camera capturing the scene with the dataset's 3D scene model and camera poses.

3.2 Human Dynamics Simulation

After reconstructing the scene, we generate natural human motion. We utilize SceneDiffuser [16], a sophisticated technology for creating sequences of human motion. This technique harnesses 3D scene information and can be combined with an initial pose to emulate human actions. Our objective is to craft a set of lifelike and physically viable human poses that remain logical and consistent amidst extensive interaction with 3D scenes. For constructing our dataset, we adhered to the SceneDiffuser protocol, inputting ScanNet scenes into the SceneDiffuser to produce continuously moving human body models. As shown in Fig. 2, our preliminary experiment found that SceneDiffuser's movements can simulate diverse motions (e.g., "sitting" and "walking") in the scene with a natural appearance, even in unfamiliar scenes.

Fig. 2. Human motion generation. The motion of the human figure is naturally generated within the 3D reconstructed scene.

3.3 Scene-Motion Synthesis

Once the human motion is generated, the generated human motion is integrated with the static scenes to synthesize a dynamic sequence. Our integration process involves rendering both static and dynamic scenes from the same perspective. This approach highlights the differences attributed to dynamic objects by comparing these two scenarios. The spatial location of the generated human motion is aligned to the static environment, but temporal alignment is required to generate the sequence. Therefore, we generated motion to match the camera frame rate. Since motion frames are shorter than camera frames, a simple playback may cause a person to instantly assume a different posture. Thus, we synthesize repeated playback and reverse playback to produce smooth motion.

We utilize the generated dynamic scenes to generate two types of sequences. One is to render the generated dynamic scene as is. This sequence is ideal because it uses a scene model and camera parameters that are optimized during the 3D reconstruction process. However, both RGB and depth images have low realism. Therefore, we generate a sequence in which the motion is combined with the original frame. The difference between the frames in which human motion is synthesized and those in which it is not can be regarded as the area affected by the dynamic object. We combine this difference with the original frame to produce a highly realistic sequence that mimics the real world.

4   Experiments

We leverage the dynamic dataset constructed in Sect. 3 to discuss the impact of dynamic objects on reconstructing the complete geometry of a scene. We first present a method for quantifying the impact of dynamic objects in a scene. Subsequently, we show both quantitative and qualitative results and look deeper into the relationships between dynamic elements and SSC. In the experiments, we used SCFusion [32] for SSC, which reconstructs incrementally complete geometry of a scene from multi-view input.

4.1   Experimental Settings

Dataset. We employ the ScanNet dataset [8] for the evaluation, which provides a sequence of RGB-D images, camera poses, 3D models, and sensor information. We extracted 142 scenes from the 312 scenes provided as the validation set[1].

We note that the camera poses for which the ScanNet dataset is provided are those predicted by BundleFusion [10]. This means that the camera poses in the RGB-D frames are estimates and not strictly ground truth. To obtain RGB-D frames with exact camera poses, we render the 3D models using the provided camera poses. We refer to this dataset as "static" to distinguish it from the original ScanNet. By integrating human models in motion into this dataset, this dataset becomes dynamic (hereafter referred to as "dynamic"). Moreover, the dataset developed by directly infusing human motion data into the real-world frames from ScanNet is termed "real world". For each scene, two different scenarios were tested: one with one person ("one") and the other with two people ("two").

Evaluation Criteria. We employ three evaluation metrics commonly used for SSC [32,33]. The first metric is precision, which evaluates the accuracy of the model in identifying true positives, such as specific objects within a scene. This metric is crucial for gauging the model's ability to correctly discern between target objects and the background or other non-target entities. The second metric is recall, which measures the model's capacity to detect all actual positives. The third metric is intersection over union (IoU), which is particularly significant in scene completion tasks as it directly pertains to the model's understanding of scene geometry and semantics. In our experiment, we analyze the impact of dynamic objects by observing the change in these metrics with the presence or absence of dynamic objects.

4.2   Quantitative Results

SSC Performance. To investigate the impact of dynamic objects on the SSC model, SCFusion [32] was applied to both static and dynamic datasets. The results are shown in Table 1. These scores constitute the aggregated averages

---

[1] Scenes with scene IDs ending in "00" were selected.

from all scenarios within the dataset. Observations indicate a proportional decrease in the precision, recall, and IoU metrics as the incorporation of dynamic entities increases. The degradation efficacy is most pronounced in scenarios where two post-rendered models of human bodies in motion are integrated. The lowest metrics in "dynamic–two" are due to the inherent data loss in part of the scene during the rendering process.

Table 1. SSC performance on each dataset.

Dataset	Precision	Recall	IoU
ScanNet	0.467	0.521	0.298
static	0.461	0.519	0.289
dynamic–one	0.398	0.482	0.251
dynamic–two	0.375	0.459	0.245
real world–one	0.437	0.501	0.260
real world–two	0.402	0.461	0.246

Impact on Class Accuracy. In order to conduct a more detailed analysis of the effects exerted by dynamic objects, we have calculated the mean values of the respective metrics in accordance with the labels assigned within the scenes. These findings are delineated in Table 2. Apart from "ceiling", SCFusion originally exhibited superior performance across various metrics on smaller objects compared to similar SSC models. However, this advantage was negated due to its inability to accurately process dynamic objects.

Impact on Area Lost. The occurrence of dynamic objects causes occlusions in the frame imagery, which we define as an area lost in our study. As depicted in Fig. 3, we calculate the area lost for each frame by subtracting the frame data containing dynamic objects from the frame data without them. The difference represents the disruption caused by dynamic objects. For each scene, we calculate the value of area lost as the overall percentage of dynamic objects present throughout all frames in the scene. This value enables us to analyze changes in SSC performance at varying levels of dynamic object presence.

Figure 4 shows the relationship between area lost and SSC performance for each scene. It demonstrates that as the lost area expands, all metrics are decreasing and are negatively correlated. Significantly, the impact on IoU and precision becomes markedly more substantial when the area lost exceeds 20% of the total area. This could be an issue caused by the characteristics of SCFusion, but the negative impact of dynamic objects on SSC have been discerned.

4.3   Qualitative Results

Figure 5 illustrates an example of the results. In this example, the first human model is at the sofa in the top-left corner, repeatedly performing the action

Table 2. Class accuracy on each dataset.

Metric	Dataset	Ceiling	Floor	Wall	Window	Chair	Bed	Sofa	Table	TV	Furni.	Object	Mean
	ScanNet	0.191	0.535	0.373	0.102	0.304	0.142	0.260	0.316	0.653	0.213	0.142	0.298
	static	0.183	0.525	0.364	0.095	0.293	0.179	0.251	0.311	0.640	0.203	0.134	0.289
IoU	dynamic−one	0.143	0.488	0.326	0.059	0.257	0.138	0.214	0.269	0.604	0.166	0.096	0.251
	dynamic−two	0.139	0.482	0.320	0.049	0.251	0.134	0.204	0.266	0.602	0.158	0.089	0.245
	real world−one	0.154	0.498	0.332	0.064	0.266	0.148	0.221	0.278	0.617	0.173	0.106	0.260
	real world−two	0.139	0.482	0.322	0.046	0.249	0.139	0.208	0.264	0.605	0.161	0.090	0.246
	ScanNet	0.431	0.679	0.590	0.247	0.527	0.303	0.377	0.504	0.770	0.409	0.299	0.467
	static	0.426	0.672	0.584	0.241	0.521	0.292	0.371	0.498	0.764	0.408	0.293	0.461
Pre-	dynamic−one	0.362	0.610	0.521	0.179	0.457	0.234	0.308	0.434	0.700	0.340	0.230	0.398
cision	dynamic−two	0.338	0.587	0.496	0.155	0.435	0.215	0.286	0.412	0.678	0.319	0.203	0.375
	real world−one	0.399	0.649	0.556	0.217	0.497	0.274	0.347	0.476	0.740	0.379	0.272	0.437
	real world−two	0.365	0.612	0.526	0.182	0.462	0.238	0.314	0.439	0.705	0.341	0.237	0.402
	ScanNet	0.342	0.718	0.516	0.389	0.453	0.666	0.713	0.496	0.839	0.346	0.255	0.521
	static	0.338	0.718	0.519	0.382	0.451	0.664	0.709	0.494	0.837	0.346	0.253	0.519
Recall	dynamic−one	0.308	0.679	0.477	0.350	0.408	0.627	0.675	0.457	0.805	0.302	0.216	0.482
	dynamic−two	0.280	0.654	0.456	0.329	0.391	0.604	0.651	0.432	0.774	0.284	0.196	0.459
	real world−one	0.324	0.697	0.493	0.369	0.433	0.646	0.696	0.476	0.818	0.328	0.233	0.501
	real world−two	0.285	0.655	0.456	0.328	0.393	0.606	0.656	0.436	0.780	0.283	0.195	0.461

(a) Static   (b) Dynamic   (c) Area Lost

Fig. 3. Dynamic object area calculation. By subtracting images without human motion from images with human motion, the area affected by the dynamic factor is derived.

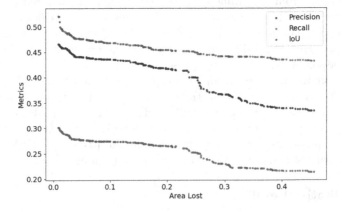

Fig. 4. Relationship between area lost and SSC performance.

of sitting down and standing up. The second human model near the bottom-right corner is performing a subtle walking action. It is apparent that parts obscured by dynamic objects are not accurately identified, and dynamic objects themselves are often erroneously classified under incorrect labels. Specifically, in the presence of dynamic objects, parts of objects near the human body, such as a "sofa", are incorrectly identified as "wall" or "window", while the human body itself is mistakenly classified as "object", "chair", or similar objects, affecting the reconstructed map's shape around them. Although it might seem reasonable for the synthesized human region to be categorized as "object", in reality, due to the movement of people and the lack of multi-view consistency, the restoration of these areas is problematic. The "sofa" should be predicted as a "sofa", not misrepresented due to the dynamic nature of the scene. This phenomenon is particularly evident in the visualization results of "real world–two".

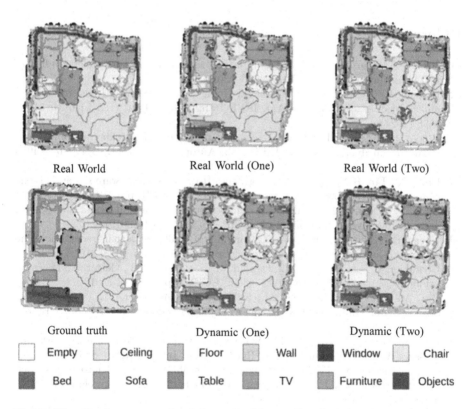

Fig. 5. Visualization case study of dynamic objects affect SSC. The images represent the results of scene0050_00 for each dataset.

5   Conclusion

We proposed a method for synthesizing a dataset of dynamic 3D scenes with moving objects (humans). The key to these techniques is the ability to naturally synthesize humans into static 3D scenes and render them through a specified camera path. We utilize this synthesized dataset to evaluate 3D reconstruction with semantic completion. By measuring indicators such as the relationship between the percentage of frames occupied by dynamic objects and the accuracy of model results, we demonstrate the impact of dynamic objects on models in this field. Although the current method doesn't include texture, it has the potential for future texturing integration. It could also be extended to incorporate expressions and subtle movements. The proposed method can serve as a benchmark for building 3D geometry models with higher robustness to dynamic objects in the future.

References

1. Behley, J., et al.: SemanticKITTI: a dataset for semantic scene understanding of LiDAR sequences. In: ICCV, pp. 9296–9306 (2019)
2. Bescós, B., Campos, C., Tardós, J.D., Neira, J.: DynaSLAM II: tightly-coupled multi-object tracking and SLAM. IEEE Rob. Autom. Lett. (RA-L) 6(3), 5191–5198 (2021)
3. Bescós, B., Fácil, J.M., Civera, J., Neira, J.: DynaSLAM: tracking, mapping, and inpainting in dynamic scenes. IEEE Rob. Autom. Lett. (RA-L) 3(4), 4076–4083 (2018)
4. Chen, X., Lin, K.Y., Qian, C., Gang Zeng, H.L.: 3D sketch-aware semantic scene completion via semisupervised structure prior. In: CVPR, pp. 4192–4201 (2020)
5. Chen, Y., Garbade, M., Gall, J.: 3D semantic scene completion from a single depth image using adversarial training. In: ICIP, pp. 1835–1839 (2019)
6. Cheng, R., Agia, C., Ren, Y., Li, X., Bingbing, L.: S3CNet: a sparse semantic scene completion network for LiDAR point clouds. In: CoRL, pp. 2148–2161 (2020)
7. Cherabier, I., Schönberger, J.L., Oswald, M.R., Pollefeys, M., Geiger, A.: Learning priors for semantic 3D reconstruction. In: ECCV, pp. 325–341 (2018)
8. Dai, A., Chang, A.X., Savva, M., Halber, M., Funkhouser, T.A., Nießner, M.: ScanNet: richly-annotated 3D reconstructions of indoor scenes. In: CVPR, pp. 2432–2443 (2017)
9. Dai, A., Diller, C., Nießner, M.: SG-NN: sparse generative neural networks for self-supervised scene completion of RGB-D scans. In: CVPR, pp. 846–855 (2020)
10. Dai, A., Niesner, M., Zollhofer, M., Izadi, S., Theobalt, C.: BundleFusion: real-time globally consistent 3D reconstruction using on-the-fly surface reintegration. ACM Trans. Graph. (ToG) 36(4), 1 (2017)
11. Dai, A., Ritchie, D., Bokeloh, M., Reed, S., Sturm, J., Niesner, M.: ScanComplete: large-scale scene completion and semantic segmentation for 3D scans. In: CVPR, pp. 4578–4587 (2018)
12. Garbade, M., Chen, Y., Sawatzky, J., Gall, J.: Two stream 3D semantic scene completion. In: CVPR, pp. 416–425 (2019)
13. Guo, Y.X., Tong, X.: Anisotropic convolutional networks for 3D semantic scene completion. In: CVPR, pp. 3348–3356 (2020)

14. Guo, Y., Wang, H., Hu, Q., Liu, H., Liu, L., Bennamoun, M.: Deep learning for 3D point clouds: a survey. IEEE Trans. Pattern Anal. Mach. Intell. (PAMI) **43**(12), 4338–4364 (2020)

15. Henein, M., Zhang, J., Mahony, R., Ila, V.: Dynamic SLAM: the need for speed. In: ICRA, pp. 2123–2129. IEEE (2020)

16. Huang, S., et al.: Diffusion-based generation, optimization, and planning in 3D scenes. In: CVPR, pp. 16750–16761 (2023)

17. Li, J., et al.: RGBD based dimensional decomposition residual network for 3D semantic scene completion. In: CVPR, pp. 7693–7702 (2019)

18. Li, S., Zou, C., Li, Y., Zhao, X., Gao, Y.: Attention-based multi-modal fusion network for semantic scene completion. In: AAAI, pp. 11402–11409 (2020)

19. Lin, D., Fidler, S., Urtasun, R.: Holistic scene understanding for 3D object detection with RGBD cameras. In: ICCV, pp. 1417–1424 (2013)

20. Liu, S., et al.: See and think: disentangling semantic scene completion. In: NeurIPS, pp. 261–272 (2018)

21. Liu, Y., et al.: Depth based semantic scene completion with position importance aware loss. Rob. Autom. Lett. (RA-L) **5**(1), 219–226 (2020)

22. Petrovich, M., Black, M., Varol, G.: Action-conditioned 3d human motion synthesis with transformer vae. In: CVPR, pp. 10985–10995 (2021)

23. Pintore, G., Mura, C., Ganovelli, F., Fuentes-Perez, L., Pajarola, R., Gobbetti, E.: State-of-the-art in automatic 3D reconstruction of structured indoor environments. Comput. Graph. Forum **39**(2), 667–699 (2020)

24. Rist, C.B., Emmerichs, D., Enzweiler, M., Gavrila, D.M.: Semantic scene completion using local deep implicit functions on LiDAR data. IEEE Trans. Pattern Anal. Mach. Intell. (PAMI) 7205–7218 (2021)

25. Rist, C.B., Schmidt, D., Enzweiler, M., Gavrila, D.M.: SCSSNet: learning spatially-conditioned scene segmentation on LiDAR point clouds. In: IV, pp. 1086–1093 (2020)

26. Roldão, L., de Charette, R., Verroust-Blondet, A.: LMSCNet: lightweight multi-scale 3D semantic completion. In: 3DV, pp. 111–119 (2020)

27. Roldao, L., de Charette, R., Verroust-Blondet, A.: 3D semantic scene completion: a survey. Int. J. Comput. Vision **130**(8), 1978–2005 (2022)

28. Silberman, N., Hoiem, D., Kohli, P., Fergus, R.: Indoor segmentation and support inference from RGBD images. In: ECCV, pp. 746–760 (2012)

29. Song, S., Yu, F., Zeng, A., Chang, A.X., Savva, M., Funkhouser, T.: Semantic scene completion from a single depth image. In: CVPR, pp. 190–198 (2017)

30. Wang, J., Xu, H., Xu, J., Liu, S., Wang, X.: Synthesizing long-term 3D human motion and interaction in 3D scenes. In: CVPR, pp. 9401–9411 (2021)

31. Wang, Y., Tan, D.J., Navab, N., Tombari, F.: Adversarial semantic scene completion from a single depth image. In: 3DV, pp. 426–434 (2018)

32. Wu, S.C., Tateno, K., Navab, N., Tombari, F.: SCFusion: real-time incremental scene reconstruction with semantic completion. In: 3DV, pp. 801–810 (2020)

33. Xia, Z., et al.: SCPNet: semantic scene completion on point cloud. In: CVPR, pp. 17642–17651 (2023)

34. Yan, X., et al.: Sparse single sweep LiDAR point cloud segmentation via learning contextual shape priors from scene completion. In: AAAI, pp. 3101–3109 (2021)

35. Yu-Xiao Guo, X.T.: View-volume network for semantic scene completion from a single depth image. arXiv preprint arXiv:1806.05361 (2018)

36. Zhang, L., et al.: Semantic scene completion with dense CRF from a single depth image. Neurocomputing **318**, 182–195 (2018)

37. Zhong, M., Zeng, G.: Semantic point completion network for 3D semantic scene completion. In: ECAI, pp. 2824–2831 (2020)
38. Zhu, W., et al.: Human motion generation: a survey. IEEE (2023)
39. Zollhofer, M., et al.: State of the art on 3D reconstruction with RGB-D cameras. Comput. Graph. Forum **37**(2), 625–652 (2018)

Framework for Measuring the Similarity of Visual and Semantic Structures in Sign Languages

Matheus Silva de Lima[1][(✉)] ⓘ, Ryota Sato[1], Erica K. Shimomoto[2]ⓘ, Suzana Rita Alves Beleza[1]ⓘ, Nobuko Kato[3]ⓘ, and Kazuhiro Fukui[1]ⓘ

[1] Department of Computer Science, University of Tsukuba, Tsukuba, Ibaraki, Japan
mlima@cvlab.cs.tsukuba.ac.jp
[2] National Institute of Advanced Industrial Science and Technology (AIST), Tokyo, Japan
[3] Faculty of Industrial Technology, Tsukuba University of Technology, Tsukuba, Ibaraki, Japan

Abstract. Sign languages are visual languages used by deaf and hard of hearing communities worldwide. As sign languages have been manually designed in an optimal visual and semantic aspect, these two representations are expected to share similar structures. This assumption is valuable due to its applicability for further analysis of the intrinsic system that empowers sign languages. By understanding the relationship between a sign and its semantic meaning, we can better design new signs. To verify this assumption, we propose a framework for measuring similarities between visual and semantic structures in sign languages. In our approach, we first introduce two vector spaces: a *visual-space*, which encodes the sign's visual features, and a *semantic-space*, which encodes the sign's semantic features. We then project data on the two spaces and generate two sets of 3D data points. Finally, we define a qualitative metric, called the *Communicability*, by measuring the structural similarity between the two sets of data points using shape-subspaces. This metric is demonstrated by measuring the mean Communicability calculated in a Japanese Sign Language dataset.

Keywords: Sign languages · structural analysis of language system · visual and semantic maps

1 Introduction

Sign Languages are visual languages used by deaf and hard of hearing communities worldwide. As new concepts emerge, there is a need to create new signs to represent their meanings. Specifically, given the fast pace of technological developments, there is an urgent need to create signs to represent new concepts in scientific and technical fields [5]. In Japanese Sign Language (JSL), new signs

ⓒ The Author(s), under exclusive license to Springer Nature Singapore Pte Ltd. 2024
G. Irie et al. (Eds.): IW-FCV 2024, CCIS 2143, pp. 93–107, 2024.
https://doi.org/10.1007/978-981-97-4249-3_8

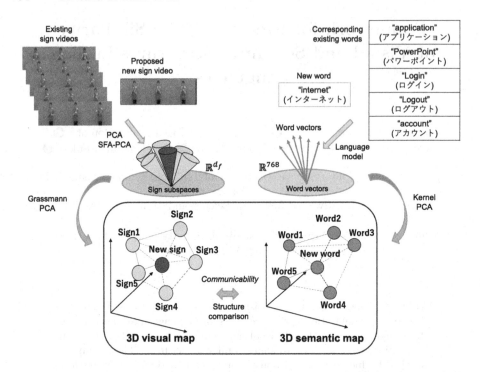

Fig. 1. Method overview. For sign videos, we convert each sign video to a low-dimensional subspace in a high-dimensional vector space. Then, we map a set of the sign subspaces onto a 3D vector space, called visual map, by using kernel PCA (Grassmann PCA). For words corresponding to signs, we convert each word to a vector by an embedding model and project the vectors on a 3D vector space, called semantic map by applying KPCA to a set of word vectors. Finally, we measure the similarity in the structures of 3D data points on the two maps by using shape subspaces as our proposed metric, Communicability.

are created every year to depict these new and existing meanings. An effective new sign must consider its ease of communication and visual interpretability.

The Japan Institute for Sign Language Studies (JISLS) creates new signs every year. Four times a year, JISLS publishes it on the web, inviting public comments before finalizing the new sign words. Users can then express their agreement and give their opinions about it. This procedure is heuristic and time-consuming and, therefore, a more quantitative method for creating new signs is necessary.

Although both communicability and interpretability can be seen as subjective and highly contextualized, the existence of locally optimal signs to depict the meaning of a given word leads us to believe that the visual and semantic spaces may have some similar structures. This assumption is valuable and applicable to further analysis of sign languages.

Given this assumption, we can effectively design a highly communicable new sign. By understanding how a new word semantically relates to existing words, we can choose a new corresponding sign which maintains the structural similarity between visual and semantic spaces. Based on this structural similarity, a sign that maximizes the *communicability* in its meaning neighbourhood should be a good guess for a new proposed sign.

To this end, we propose a framework for measuring the similarity between visual and semantic structures of sign languages as shown in Fig. 1. In our framework, each sign is represented by a video, i.e., visual information, and a word, i.e., semantic information. Videos are represented as low-dimensional subspaces in a high-dimensional vector space [7] modeled from video features, and the words are represented as word vectors extracted using a language model.

We model 3D principal component spaces for each modality, namely the *visual-space* and the *semantic-space*, using kernel PCA [13]. To generate the *visual-space*, we use the Grassmann kernel to encode the relationship information between the sign subspaces. To generate the *semantic-space*, we use the linear kernel (i.e., cosine similarity) to encode the semantic relationship between words. Sign subspaces and word vectors are then projected on to their respective spaces, leading to a 3D map of their distributions, the 3D visual map and the 3D semantic map.

We then define a qualitative metric, called the *Communicability*, by measuring the structural similarity between the data distributions in the *visual-space* and its corresponding *semantic-space*. This naming is derived from our assumption that the higher similarity between the two structures indicates the higher communicability ability of the sign set. Each 3D map is modeled as a shape subspace [11,16] and their structural similarity is measured using the canonical angles between the two shape subspaces. The *communicability* metric between the two spaces may vary depending on the features used to represent the videos and the words. Therefore, we investigate different approaches for generating both vector spaces, analysing how each approach affects the mean behaviour of the *communicability*.

The main contributions of the paper are summarised as follows:

- We propose a framework for measuring the similarity between visual and semantic structures of sign languages for the future detailed analysis of sign language.
- We introduce a metric for measuring the similarity using canonical angles between two shape subspaces.
- We created a dataset of Japanese Sign Language with IT-related terms, containing multiple selected signs as performed by deaf and hard-of-hearing signers.
- We demonstrate our metric and examine its mean characteristics on our dataset.

The rest of the paper is structured as follows: In Sect. 2, we give a brief explanation on fundamental theoretical background on which our proposed method is based; In Sect. 3, we describe in details how *visual-space* and *semantic-space* are generated, and how the communicability metric is calculated; In Sect. 4, we describe our experimental setting and report the results from our analysis. Finally, we conclude the paper in Sect. 5.

2   Theoretical Background

This section describes the theoretical background on key components in our framework. First, we explain how to model the subspace representation from a sign language video using PCA and PCA-SFS [1,2]. Then, we explain the three main types of visual features used to generate the *visual-space*. Finally, we overview how to represent words in a high-dimensional vectors, used to generate the *semantic-space*.

2.1   Subspace Representation for Sign Language Video

Subspace representation has been widely used to compactly represent a set of frames, i.e., images, from a video [6,7]. The orthonormal basis vectors of such a subspace is obtained by applying the principal component analysis (PCA) without data centring to the image set.

Given a set of T image feature vectors $\{\mathbf{x}_t\}_{t=1}^{T}$, where an image feature with $w \times h$ pixels is regarded as an $d(=wh)$ dimensional vector $\mathbf{x}$, the orthonormal basis vectors $\{\mathbf{u}_i\}_{i=1}^{m}$ of a m-dimensional subspace $\mathcal{A}$ is obtained as follows:

1. An $d \times d$ auto-correlation matrix is computed as $\mathbf{R} = \frac{1}{T}\sum_{t=1}^{T}\mathbf{x}_t\mathbf{x}_t^{\top}$.
2. The orthonormal basis $\{\mathbf{u}_i\}_{i=1}^{m}$ of the m-dimensional subspace is obtained as the unit eigenvectors corresponding to the m largest eigenvalues of $\mathbf{R}$.

The above standard PCA discards the order information of the feature vectors. To address this issue, we also use a variant of PCA, PCA-SFS [1,2] to generate the slow feature subspace that considers the order information.

2.2   Video Features for Sign Subspaces

In our proposed framework, given a sequence of T frames in a video $\{\mathbf{x}_t\}_{t=1}^{T} \in \mathbb{R}^d$, we first extract its visual features $\mathbf{X} \in \mathbb{R}^{d_f \times T}$ to generate the subspace $\mathcal{S}$ representation for sign videos using PCA and PCA-SFS.

We selected three main groups of features: first, we generate the subspaces with no feature extraction and no additional pre-processing, i.e., raw images; then, we experiment using image features extracted from deep convolutional neural networks; and finally, we experiment using optical-flow information, extracted by using RAFT [15]. In the following, we give a detailed explanation of how to encode them according to each proposed approach.

Raw Images. In this approach, we don't perform any additional pre-processing or extract any features prior to generating subspaces. As such, we directly encode T frames $\{\mathbf{x}_t\}_{t=1}^{T}$ as the columns of the feature matrix

$$\mathbf{X} = \begin{bmatrix} \mathbf{x}_1 \ldots \mathbf{x}_T \end{bmatrix} \in \mathbb{R}^{d \times T}. \tag{1}$$

This approach is the simplest and most explainable. It can be seen as an ablation baseline for the different features used in this research.

Deep Features. In this case, we extract deep features using pre-trained convolutional neural networks. This approach sacrifices feature explainability to some degree, but benefits from the high level of abstraction and generalization of such networks. We extract feature vectors $\mathbf{h} \in \mathbb{R}^{d_f}$ from such networks, where d_f corresponds to the hidden layer dimension of the CNN. Then, we encode them as the columns of the feature matrix

$$\mathbf{X}_h = \begin{bmatrix} \mathbf{h}_1 \ldots \mathbf{h}_T \end{bmatrix} \in \mathbb{R}^{d_f \times T}. \tag{2}$$

We experiment with features extracted using the VGG16 [14] and ResNet-50 [10], both pre-trained on the ImageNet [3].

Optical-Flow Information. We generate subspaces using the optical-flow information extracted by using RAFT [15]. The motivation to use this method lies on the assumption that the general body movement has enough information to represent the sign meaning.

By applying RAFT to the raw image feature matrix $\mathbf{X} \in \mathbb{R}^{d \times T}$, we obtain the horizontal and vertical displacement matrices, $\{(\mathbf{H}_t, \mathbf{V}_t)\}_{t=1}^{T}$, where $\mathbf{H}_t, \mathbf{V}_t \in \mathbb{R}^{h \times w}$. We transform this data into three different representations:

Intensity: We encode the flow direction information in given $\mathbf{H}_i$ and $\mathbf{V}_i$ into an RGB image, where each color represents a direction and similar colors indicate similar flow directions. Then, we convert this image to grayscale and encode pixels intensity levels as the columns of the feature matrix $\mathbf{X}_g \in \mathbb{R}^{d \times T}$.
Vector Field: We treat the displacement information in $\mathbf{H}_t, \mathbf{V}_t$ as a complex vector field by encoding them in the form

$$\mathbf{F}_t = \mathbf{H}_t + j\mathbf{V}_t = \begin{bmatrix} x_{11} + jy_{11} & \ldots & x_{1w} + jy_{1w} \\ & \ddots & \vdots \\ h_1 + jy_{h1} & \ldots & x_{hw} + jy_{hw} \end{bmatrix} \in \mathbb{C}^{h \times w}, \tag{3}$$

where j represents the imaginary unit vector. Then, we encode multiple fields as the columns of the feature matrix $\mathbf{X}_F \in \mathbb{C}^{(h \times w) \times T}$.
In this approach, we preserve both the movement magnitude and direction information.

Trajectory: We use the displacement vector field to estimate the trajectory of $M \leq hw$ uniformly sampled pixels. Consider the coordinates of M pixels in frame t, (x_{it}, y_{it}) where $i = 1, \ldots, M$. We arrange them as a column vector $\mathbf{r}_t \in \mathbb{R}^{2M}$ so that the x-coordinates populate the first half of the vector and the y-coordinates, the second half, $\mathbf{r}_t = [x_{1t}, \ldots, x_{Mt}, y_{1t}, \ldots, y_{Mt}]^{\top}$. Similarly, we arrange the correspondent displacements in $\mathbf{H}_t$ and $\mathbf{V}_t$ as a column vector $\mathbf{f}_t = [h_{1t}, \ldots, h_{Mt}, v_{1t}, \ldots, v_{Mt}]^{\top}$.

We then estimate the trajectory of the selected M pixels at each time t by the following equation:

$$\mathbf{r}_{t+1} = \mathbf{r}_t + \mathbf{f}_t \Delta t, \Delta t = 1. \tag{4}$$

Finally, we encode the position of all M tracked pixels across T frames as a measurement matrix $\mathbf{X}_R \in \mathbb{R}^{2M \times T}$.

2.3 Vector Representation of Words

In this work, we use a pre-trained BERT language model [4] to embed the target meanings into a vector space. BERT is a transformer-based model capable of embedding full sentences, and thus, its word vector representation are context-aware, i.e., they change according to the surrounding words.

Given a word w, we obtain its vector representation $\mathbf{w} \in \mathbb{R}^{768}$ by summing the representation vectors from the last four layers. Since BERT works with sub-word tokens, a single word might be split into several tokens. In this case, we average the representations for all tokens to represent the word w.

In this work, we use pre-trained weights on a Japanese corpus made available by the Tohoku NLP Group[1]

3 Proposed Method

In this section, we describe our proposed framework for compare the visual and semantic features of a sign in sign language. Each sign is represented by a video, i.e., visual information, and a word, i.e., semantic information. We model the distribution of videos and words by using the kernel PCA with the appropriate kernel function and obtain 3D maps for visual and semantic features. We model these 3D features into shape subspaces and compare them using our proposed metric called the *Communicability*.

The rest of the section proceeds as follows: First, we explain how to model the *visual-space* $\mathcal{S}_v$ and the *semantic-space* $\mathcal{S}_s$, and how to obtain the 3D visual and semantic maps of signs' videos and words. Then, we introduce a qualitative metric called the *Communicability*, and define it in terms of similarity between the shape subspaces modeled from the data points in the 3D visual and semantic maps.

---

[1] Model cl-tohoku/bert-base-japanese, from https://huggingface.co/cl-tohoku.

3.1   3D Visual and Semantic Maps on the Visual and Semantic Spaces

3D Visual Map: We first obtain a set of n subspaces $\{\mathcal{A}_i\}_{i=1}^n$, where each subspace models one sign video. We model these subspaces using any of the features described in Sect. 2.2.

We map the distribution of the sign subspaces by approximating their representation on the Grassmann manifold. The Grassmann manifold $\mathbb{G}(d, m)$ is the set of all m-dimensional subspaces in $\mathbb{R}^d$ Euclidean space, where a subspace $\mathcal{A}$ is regarded as a point on the Grassmann manifold. The Grassmann PCA [9], a variant of the the kernel PCA [13], allows us to approximately represent subspaces as points on the manifold.

Given the set of video subspaces, we first calculate the gram matrix $\mathbf{G}_v$ using the Grassmann kernel function $K_g()$ [9] as follows:

$$\mathbf{G}_v = \begin{bmatrix} K_g(\mathcal{A}_1, \mathcal{A}_1) & \cdots & K_g(\mathcal{A}_1, \mathcal{A}_n) \\ \vdots & \ddots & \vdots \\ K_g(\mathcal{A}_n, \mathcal{A}_1) & \cdots & K_g(\mathcal{A}_n, \mathcal{A}_n) \end{bmatrix}, \tag{5}$$

where $K_g(\mathcal{A}_i, \mathcal{A}_j) = \frac{1}{m}\sum_{k=1}^m \cos^2 \theta_k$ and θ_k is the k-th canonical angle between subspaces $\mathcal{A}_i$ and $\mathcal{A}_j$. The cosine of the canonical angle, $\cos\theta_k$, can be calculated as the k-th largest singular value σ_k of the matrix $\mathbf{A}_i^T\mathbf{A}_j$ [8], where $\mathbf{A}_i$ and $\mathbf{A}_j$ are the orthonormal basis of the subspaces $\mathcal{A}_i$ and $\mathcal{A}_j$.

Then, we calculate the projection $\eta(\mathcal{A}_i)$ of i-th data point (i.e., the subspace $\mathcal{A}_i$), $i = 1, \ldots, n$, onto the k-th principal component vector of $\mathbf{G}_v$ by using the following equation:

$$\eta_k(\mathcal{A}_i) = \sum_{j=1}^n \alpha_{kj} K_g(\mathcal{A}_i, \mathcal{A}_j), \tag{6}$$

where α_{kj} is the j-th component of the eigenvector $\boldsymbol{\alpha}_k$ corresponding to the k-th largest eigenvalue λ_k of $\mathbf{G}_v$. The vector $\boldsymbol{\alpha}_k$ is normalized to satisfy that $\lambda_k(\boldsymbol{\alpha}_k^\top \boldsymbol{\alpha}_k) = 1$.

Finally, we obtain the coordinates of the projection of $\mathcal{A}_i$ onto the m_p-dimensional *visual-space* $\mathcal{S}_v$ as $[\eta_1(\mathcal{A}_i), \eta_2(\mathcal{A}_i), \ldots, \eta_{m_p}(\mathcal{A}_i)]^\top$. For the purposes of this work, we set $m_p = 3$ to allow 3D visualization.

3D Semantic Map: Similarly, we generate a 3D Semantic map by applying kernel PCA to a set of n word vectors corresponding to the sign language videos. All the word vectors are normalized to unit norm.

First, we calculate the Gram matrix $\mathbf{G}_s$ using the simple kernel function:

$$\mathbf{G}_s = \begin{bmatrix} K_s(\mathbf{w}_1, \mathbf{w}_1) & \cdots & K_s(\mathbf{w}_1, \mathbf{w}_n) \\ \vdots & \ddots & \vdots \\ K_s(\mathbf{w}_n, \mathbf{w}_1) & \cdots & K_s(\mathbf{w}_n, \mathbf{w}_n) \end{bmatrix}, \tag{7}$$

where $K_s(\mathbf{w}_i, \mathbf{w}_j) = cos^2\theta_{ij}$ and θ_{ij} is the angle between word vectors $\mathbf{w}_i$ and $\mathbf{w}_j$.

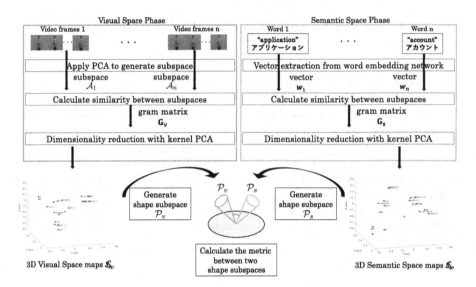

Fig. 2. Detailed framework on the calculation of Communicability C. On the visual side, we extract image features and generate a set of subspace representations. On the semantic side, we calculate word embeddings for the sign labels and obtain a set of word vectors. We independently apply the Grassmann PCA on both spaces, and project their Gram matrices $\mathbf{G}_v$ and $\mathbf{G}_s$ onto their respective principal components, obtaining the 3D mapping of videos onto the *visual-space* $\mathcal{S}_v$ and 3D mapping of words onto the *semantic-space* $\mathcal{S}_s$. Finally, we model these mappings as shape subspaces $\mathcal{P}_v$ and $\mathcal{P}_s$, and calculate $C(\mathcal{P}_v, \mathcal{P}_s)$.

Then, we calculate the projection $\beta(\mathbf{w}_i)$ onto the k-th principal component vector of $\mathbf{G}_s$ by using the following equation:

$$\beta_k(\mathbf{w}_i) = \sum_{j=1}^{n} \alpha_{kj} K_s(\mathbf{w}_i, \mathbf{w}_j), \tag{8}$$

where α_{kj} is the j-th component of the eigenvector $\boldsymbol{\alpha}_k$ corresponding to the k-th largest eigenvalue λ_k of $\mathbf{G}_s$. The vector $\boldsymbol{\alpha}_k$ is normalized to satisfy that $\lambda_k(\boldsymbol{\alpha}_k^T \boldsymbol{\alpha}_k) = 1$.

Finally, we obtain the coordinates of the projection of $\mathbf{w}_i$ onto the 3-dimensional principal component space $\mathcal{S}_s$ as $[\beta_1(\mathbf{w}_i), \beta_2(\mathbf{w}_i), \beta_3(\mathbf{w}_i)]^T$.

3.2   Calculation of Communicability Metric

The Communicability C is a metric of similarity between two structures of data points, represented by two shape subspaces, $\mathcal{P}_v$ and $\mathcal{P}_s$ [11, 16] modeled from 3D data points mapped to the *visual-space* $\mathcal{S}_v$ and the *semantic-space* $\mathcal{S}_s$ as shown in Fig. 2.

To generate the shape subspace $\mathcal{P}_v$, we first calculate the following matrix that consists of the coordinates of each 3D point and their gravity center of all points $[m_1, m_2, m_3]^T$ as follows:

$$
\mathbf{T}_v = \begin{bmatrix} \eta_1(\mathcal{A}_1) - m_1 & \eta_2(\mathcal{A}_1) - m_2 & \eta_3(\mathcal{A}_1) - m_3 \\ \eta_1(\mathcal{A}_2) - m_1 & \eta_2(\mathcal{A}_2) - m_2 & \eta_3(\mathcal{A}_2) - m_3 \\ \vdots & \vdots & \vdots \\ \eta_1(\mathcal{A}_n) - m_1 & \eta_2(\mathcal{A}_n) - m_2 & \eta_3(\mathcal{A}_n) - m_3 \end{bmatrix}, \tag{9}
$$

where $m_k = \frac{1}{n} \sum_{i=1}^{n} \eta_k(\mathcal{A}_i)$. The orthonormal basis vectors of the 3-dimensional shape subspace $\mathcal{P}_v$ in n-dimensional vector space are obtained by applying the Gram-Schmidt orthonormalization to $\mathbf{T}_v$.

Similarly, we generate the shape subspace $\mathcal{P}_s$ from a set of 3D data points mapped on the *semantic space* $\mathcal{S}_s$.

$$
\mathbf{T}_s = \begin{bmatrix} \beta_1(\mathbf{w}_1) - m_1 & \beta_2(\mathbf{w}_1) - m_2 & \beta_3(\mathbf{w}_1) - m_3 \\ \beta_1(\mathbf{w}_2) - m_1 & \beta_2(\mathbf{w}_2) - m_2 & \beta_3(\mathbf{w}_2) - m_3 \\ \vdots & \vdots & \vdots \\ \beta_1(\mathbf{w}_n) - m_1 & \beta_2(\mathbf{w}_n) - m_2 & \beta_3(\mathbf{w}_n) - m_3 \end{bmatrix}, \tag{10}
$$

where $m_k = \frac{1}{n} \sum_{i=1}^{n} \beta_k(\mathbf{w}_i)$. The orthonormal basis vectors of the 3-dimensional shape subspace $\mathcal{P}_s$ in k-dimensional vector space are obtained by applying the Gram-Schmidt orthonormalization to $\mathbf{T}_s$.

The Communicability C is defined as the following equation:

$$
C(\mathcal{P}_v, \mathcal{P}_s) = \frac{1}{3} \sum_{k=1}^{3} \cos^2 \theta_k, \tag{11}
$$

where θ_k is the k-th canonical angle between the shape subspaces $\mathcal{P}_v$ and $\mathcal{P}_s$.

The proposed framework is summarized as follows:

1. Extract visual features X_i and generate per-sign subspace representations $\{\mathcal{A}_i\}_{i=1}^{n}$.
2. Calculate the Gram matrix of subspace similarities $\mathbf{G}_v$.
3. Obtain the 3D visual map by projecting all the subspaces on to the *visual-space* $\mathcal{S}_h$ by using the Grassmann PCA with $\mathbf{G}_v$.
4. Extract the word embeddings $\{\mathbf{w}_i\}_{i=1}^{n}$ from the signs's words, and calculate the Gram matrix $\mathbf{G}_s$.
5. Obtain the 3D semantic map by projecting all the word vectors on to the *semantic-space* by using the kernel PCA with the Gram matrix $\mathbf{G}_s$.
6. Generate the respective shape subspaces $\mathcal{P}_v$ and $\mathcal{P}_s$ from the sets of 3D visual maps, respectively.
7. Calculate the Communicability C as the mean of the three canonical angles between $\mathcal{P}_v$ and $\mathcal{P}_s$.

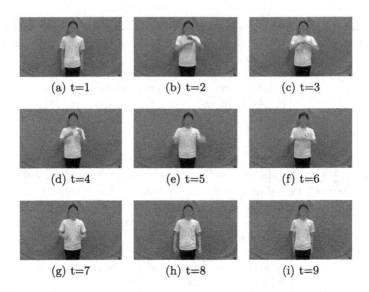

Fig. 3. Sample data from the Tsukuba New Signs Dataset, depicting a variation for the sign "internet".

3.3 Tsukuba New Signs Dataset

To demonstrate our framework and the Communicability metric C, we created a dataset on Japanese Sign Language, called the Tsukuba New Signs Dataset, as a joint effort between the University of Tsukuba and the Tsukuba University of Technology. It contains 3 repetitions of 31 selected signs, representing 19 different words. A total of 10 signs contain alternative versions, giving a total of 2304 possible sign combinations. All signs are related to information technology vocabulary, such as "internet", "URL", and "email". It has 9 participants and a total of 837 short videos. 7 out of the 9 participants are right-handed, and 2 are left-handed. 6 of the participants are males and 3 are females. Every participant has different clothes, height, and form of expressing the same sign, with varying speed and range of motion. A sample of the dataset can be seen in Fig. 3.

4   Experimental Results

We begin the experimental results section with the visualization of 3D Visual/Semantic maps generated by our framework, offering insights about the sign-semantic relationships. Then, we showcase the principal components of the subspaces generated by PCA and PCA-SFS. Finally, we report the mean Communicability C obtained from both subspace representations in our dataset.

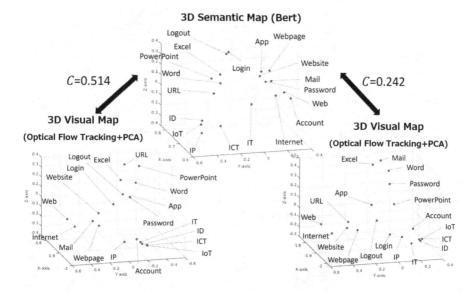

Fig. 4. Visualization of two 3D Visual maps compared to a 3D Semantic map. Using the same subspace representation, the structure of two Visual spaces is different based on which candidate signs get chosen as new signs. It's desirable to choose candidate signs that maximize the Communicability. This comparison framework is our main contribution. Labels shown in English.

4.1   Visualization of 3D Visual and Semantic Maps

In this experiment, we propose a direct visualization of Visual and Semantic spaces as a 3D point cloud map. This is useful for understanding the relationship between signs and their semantic meanings.

Figure 4 depicts a use-case of our framework. Given a Semantic map, a subspace representation and a set of candidate signs, we can chose which combination of signs better matches the Semantic map by measuring their communicability C. In a practical aspect, a map with a high communicability would support the creation of a new sign by using the information available in the neighborhood signs that have a strong relationship with their semantic meanings. In this way, when a sign is mapped to a region that is uncorrelated to its intended semantic meaning, it may indicate the need to improve the design of the sign.

4.2   Visualization of Extracted Image Features

We experimented using different visual features and subspace representations in our framework. In this section, we visualize some samples of these features, and discuss where they can be used.

As an initial baseline, we generate subspace representations using the image set without extracting visual features. The principal components obtained from both PCA and PCA-SFS can be seen in Fig. 5.

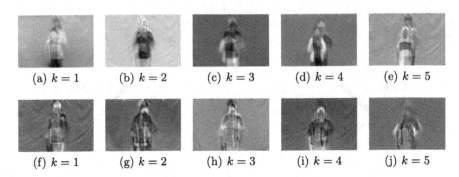

(a) $k = 1$ (b) $k = 2$ (c) $k = 3$ (d) $k = 4$ (e) $k = 5$

(f) $k = 1$ (g) $k = 2$ (h) $k = 3$ (i) $k = 4$ (j) $k = 5$

Fig. 5. k-first principal components of the "internet" sign. The top row from (a) to (e) illustrates the principal components of PCA, while the bottom row from (f) to (j) shows the principal components of PCA-SFS.

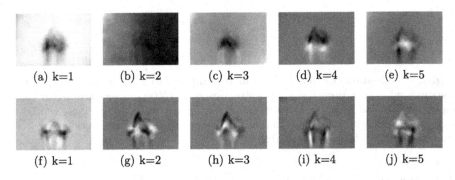

(a) k=1   (b) k=2   (c) k=3   (d) k=4   (e) k=5

(f) k=1   (g) k=2   (h) k=3   (i) k=4   (j) k=5

Fig. 6. k-first principal components of the "internet" sign. The subspaces were generated from the optical flow representation of the video frames. The top row from (a) to (e) illustrates the principal components of PCA, while the bottom row from (f) to (j) shows the principal components of PCA-SFS.

Although no prior feature extraction is performed, this subspace representation carries much information. As such, we expect these to reasonably represent the semantic aspects of the language, even if not optimally. For this reason, it can be seen here as an ablation case for analyzing different proposed features in this framework.

As movement is a key aspect of many signs, we also proposed to generate subspaces from their optical flow representations. Each of the three described procedures can be visualized in an explainable way, which is key to our framework. For example, Fig. 6 shows the principal components extracted from the optical flow's "intensity" image representation.

The optical flow information may not be able to capture detailed information at the pixel level, but it is proposed here for two different reasons: first, we believe that the general movement of signs is a key component for understanding it, being capable of giving insights on how different movements are related to different meanings. And second, it is an effective way of abstracting the

Table 1. Mean Communicability C per features and subspace representation.

Visual features	Subspace	Mean C
Images	PCA	0.330
Deep Features VGG16	PCA	0.343
Deep Features ResNet50	PCA	0.297
Optical Flow Intensity	PCA	0.303
Optical Flow Vector Field	PCA	0.294
Optical Flow Tracking	PCA	0.352
Images	PCA-SFS	0.347
Deep Features VGG16	PCA-SFS	0.312
Deep Features ResNet50	PCA-SFS	0.262
Optical Flow Intensity	PCA-SFS	0.328
Optical Flow Vector Field	PCA-SFS	0.316
Optical Flow Tracking	PCA-SFS	0.349

subjects' identities. For example, by comparing the principal components depicted in Figs. 5 and 6, we can visually see how optical flow is capable of capturing abstract information, while still being well explained. We propose that these may be useful features, especially in low-data scenarios, for capturing meaningful aspects of the language.

On the other side, we also experiment with using deep features extracted from pre-trained neural networks. Such features are known to be dense and non-trivially interpretable, but efficient in leveraging highly abstract information. Although interpretability may be hindered, we believe it's a natural and necessary approach to be considered for such a framework.

4.3 Evaluation of the Communicability Metric

In this section, we report the mean Communicability C obtained using the previously discussed representations.

To assess our proposed framework and the communicability of different subspace representations, we calculated all possible permutations of signs in our dataset, with non-repeated words, and measured C between those and a fixed Semantic map. This gave us a total of 2304 combinations. We proceeded to calculate the mean Communicability on all these combinations of signs. Results can be seen in Table 1.

Our results suggest that all the features have a similar mean Communicability, with minor deviations. This is an interesting result and indicates that perhaps they can be used interchangeably, being chosen depending on which characteristics are the most interesting in a given situation. For example, the usage of optical flow information to track pixel trajectories may not be suitable for processing fingerspelling, as pixel-level may be necessary in this context. However, it may be useful on other places where the general movement alone is able to well represent it. Using these features in an ensemble manner may be sufficient to leverage sign-meaning relationships, and support the creation process of new signs.

5   Conclusion

In this work, we proposed a framework to measure similarities between visual and semantic structures in sign languages. To do that, we first introduced two vector spaces: a 3D Visual map $\mathcal{S}_h$, which encodes the sign's visual features, and a 3D Semantic map $\mathcal{S}_e$, which encodes the sign's semantic features. We then define a qualitative metric, called the Communicability C, to measure the structural similarity between the data distributions of the shape subspaces $\mathcal{P}_h$, calculated from $\mathcal{S}_h$, and $\mathcal{P}_e$, calculated from $\mathcal{S}_e$.

We showed how we can use the 3D Visual and Semantic maps to visualize the structure of the signs distributions comparatively to their semantic structure (meanings), and how this can be helpful for designing new signs in sign languages.

We created a new dataset for Japanese Sign Language, and demonstrated our proposed framework on it.

As future research, it might be interesting to use image-text features trained in a multi-modal learning framework. For example, using image and text encoding extracted from CLIP [12] might be an interesting approach towards improving the visual-semantics mapping. It might also be interesting to experiment with using skeleton-based pose estimation features of video-frames.

Acknowledgment. This work was supported by JSPS KAKENHI Grant Number JP21K18481 and the Mext Scholarship. The authors have no competing interests to declare that are relevant to the contents of this article.

References

1. Beleza, S.R.A., Fukui, K.: Slow feature subspace for action recognition. In: Pattern Recognition. ICPR International Workshops and Challenges: Virtual Event, 10–15 January 2021, Proceedings, Part III, pp. 702–716 (2021)
2. Beleza, S.R.A., Shimomoto, E.K., Souza, L.S., Fukui, K.: Slow feature subspace: a video representation based on slow feature analysis for action recognition. Mach. Learn. Appl. **14**, 100493 (2023)
3. Deng, J., Dong, W., Socher, R., Li, L.J., Li, K., Fei-Fei, L.: Imagenet: a large-scale hierarchical image database. In: 2009 IEEE Conference on Computer Vision and Pattern Recognition, pp. 248–255 (2009)
4. Devlin, J., Chang, M.W., Lee, K., Toutanova, K.: Bert: pre-training of deep bidirectional transformers for language understanding (2019)
5. Enderle, P., Cohen, S., Scott, J.: Communicating about science and engineering practices and the nature of science: an exploration of American sign language resources. J. Res. Sci. Teach. **57**(6), 968–995 (2020)
6. Fukui, K.: Subspace Methods. Springer, Heidelberg (2020)

7. Fukui, K., Maki, A.: Difference subspace and its generalization for subspace-based methods. IEEE Trans. Pattern Anal. Mach. Intell. **37**, 2164–2177 (2015)
8. Fukui, K., Yamaguchi, O.: The kernel orthogonal mutual subspace method and its application to 3d object recognition. In: Computer Vision – ACCV 2007, pp. 467–476 (2007)
9. Hamm, J., Lee, D.: Extended grassmann kernels for subspace-based learning. In: Koller, D., Schuurmans, D., Bengio, Y., Bottou, L. (eds.) Advances in Neural Information Processing Systems, vol. 21 (2008)
10. He, K., Zhang, X., Ren, S., Sun, J.: Deep residual learning for image recognition. arXiv preprint arXiv:1512.03385 (2015)
11. Igarashi, Y., Fukui, K.: 3D object recognition based on canonical angles between shape subspaces. In: Computer Vision – ACCV 2010, pp. 580–591 (2011)
12. Radford, A., et al.: Learning transferable visual models from natural language supervision. In: Meila, M., Zhang, T. (eds.) Proceedings of the 38th International Conference on Machine Learning. Proceedings of Machine Learning Research, vol. 139, pp. 8748–8763. PMLR (2021)
13. Schölkopf, B., Smola, A., Müller, K.R.: Nonlinear principal component analysis as a kernel eigenvalue problem. Neural Comput. **10**, 1299–1319 (1998)
14. Simonyan, K., Zisserman, A.: Very deep convolutional networks for large-scale image recognition. CoRR arxiv:1409.1556 (2014)
15. Teed, Z., Deng, J.: Raft: recurrent all-pairs field transforms for optical flow (2020)
16. Yoshinuma, T., Hino, H., Fukui, K.: Personal authentication based on 3D configuration of micro-feature points on facial surface. In: Image and Video Technology - 7th Pacific-Rim Symposium, PSIVT 2015, vol. 9431, pp. 433–446 (2015)

Human Facial Age Group Recognizer Using Assisted Bottleneck Transformer Encoder

Adri Priadana⬥, Duy-Linh Nguyen⬥, Xuan-Thuy Vo⬥,
and Kanghyun Jo$^{(\boxtimes)}$⬥

Department of Electrical, Electronic and Computer Engineering, University of Ulsan,
Ulsan, South Korea
{priadana3202,ndlinh301}@mail.ulsan.ac.kr, xthuy@islab.ulsan.ac.kr,
acejo@ulsan.ac.kr

Abstract. Recognizing age from facial images has attracted considerable attention because of its wide array of applications and practical utilities. These include support for advertising platforms, access control, forensic objectives, and video surveillance. Efficient facial age recognition for these varied purposes is essential, necessitating smooth operation on low-cost devices or, at the very least, on a CPU to minimize implementation costs. This work proposes a lightweight CNN architecture efficiently integrated with a transformer encoder to perform facial age group recognition. An assisted bottleneck transformer encoder (ABTE) is introduced to enhance the feature extractor, generating only a few parameters and requiring low computation. As a result, the proposed architecture can achieve competitive performance on the two benchmark datasets, UTK-Face and FG-NET. Moreover, this recognizer can attain real-time speed at 147 and 136 frames per second (FPS) with a single and double utilization of the ABTE, respectively, on a CPU device with Intel Core i7-9750H 2.6 GHz and 20 GB of RAM while maintaining its performance.

Keywords: Age Group Recognition · Assisted Bottleneck Transformer · Convolutional Neural Network (CNN) · Facial Age Recognition · Transformer Encoder

1 Introduction

Age estimation from facial images has garnered significant interest due to its broad range of applications and practical uses, including support for advertising platforms [16,22], access control [7], forensic applications and video surveillance [2]. In advertising applications, it can assist platforms in audience segmentation and delivering relevant ads and products. For example, in some countries, vending machines can suggest beverages like alcohol or tobacco based on facial age estimation, ensuring compliance with age restrictions for specific items. In forensic applications, it can be used to determine victim or criminal profiles.

© The Author(s), under exclusive license to Springer Nature Singapore Pte Ltd. 2024
G. Irie et al. (Eds.): IW-FCV 2024, CCIS 2143, pp. 108–121, 2024.
https://doi.org/10.1007/978-981-97-4249-3_9

In the context of surveillance and access control, it can be employed to restrict access to specific areas for individuals of particular age groups. Age recognition involves automatically predicting a person's exact age [26] or categorizing them based on face into age groups [13,16] such as child, teen, adult, and old.

As a popular deep learning technique, Convolutional Neural Networks (CNNs) have demonstrated remarkable performance in age estimation based on facial images. Many studies [1,5,11,20,25] have utilized and proposed deeper CNN architectures to enhance their performance. However, it frequently yields architectures with a significant parameter count, potentially causing operational inefficiency. This limitation can hinder implementation on platforms or machines that utilize low-cost or CPU devices. Hence, the need for efficient architectures with reduced computational demands is evident.

Recently, several efforts have been directed towards designing CNN architectures that are more efficient [16,18] and faster [15], generating few parameters and low operation for enhanced overall efficiency and speed. Moreover, the Vision Transformer (ViT) technique [6] and its variant, inspired by the Transformer architecture [24], initially designed for machine translation tasks, has become dominant and proven to offer high classification performance in computer vision tasks. However, Transformer-based architectures often prioritize accuracy over computational efficiency, which is critical for operation on resource-constrained devices, such as CPUs or mobile platforms. By combining CNN architectures with the Transformer encoder in an efficient manner, it is possible to create models with fewer parameters and reduced computational demands while maintaining or even improving performance. Therefore, it can be satisfactorily performed on a lower-cost device and contribute more to procurement cost reduction.

This work proposes a lightweight CNN architecture integrated efficiently with a transformer encoder to perform a facial age group recognition task. A novel assisted bottleneck transformer encoder, improved from [14], is introduced to enhance the feature extractor used in the recognizer. It generates few parameters and low computation. As a result, the age group recognizer can operate more efficiently and rapidly when identifying age groups based on facial features. To summarize, the notable contributions of the present study include the following:

1. A lightweight CNN architecture integrated with a transformer encoder to perform age group recognition based on facial features. It demonstrates highly competitive performance on UTKFace [29] and FG-NET [10] benchmark datasets.
2. A novel assisted bottleneck transformer encoder (ABTE), inspired by [14], is offered as a strategy to capture spatial relationship representations within the feature maps. The enhancement significantly improves the quality of feature maps, leading to enhanced recognition performance.
3. A facial age group recognizer capable of swift operation on a CPU device. It can achieve real-time performance at 147 and 136 frames per second (FPS) with one and two times assisted bottleneck transformer encoder, respectively, on a CPU device with Intel Core i7-9750H 2.6 GHz and 20 GB of RAM.

2   Related Work

Due to the exceptional capabilities of Convolutional Neural Networks (CNNs), the majority of studies in recent years have adopted this approach for age recognition based on human faces. For example, Li et al. [11] introduced BridgeNet, which incorporates local regressors in learning continuity-aware weights for age recognition from facial images. Badr et al. [1] adopted ResNet-34 as a foundation to develop a system called landmark ratios with task importance (LRTI) for age estimation. Another researcher [5] presented a feature constraint reinforcement network (FCRN) for leveraging the influence of gender constraints on age estimation. Meanwhile, Shin et al. [20] utilized the VGG architecture as an encoder, introducing a novel moving window regression algorithm designed to estimate facial age precisely. Wang et al. [25] adopted the ResNet34 and proposed a meta-set learning (MSL) approach for exploiting the unfairness of face-aging datasets.

There has been a trend in developing lightweight CNN architectures to consider efficient computation applied for mobile or CPU-based devices. Savchenko [18] employed MobileNet for estimating facial age in mobile applications, producing a model with 3.5 million parameters. In a different study [16], an efficient CNN architecture was introduced, boasting a mere four hundred thousand parameters. This architecture comprises two branches of feature extractors boosted by an innovative attention mechanism. In the most recent advancement [15], a novel efficient CNN architecture is presented, integrating a lightweight backbone featuring a combination of different mini-feature map levels stimulated by a slight attention block. This network can perform real-time facial age recognition on CPU devices.

3   The Proposed Method

The proposed CNN model is designed with proficient feature extraction and classification phases, as illustrated in Fig. 1. This architecture stands out for its efficiency, boasting a mere 446,468 parameters and approximately 24 million floating-point operations (MFLOPs).

3.1   The Feature Extraction Module

Following a common optimal design approach, the proposed seamless feature extraction strategically utilizes a shallow convolution layer, each employing a 3×3 filter size for precision and effectiveness. It initiates with 16 channels, followed by increments to 32 and, ultimately, to 64. This deliberate design intention aims to minimize the number of parameters and computational burden within the architecture. Additionally, the architecture utilizes batch normalization (BN) after each convolution operation, followed by sigmoid linear units (SiLU) activation, to address gradient-related issues. It incorporates three max-pooling operations as pivotal for downsampling the feature map effectively. These operations

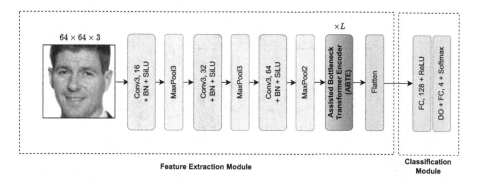

Fig. 1. The proposed lightweight CNN architecture integrated efficiently with a assisted bottleneck transformer encoder to perform facial age group recognition. Conv3 indicates 3×3 convolution operation with stride 1. MaxPool3 and Maxpool2 denote 3×3 and 2×2 max pooling operations with stride 2, respectively. BN, DO, and FC are batch normalization, dropout, and fully connected layers.

employ two 3×3 and one 2×2 kernel sizes, each with strides set at 2. The careful selection of these parameters facilitates a systematic reduction in the spatial dimensions of the feature map, contributing to enhanced efficiency in subsequent processing stages. The downsampling mechanism is strategically positioned to optimize the overall computational load, ensuring the architecture's responsiveness to real-time demands. It is important to note that opting for fewer convolution layers can result in a shallower network, which impacts its performance. In response, we introduce an assisted bottleneck transformer encoder (ABTE) to capture spatial relationship representations within the feature maps by applying self-attention as the core operation, enhancing recognition performance. The proposed architecture situates this encoder between the final max-pooling and flattening operation in the layer sequence.

3.2   The Assisted Bottleneck Transformer Encoder (ABTE)

Nowadays, Vision Transformer (ViT) [6] with self-attention has shown impressive performance in image classification tasks. The self-attention mechanism allows the model to capture relationships between different parts of the input image using a global context. It makes the architecture particularly effective for tasks that require understanding long-range relationships within an image. ViT has achieved state-of-the-art performance on various image classification benchmarks. It attains competitive accuracy with fewer parameters. However, the computational efficiency of ViT still becomes a concern because the self-attention mechanism has a quadratic complexity regarding the input sequence length. Many researchers have proposed various techniques to address these issues. This work proposes an assisted bottleneck transformer encoder (ABTE). It consists of an efficient transformer encoder, assisted by an enhanced efficient convolution module shown in Fig. 2. Following the efficient transformer encoder in [14], a

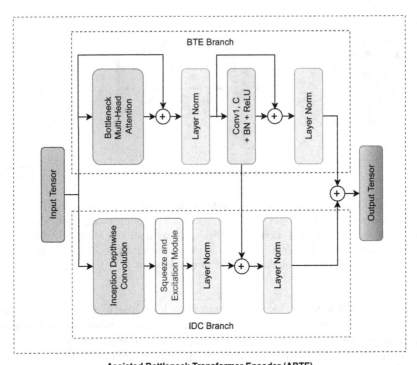

Fig. 2. The proposed assisted transformer encoder consists of an efficient transformer encoder, assisted by an efficient inception depthwise convolution module.

bottleneck transformer encoder (BTE) is applied to enhance the computational efficiency of the encoder. BTE employs a reduction channel denoted as r and a multi-head mechanism with $NumHead$ to generate a more streamlined input tensor of dimensions $H \times W \times ((\frac{C}{NumHead})/r)$ before transforming it into a query ($\mathbf{Q}$), key ($\mathbf{K}$), and value ($\mathbf{V}$). The implementation of scaled dot-product attention, as depicted in Fig. 3, is similar to the structure of the original transformer encoder and is defined by the following definition:

$$\text{Attention}(\mathbf{Q}, \mathbf{K}, \mathbf{V}) = \text{softmax}\left(\frac{\mathbf{Q}\mathbf{K}^{\mathrm{T}}}{\sqrt{d_k}}\right)\mathbf{V}, \tag{1}$$

where T is a transpose matrix operation and d_k indicates a scaling factor to control the softmax temperature. Improved from BTE, we apply an inception depthwise convolution (IDC) module from InceptionNeXt [28] in parallel structure to assist the BTE. This module decomposes multi-kernel depthwise convolution into four parallel branches along the channel dimension. It splits the input feature map $\mathbf{X}$ into four elements $[\mathbf{X_1}, \mathbf{X_2}, \mathbf{X_3}, \mathbf{X_4}]$ based on channel axes and applies small square kernels (3×3), two orthogonal band kernels (11×1 and

1×11), and an identity mapping, respectively, defined as follows:

$$\text{IDC}(\mathbf{X}) = \text{Concat}[\text{DW}_{3\times3}(\mathbf{X_1}), \text{DW}_{1\times11}(\mathbf{X_2}), \text{DW}_{11\times1}(\mathbf{X_3}), \mathbf{X_4}], \qquad (2)$$

where Concat and $\text{DW}_{m\times n}$ indicate concatenation and depthwise convolution operations with $m \times n$ kernel size, respectively. IDC module function to preserve performance by efficiently applying multi-scale and large-kernel-based convolution. We also utilize squeeze-and-excitation (SE) [9] module and layer normalization to enhance and normalize the feature maps resulting from the IDC module. Figure 4 shows the IDC and SE modules in more detail. In this work, ABTE performs interaction or connection between BTE and IDC branches to share information by adding the feature map resulting from the convolution operation in the BTE branch to the IDC branch using an element-wise addition operation. The proposed encoder also uses this mechanism to allocate a more significant portion to BTE in extracting information. Based on the model analysis results described in the ablation study subsection in the next section, BTE contributes more performance than IDC when performing individually. Moreover, this ABTE combines the BTE and IDC branches by applying an element-wise addition operation in the last layer.

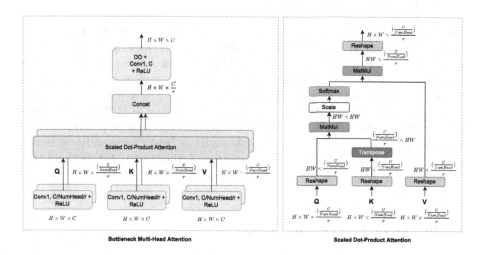

Fig. 3. The detail design of the bottleneck multi-head attention [14].

3.3 The Classification Module

In the final phase, the features of the instance face coming from the backbone phase are inputted into the classification module to calculate the probability for individual group classes. This component assists in determining whether the instance input belongs to which class individual. It consists of two multi-layer perceptron layers, following the classification module from [15].

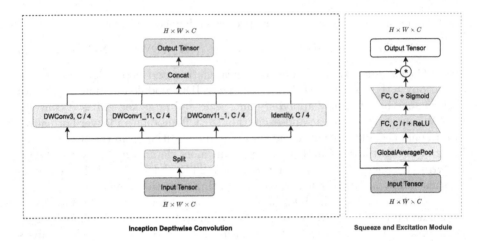

Fig. 4. The inception depthwise convolution (IDC) and squeeze and excitation (SE) modules.

4 Implementation Settings

Following the previous setting [15], the proposed architecture undergoes training on UTKFace and FG-NET datasets with an initial learning rate of 1×10^{-3} with a batch size of 256 trained over 300 epochs and Adam optimizer. In this configuration, the reduce learning rate mechanism is implemented to modulate the learning rate based on changes in validation accuracy. The rate is decreased by a factor of 0.75 after 20 epochs of stagnant accuracy, contributing to adaptive learning in the training process. It utilizes an Nvidia GeForce GTX 1080Ti featuring GPUs with 11 GB of memory through the Tensorflow and Keras framework. An Intel Core i7-9750H CPU running at 2.6 GHz with 20 GB of RAM is employed to evaluate the FPS for both the proposed architecture and the recognizer.

5 Experiments and Results

5.1 Evaluation on Datasets

UTKFace. This dataset is a widely utilized resource in the field of computer vision, particularly for research on age and gender estimation. It comprises 23,708 facial images annotated with valuable information such as age, gender, and ethnicity. Notably, the age range covered by the dataset spans from 0 to 116 years, and it incorporates diverse images with variations in pose, illumination, expression, and other factors. This work applies two configurations for the dataset as an evaluation. Following the prior studies [3,4], this dataset is divided into training (80%) and testing (20%) sets for the first configuration, denoted as Setting I. The evaluation of the offered architecture's performance involves the calculation

Table 1. The results of the assessment on the UTKFace dataset under Setting I.

Architectures	Params (M)	Mean Absolute Error ↓
CORAL [4]	21.11	5.47
Savchenko [18]	3.50	5.44
LRTI [1]	21.11	4.55
Berg et al. [3]	23.60	5.14
FCRN [5]	23.60	4.47
2PDG [16]	0.46	4.44
AggerCPU [15]	0.49	4.38
MWR (based on VGG16) [20]	39.79	4.37
MSL (based on ResNet34) [25]	21.11	**4.31**
Proposed $(L = 2)$	**0.45**	**4.37**

Table 2. The results of the assessment on the UTKFace dataset under Setting II.

Architectures	Params (M)	Validation Accuracy ↑ (%)
ResNet50 [8]	23.60	88.43
InceptionNeXt-N16 [28]	0.36	90.08
2PDG [16]	0.46	90.12
VGG16 [21]	39.79	90.34
InceptionNeXt-N24 [28]	0.80	90.81
AggerCPU [15]	0.46	90.90
BTE [14]	0.57	91.08
Proposed $(L = 2)$	**0.45**	**91.33**

of the mean absolute error (MAE) on the testing set within this configuration. The proposed architecture, comprising only around 450,000 parameters, achieves the second-best performance with the mean absolute error (MAE) of 4.37, as shown in Table 1. The result is marginally lower by only 0.06 compared to the top-performing model [25]. The proposed architecture proves significantly more efficient than [25] considering the number of parameters.

Similarly, following the methodology of a prior study [15], we divided the dataset into training (90%) and testing (10%) sets for the second configuration, identified as Setting II. The class target comprises four age groups: children, teens, adults, and old. Validation accuracy (VA) is utilized in evaluating the proposed architecture in this setting. The offered architecture achieves the VA of 91.33%, surpassing the state-of-the-art, as shown in Table 2. This experiment also compares our proposed model with InceptionNeXt [28] model, -N16 and -N24, which means applied 16 and 24 as initial embedding dimensions, respectively, of InceptionNeXt T model configuration and used only the last stage, to generate

Table 3. The results of the assessment on the FG-NET dataset.

Architectures	Params (M)	Mean Absolute Error ↓
DRF based on VGG16 [19]	14.00	3.41
DAG-VGG16 [23]	24.00	3.08
ADPF [26]	14.00	2.86
2PDG [16]	0.46	2.75
MSFCL [27]	15.00	2.71
AggerCPU [15]	0.49	2.71
BridgeNet [11]	120.00	**2.56**
MWR based on VGG16 [20]	40.00	**2.23**
Proposed $(L = 2)$	**0.45**	**2.67**

the InceptionNeXt [28] variant that has a comparable number of parameters with our proposed model.

FG-NET. This dataset comprises 1,002 facial images collected from 82 subjects, featuring variations in pose, expression, and illumination. Following established settings [12,19], the dataset employs k-fold cross-validation and leave-one-person-out (LOPO) methodologies. In each fold, facial images from one subject are reserved for testing, while the images of the remaining subjects are used for training. This process is repeated 82 times, with each subject applied as a training set, corresponding to the 82 subjects in the dataset. Given the diverse distribution of instances among individuals in the dataset, the number of instances for both training and testing sets exhibits variability across each fold. It is important to note that this evaluation process computes results based on average values using the mean absolute error (MAE) metric. The proposed architecture achieves the MAE of 2,67, attaining the third-best performance, deviating by 0.44 and 0.11 from the best [20] and second-best [11], respectively, as shown in Table 3. However, the parameters of the proposed CNN model are significantly lower than both.

5.2 Model Analysis

This section investigates the contribution of each component of the proposed module to the recognition performance on the UTKFace dataset. Firstly, we perform an ablation study by removing each module from the proposed model and then comparing its performance to reveal the influence of the existence of each module. Secondly, channel reduction analysis examines the optimal channel reduction value on the BTE. Lastly, we analyzed how many times the ABTE (the number of L) should be applied to produce the best performance.

Table 4. Ablation study of the proposed architecture with $L = 2$ on the UTKFace dataset under Setting II.

Baseline	IDC Branch	BTE Branch	Connection between IDC and BTE	MFLOPs	Params	Validation Accuracy (%)
✓				22.15	426,084	90.25
✓	✓			22.33	428,452	90.60
✓		✓		23.95	443,844	90.73
✓	✓	✓		24.13	446,212	90.99
✓	✓	✓	✓	**24.18**	**446,468**	**91.33**

Table 5. Channel reduction analysis of the proposed ABTE with $L = 2$ on the UTK-Face dataset under Setting II.

Value of Reduction r	MFLOPs	Params	Validation Accuracy (%)
1	27.38	471,332	90.94
2	25.15	454,756	91.12
4	**24.18**	**446,468**	**91.33**
8	23.74	442,324	90.86

Ablation Study. Table 4 shows the reported results of the ablation study based on validation accuracy metrics. The report shows that using IDC and BTE modules individually can escalate performance based on accuracy by 0.35% and 0.48%, respectively, from the baseline based on accuracy. Combining IDC and BTE modules can upgrade performance by 0.74% from the baseline. Moreover, combining IDC and BTE modules with a connection can enhance performance by 1.08% from the baseline. These results confirm that the IDC module can assist the BTE in providing higher performance.

Channel Reduction Analysis. This study explores the impact of different channel reduction values on the performance of the proposed ABTE in facial recognition. The findings, as presented in Table 5, suggest that channel reduction values of one or eight do not yield significant performance improvements. The optimal recognition performance is achieved by the proposed ABTE when employing a channel reduction value of four. In this configuration, the model attains the highest validation accuracy, reaching 91.33%, while maintaining a moderate parameter count of 446,468 and a computational load of 24.18 MFLOPs.

Table 6. Number of L analysis on the UTKFace dataset under Setting II.

Number of L	MFLOPs	Params	Validation Accuracy (%)	Age (FPS)	Face + Age (FPS)
1	23.17	436,276	91.07	**335.99**	**147.53**
2	24.18	446,468	**91.33**	285.67	135.48
3	25.20	456,660	90.85	250.43	127.52

Table 7. The efficiency of runtime, as measured on the UTKFace dataset with the same CPU configuration, is specifically evaluated under Setting II.

Architectures	MFLOPs	Params	Validation Accuracy (%)	Age (FPS)	Face + Age (FPS)
VGG16 [21]	2,290	39,782,722	90.34	42.40	36.28
ResNet50 [8]	633	23,595,908	88.43	54.21	44.54
InceptionNeXt-N24 [28]	1,391	796,564	90.81	57.44	46.87
InceptionNeXt-N16 [28]	625	359,012	90.08	89.09	65.99
Proposed ($L = 2$)	**24**	**446,468**	**91.33**	**285.67**	**135.48**
AggerCPU [15]	41	486,822	90.90	330.66	144.49
BTE [14]	25	556,028	91.08	335.41	146.25
Proposed ($L = 1$)	**23**	**436,276**	**91.07**	**335.99**	**147.53**

Number of Transformer Encoder Analysis. This part analyzes the most effective number of L (how many times applying ABTE) on the proposed model regarding recognition performance. Table 6 reveals that using ABTE one time can make the model run faster. However, the proposed model with two times ABTE achieves the highest validation accuracy in this study. This setting can deliver a validation accuracy of 91.33% with 446,468 parameters and 24.18 MFLOPs at a sufficient speed based on FPS. Age (FPS) denotes the speed of age group recognition, and Face + Age (FPS) indicates the speed of age group recognition integrated with face detection [17].

5.3   Runtime Efficiency

The practical implementation prioritizes a recognizer capable of real-time performance on cost-effective devices, ideally on a CPU setup, to reduce expenses during system procurement. The offered architecture, featuring two times of ABTE ($L = 2$), demonstrates real-time efficiency on a CPU with a modest parameter count of 446,468 and a computational load of 24.18 MFLOPs. It excels in classification tasks, achieving a speed of 286 and 135 frames per second for age group recognition and integrated with face detection [17] (Face + Age), respectively, as detailed in Table 7.

This work also presents a recognizer that performs ABTE only once ($L = 1$) utilizing 436,276 parameters and 23.17 MFLOPs to provide faster recognition with a performance that still surpasses the current state-of-the-art models. The proposed recognizer, leveraging a single ABTE operation, emerges as the fastest among competitors, achieving a remarkable speed of 336 frames per second for age group recognition (Age) and 148 frames per second for age group recognition integrated with face detection [17] (Face + Age). The recognition outcomes of the proposed model are illustrated in Fig. 5, where green, yellow, blue, and red bounding boxes signify the faces of children, teens, adults, and old, respectively.

Fig. 5. The example of the recognition results of the proposed recognizer.

6   Conclusion

Addressing the need for improved feature extraction in age group recognition from human faces, this work introduces the concept of ABTE. By incorporating a bottleneck mechanism and employing inception depthwise convolution (IDC) in parallel structure, the proposed encoder efficiently enhances the transformer encoder's capabilities while maintaining a minimal parameter count and low computational requirements. Demonstrating competitive performance on UTK-Face and FG-NET datasets, the proposed architecture doubles as a recognizer, achieving real-time speeds of 147 and 136 FPS with a single and double utilization of the assisted bottleneck transformer encoder, respectively. As part of future endeavors, the proposed facial age group recognizer will be extended to operate on more cost-effective devices, further supporting applications in Robot Vision.

Acknowledgment. This result was supported by "Regional Innovation Strategy (RIS)" through the National Research Foundation of Korea(NRF) funded by the Ministry of Education(MOE)(2021RIS-003).

References

1. Badr, M.M., Elbasiony, R.M., Sarhan, A.M.: Lrti: landmark ratios with task importance toward accurate age estimation using deep neural networks. Neural Comput. Appl. **34**(12), 9647–9659 (2022)
2. Becerra-Riera, F., Morales-González, A., Méndez-Vázquez, H.: A survey on facial soft biometrics for video surveillance and forensic applications. Artif. Intell. Rev. **52**(2), 1155–1187 (2019)
3. Berg, A., Oskarsson, M., O'Connor, M.: Deep ordinal regression with label diversity. In: 2020 25th International Conference on Pattern Recognition (ICPR), pp. 2740–2747. IEEE (2021)
4. Cao, W., Mirjalili, V., Raschka, S.: Rank consistent ordinal regression for neural networks with application to age estimation. Pattern Recogn. Lett. **140**, 325–331 (2020)
5. Chen, G., Peng, J., Wang, L., Yuan, H., Huang, Y.: Feature constraint reinforcement based age estimation. Multimedia Tools Appl. **82**(11), 17033–17054 (2023)
6. Dosovitskiy, A., et al.: An image is worth 16×16 words: transformers for image recognition at scale. arXiv preprint arXiv:2010.11929 (2020)
7. Gupta, S.K., Nain, N.: Single attribute and multi attribute facial gender and age estimation. Multimedia Tools Appl. **82**(1), 1289–1311 (2023)
8. He, K., Zhang, X., Ren, S., Sun, J.: Deep residual learning for image recognition. In: 2016 IEEE Conference on Computer Vision and Pattern Recognition (CVPR), pp. 770–778. IEEE (2016)
9. Hu, J., Shen, L., Albanie, S., Sun, G., Wu, E.: Squeeze-and-excitation networks. IEEE Trans. Pattern Anal. Mach. Intell. **42**(8), 2011–2023 (2019)
10. Lanitis, A., Taylor, C.J., Cootes, T.F.: Toward automatic simulation of aging effects on face images. IEEE Trans. Pattern Anal. Mach. Intell. **24**(4), 442–455 (2002)
11. Li, W., Lu, J., Feng, J., Xu, C., Zhou, J., Tian, Q.: Bridgenet: a continuity-aware probabilistic network for age estimation. In: Proceedings of the IEEE/CVF Conference on Computer Vision and Pattern Recognition, pp. 1145–1154 (2019)
12. Liu, H., Lu, J., Feng, J., Zhou, J.: Label-sensitive deep metric learning for facial age estimation. IEEE Trans. Inf. Forensics Secur. **13**(2), 292–305 (2017)
13. Mai, A.T., Nguyen, D.H., Dang, T.T.: Real-time age-group and accurate age prediction with bagging and transfer learning. In: 2021 International Conference on Decision Aid Sciences and Application (DASA), pp. 27–32. IEEE (2021)
14. Priadana, A., Putro, M.D., An, J., Nguyen, D.L., Vo, X.T., Jo, K.H.: Gender recognizer based on human face using cnn and bottleneck transformer encoder. In: 2023 International Workshop on Intelligent Systems (IWIS), pp. 1–6. IEEE (2023)
15. Priadana, A., Putro, M.D., Nguyen, D.L., Vo, X.T., Jo, K.H.: Age group recognizer based on human face supporting smart digital advertising platforms. In: 2023 IEEE 32nd International Symposium on Industrial Electronics (ISIE), pp. 1–7. IEEE (2023)

16. Priadana, A., Putro, M.D., Vo, X.T., Jo, K.H.: An efficient face-based age group detector on a CPU using two perspective convolution with attention modules. In: 2022 International Conference on Multimedia Analysis and Pattern Recognition (MAPR), pp. 1–6. IEEE (2022)

17. Putro, M.D., Nguyen, D.L., Jo, K.H.: Lightweight convolutional neural network for real-time face detector on CPU supporting interaction of service robot. In: 2020 13th International Conference on Human System Interaction (HSI), pp. 94–99. IEEE (2020)

18. Savchenko, A.V.: Efficient facial representations for age, gender and identity recognition in organizing photo albums using multi-output convnet. PeerJ Comput. Sci. **5**, e197 (2019)

19. Shen, W., Guo, Y., Wang, Y., Zhao, K., Wang, B., Yuille, A.: Deep differentiable random forests for age estimation. IEEE Trans. Pattern Anal. Mach. Intell. **43**(2), 404–419 (2019)

20. Shin, N.H., Lee, S.H., Kim, C.S.: Moving window regression: a novel approach to ordinal regression. In: Proceedings of the IEEE/CVF Conference on Computer Vision and Pattern Recognition, pp. 18760–18769 (2022)

21. Simonyan, K., Zisserman, A.: Very deep convolutional networks for large-scale image recognition. arXiv preprint arXiv:1409.1556 (2014)

22. Suman, S., Urolagin, S.: Age gender and sentiment analysis to select relevant advertisements for a user using CNN. In: Jacob, I.J., Shanmugam, S.K., Bestak, R. (eds.) Data Intelligence and Cognitive Informatics: Proceedings of ICDICI 2021, pp. 543–557. Springer, Heidelberg (2022). https://doi.org/10.1007/978-981-16-6460-1_42

23. Taheri, S., Toygar, Ö.: On the use of dag-cnn architecture for age estimation with multi-stage features fusion. Neurocomputing **329**, 300–310 (2019)

24. Vaswani, A., et al.: Attention is all you need. Adv. Neural Inf. Process. Syst. **30** (2017)

25. Wang, C., Li, Z., Mo, X., Tang, X., Liu, H.: Exploiting unfairness with meta-set learning for chronological age estimation. IEEE Trans. Inf. Forensics Secur. **18**, 5678–5690 (2023)

26. Wang, H., Sanchez, V., Li, C.T.: Improving face-based age estimation with attention-based dynamic patch fusion. IEEE Trans. Image Process. **31**, 1084–1096 (2022)

27. Xia, M., Zhang, X., Weng, L., Xu, Y., et al.: Multi-stage feature constraints learning for age estimation. IEEE Trans. Inf. Forensics Secur. **15**, 2417–2428 (2020)

28. Yu, W., Zhou, P., Yan, S., Wang, X.: Inceptionnext: when inception meets convnext. arXiv preprint arXiv:2303.16900 (2023)

29. Zhang, Z., Song, Y., Qi, H.: Age progression/regression by conditional adversarial autoencoder. In: 2017 IEEE Conference on Computer Vision and Pattern Recognition (CVPR), pp. 4352–4360. IEEE (2017)

Efficient Detection Model Using Feature Maximizer Convolution for Edge Computing

Jehwan Choi⬤, Youlkyeong Lee⬤, and Kanghyun Jo$^{(\boxtimes)}$⬤

Department of Electrical, Electronic and Computer Engineering, University of Ulsan, Ulsan, South Korea
{cjh1897,yklee00815,acejo}@ulsan.ac.kr
http://islab.ulsan.ac.kr

Abstract. Deep learning is heavily influenced by the quantity and quality of data. Moreover, most deep learning models are developed and tested on servers equipped with high-performance GPUs and large memory capacities. However, for practical application in industrial fields or real-world scenarios, optimal performance must be achieved using limited resources and equipment. Therefore, this paper proposes the FMC (Feature Maximizer Convolution). This method aims to enhance performance with limited data by extracting as diverse features as possible and assigning more weight to crucial feature maps, which are then passed on to the next layer. Additionally, to ensure real-time performance on limited hardware, DSC (Depthwise Separable Convolution) is employed instead of standard convolution to reduce computational load. The approach is applied to deep learning models on datasets such as COCO, VisDrone, VOC, and xView, and its performance is compared with existing networks. Inference experiments are also conducted on the edge device Odroid H3+. The proposed network shows a 30% average reduction in the number of parameters compared to existing networks and a 5% increase in inference speed. On the Odroid H3+, the inference speed improved by an average of 2.5 ms, resulting in an increase from 19 FPS to 20 FPS.

Keywords: Computer vision · deep learning · edge computing · lightweight

1 Introduction

As deep learning rapidly evolves, it has begun to be applied across various industries. A typical deep learning process involves extracting features from data through Convolution operations, computing these features to produce probabilistic outcomes, and then determining the most probable formula by comparing these outcomes with the Ground Truth. This process signifies that the deep learning process is influenced by the accuracy and characteristics of the data.

© The Author(s), under exclusive license to Springer Nature Singapore Pte Ltd. 2024
G. Irie et al. (Eds.): IW-FCV 2024, CCIS 2143, pp. 122–133, 2024.
https://doi.org/10.1007/978-981-97-4249-3_10

Consequently, in recent years, many countries have been focusing on acquiring and constructing data, and research into learning methods such as Data Augmentation [1,2], semi-supervised learning [3], and Few-shot learning [4] that yield good results with limited data has been extensive. Moreover, from the perspective of computer vision, object detection, which deals with various datasets (COCO [5], VOC [6], xView [7], VisDrone [8], etc.), is a significant challenge. These datasets include objects of various appearances and sizes, from those that are clearly visible to those that are hardly discernible due to high altitude or distance. Therefore, it is common to use pre-trained models on various datasets and apply transfer learning according to specific conditions and tasks. However, to enhance the performance of transfer learning, the pre-trained model itself must also be high-performing. To ensure good performance in any task, a network capable of effectively extracting features of various sizes and shapes is necessary. Faster R-CNN improved accuracy by quickly generating candidate regions for objects using the RPN (Region Proposal Network) [9], while the SSD (Single Shot MultiBox Detector) [10] and YOLO (You Only Look Once) [11–13] series demonstrated good performance on objects of various sizes using feature maps of different scales. In this paper, we propose the FMC (Feature Maximizer Convolution) module, which maximizes the diversity of limited features and effectively extracts features through computations among feature maps, utilizing superior feature maps.

As mentioned earlier, extracting features effectively from data and the quantity and quality of data are crucial for enhancing the performance of deep learning. However, the amount and quality of data are expected to increase over time, leading to improved learning outcomes. Yet, deploying these data-driven models in real-world applications presents another challenge. This is because inference using servers with high-performance GPUs and large memory capacities is difficult to apply in actual industries. In reality, devices such as smartphones, autonomous vehicles, and CCTV cameras do not have servers equipped with high-performance GPUs or large memory capacities. Therefore, to use deep learning efficiently in real-world scenarios, it is necessary to achieve good performance with limited power and hardware specifications. This task is referred to as Edge Computing or Edge AI. With the growing trend of edge computing, there is an increasing need for lightweight yet powerful models that can operate efficiently on edge devices. Recent research focuses on enhancing the practicality and efficiency of deep learning technologies in Edge Computing and Edge AI. For example, Lian et al. (2023) [14] proposed a new method for testing and strengthening the vulnerability of deep learning models in Edge Computing environments. This suggests that Edge AI can play a significant role in enhancing reliability and efficiency in real-world settings. Additionally, Zeng et al. (2023) [15] developed a new task scheduling algorithm for efficiently allocating large and dynamic workloads on Edge Computing nodes. These studies contribute significantly to improving the efficiency and performance of Edge AI. In this paper, we propose applying DSC (Depthwise Separable Convolution) instead of standard convolution operations to the main modules of the Object Detection model

YOLOv5, reducing computational load for efficient operation on Edge Devices. We also introduce experimental results showing the improved performance of the proposed model implemented on the Edge Device Odroid H3+ compared to existing models. The main contributions of this article are summarized as follows:

- We propose the FMC (Feature Maximizer Convolution) module to extract as diverse features as possible from limited feature maps and to use only the most effective features.
- We implement model lightening by applying DSC (Depthwise Separable Convolution) instead of standard convolution operations in the main modules of YOLOv5.
- We conduct experiments and analyze the performance changes compared to existing models using the Edge device Odroid H3+.

2   Related Work

2.1   Edge Computing

Edge Computing (EC) is a technology that can overcome the limitations of Cloud Computing (CC). The typical limitations of cloud computing include: a. the latency involved in sending data to a server capable of computation, processing it, and then receiving the results, b. the increased costs and network congestion due to the high bandwidth required to transfer large volumes of data to the cloud, and c. cyber security issues that can arise during data transmission. The core technologies of EC to solve these problems include: a. real-time response by processing data immediately at the site of data generation, b. distributed processing that reduces system load and increases efficiency by distributing data across multiple edge devices, and c. enhanced security by processing data on-site, thereby protecting against data breaches and hacking. In terms of recent research in computer vision, Guanchu Wang et al. (2022) [16] demonstrated a system called BED (oBject detection system for Edge Devices), which creates a small DNN (Deep Neural Network) model of 300kb through an end-to-end pipeline of model training, quantization, synthesis, and deployment. Shihan Liu et al. (2023) [17] achieved results of over 30FPS on Nvidia jetson AGX Xavier using Data Augmentation with Mosaic and an Efficient Decoupled Head. This paper also improves results by efficiently adjusting the feature map.

2.2   Efficient Feature Extraction

Efficient feature extraction is a crucial research topic in the fields of deep learning and computer vision, particularly in real-time image processing and object detection on edge devices with limited computing resources. Recent studies focus on maintaining high performance while reducing model complexity. Notably, in the MobileNet series by Andrew G. Howard et al. (2017) [18], techniques like DSC were used to reduce the number of parameters and increase computational efficiency. Tsung-Yi Lin et al. (2017) proposed the FPN [19], extracting feature maps of various scales to achieve significant results in detecting small objects. The reason for applying these methods is to achieve good performance and fast inference speed in limited environments and data. Reducing computational load while maintaining object detection performance can speed up inference, ensuring real-time processing. Conversely, improving object detection performance while maintaining computational load allows for more effective application of models in real life and industry. The DSC used in this paper can be seen in Fig. 1.

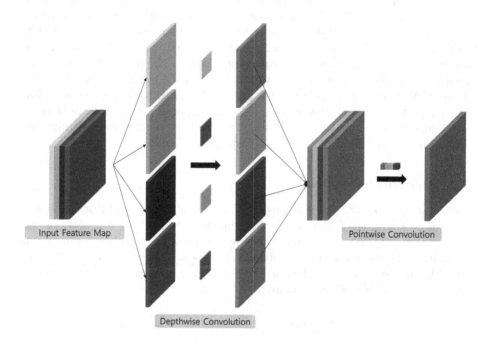

Fig. 1. The Computational Process of Depthwise Separable Convolution (DSC)

3   Proposed Method

In this paper, YOLOv5 is used as the base model. Instead of the core C3 module of YOLOv5, the FMC module is used to extract more diverse features from the feature map. To reduce computational load, DSC (Depthwise Separable Convolution) is employed instead of standard convolution operations.

3.1   Feature Maximizer Convolution

In this paper, the C3 module used in YOLOv5, which consists of multiple layers of convolution operations, is discussed. The C3 module is based on the CSP

(Cross Stage Partial) structure. This structure divides the input feature map into two parts, applies convolution operations intensively to one part, and then merges them back together. However, most of these operations are carried out using 1×1 convolutions. While 1×1 convolutions have the advantage of combining features across channels and reducing dimensions with less computational load, they are limited in capturing spatial information. To address this, the FMC is proposed in this paper. Like the C3 module, the FMC also consists of two branches. The first branch applies a 3×3 convolution to the input feature map to compensate for the shortcomings of 1×1 convolutions, but uses DSC to reduce computational load. It does not reduce the channel dimension to retain as diverse features as possible. Then, the feature map processed by 3×3 DSC and the input feature map are concatenated, followed by a 1×1 convolution to adjust the weights for extracting important features. The second branch applies another 3×3 DSC to the feature map processed by the first branch's 3×3 DSC. Finally, the first and second branches are concatenated to output the final feature map. This configuration is designed to generate as diverse feature maps as possible and extract features that effectively enhance performance with limited data. The C3 and FMC modules are illustrated in Fig. 2.

3.2 Lightweight Strategy

The existing YOLOv5 pipeline consists of a sequence of C3 and Conv modules. As seen in Fig. 2, the C3 module predominantly applies 1×1 convolutions. As shown in Eq. (1), 1×1 convolution is the operation with the least number of parameters among standard convolution operations. Therefore, as indicated in Eq. (2), applying DSC with the same kernel size increases the number of parameters by the number of input channels.

$$k * k * c_{in} * c_{out} = 1 * 1 * c_{in} * c_{out} = c_{in} * c_{out} \tag{1}$$

$$k * k * c_{in} + 1 * 1 * c_{in} * c_{out} = 1 * 1 * c_{in} + 1 * 1 * c_{in} * c_{out} = c_{in}(1 + c_{out}) \tag{2}$$

k represents the kernel size, while c_{in} and c_{out} denote the number of input and output channels, respectively. As per the above formula, the number of parameters for the C3 and FMC modules can be calculated as shown in Eqs. 3 and 4, respectively.

$$c_{out}(c_{in} + 2.25 * c_{out}) \tag{3}$$

$$c_{in}(18 + c_{in} + 1.5 * c_{out}) \tag{4}$$

To compare Eqs. (3) and (4), let's assume that the number of input and output channels are the same ($c_{in} = c_{out} = C$). As a result, the number of parameters for the C3 module is $3.25C^2$, and for the FMC module, it is $2.5C^2 + 18C$. Upon comparison, it is evident that the C3 module has more parameters when $C > 24$, and the FMC module has more when $C < 24$. Since most deep learning networks typically have more than 32 channels, it can be inferred that the FMC module has fewer parameters than the C3 module.

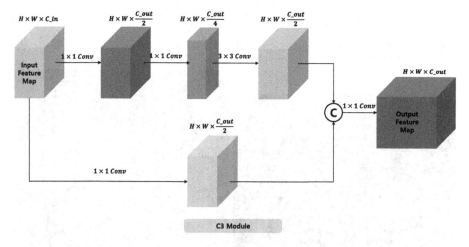

(a) C3 module used in YOLOv5

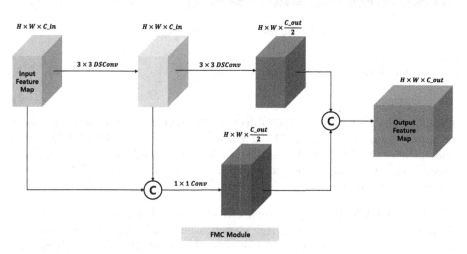

(b) Proposed FMC (Feature Maximizer Convolution) module

Fig. 2. Images of the computational processes of the C3 and FMC modules

The Conv module involves standard convolution operations followed by batch normalization and an activation function. However, in YOLOv5, most Conv operations have a kernel size of 3. If k is applied as 3 in Eqs. (1) and (2), standard convolution is calculated as shown in Eq. (5), and DSC is calculated as shown in Eq. (6), indicating that DSC has fewer parameters. Therefore, in this paper, all Conv modules in the YOLOv5 Backbone have been modified to DSC modules for model lightening.

$$k * k * c_{\text{in}} * c_{\text{out}} = 3 * 3 * c_{\text{in}} * c_{\text{out}} = 9 * c_{\text{in}} * c_{\text{out}} \qquad (5)$$

$$k * k * c_{\text{in}} + 1 * 1 * c_{\text{in}} * c_{\text{out}} = 3 * 3 * c_{\text{in}} + 1 * 1 * c_{\text{in}} * c_{\text{out}} = c_{\text{in}}(9 + c_{\text{out}}) \quad (6)$$

Fig. 3. The result image of xView dataset

4   Experiment

4.1   Dataset

COCO: The COCO (Common Objects in Context) dataset contains a variety of objects found in everyday life. It consists of approximately 200,000 images and includes 80 different classes. COCO is widely used for various computer vision tasks such as object detection, segmentation, and keypoint detection, and is characterized by its complex backgrounds and a range of object sizes.

VOC: The PASCAL VOC (Visual Object Classes) dataset is a benchmark dataset for object detection, image classification, and object segmentation. It includes 20 object categories and has evolved through the VOC challenge. Its main features and challenges are the variety of object sizes, overlapping objects, and diverse poses and backgrounds.

VisDrone: The VisDrone dataset is based on images and videos captured by drones for object detection and tracking. It includes high-resolution images and videos shot in various urban, rural, and coastal areas. The main challenges of this dataset are small objects captured from high altitudes, varying lighting conditions, and blur caused by camera movement (Figs. 4, 5, 6 and 7).

xView: The xView dataset is for object detection based on satellite imagery. It contains over one million object instances and more than 60 object categories. Providing data captured in various geographical locations through high-resolution satellite imagery, its main challenges are detecting small objects and handling objects of various scales.

Fig. 4. The result of big size human, YOLOv5n (Left) Proposed method (Right)

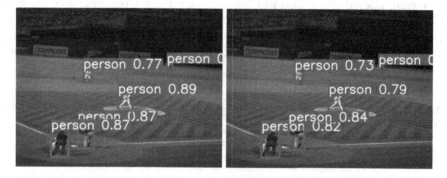

Fig. 5. The result of small size human, YOLOv5n (Left) Proposed method (Right)

Fig. 6. The result of various object, YOLOv5n (Left) Proposed method (Right)

Fig. 7. The result of many objects, YOLOv5n (Left) Proposed method (Right)

4.2   Evaluation Metric

For the evaluation metric, we measure the number of parameters, which affects the computational speed, and FLOPS (Floating Point Operations Per Second). Additionally, to assess the object detection accuracy of the generated model, we set mAP50 and mAP50-95 as indicators. Finally, to determine if the conditions are suitable for operation on Edge Devices, we compare the size of the generated model (in Mb) and the inference speed.

Table 1. Comparison of YOLOv5 and Proposed Network Performance Results on Four Datasets

Dataset	Result	Model		
		YOLOv5 nano	Proposed nano	Change
COCO	Parameters	1,867,405	1,309,673	−29.87%
	GFLOPS	4.5	3.2	−28.89%
	mAP50	40.9	35.3	−5.6%
	mAP50-95	24	20.2	−3.8%
VOC	Parameters	1,786,225	1,228,493	−31.22%
	GFLOPS	4.2	2.9	−30.95%
	mAP50	64.2	62.5	−1.7%
	mAP50-95	37.5	35.7	−1.8%
VisDrone	Parameters	1,772,695	1,214,963	−31.46%
	GFLOPS	4.2	2.9	−30.95%
	mAP50	18.2	16.1	−2.1%
	mAP50-95	8.77	7.11	−1.66%
xView	Parameters	1,840,345	1,282,613	−30.31%
	GFLOPS	4.4	3.1	−29.55%
	mAP50	0.141	0.143	+0.002%
	mAP50-95	0.0465	0.0474	+0.0009%

4.3   Experimental Setting

All training was conducted under the same environment and conditions, and the model training was carried out on a server equipped with an Intel Core i9-9960X,

Nvidia RTX 2080 Ti x 4EA, and 125.5 GB of memory. The best-performing results out of 100 epochs were used for all models. Model performance evaluation was conducted on both the training server and the edge device, Odroid H3+.

Table 2. Comparison of YOLOv5 and Proposed Network Performance Results on Four Datasets

Dataset	Result	Model		
		YOLOv5 nano	Proposed nano	Change
COCO	Model size(Mb)	3.82	2.74	−28.27%
	Inference time(ms/image)	55.21	53.12	−3.79%
VOC	Model size(Mb)	3.68	2.61	−29.08%
	Inference time(ms/image)	50.94	47.67	−6.42%
VisDrone	Model size(Mb)	3.65	2.57	−29.59%
	Inference time(ms/image)	42.38	40.42	−4.62%
xView	Model size(Mb)	3.87	2.79	−27.91%
	Inference time(ms/image)	62.28	59.62	−4.27%

4.4 Result

The experiment used four datasets on two networks: the original YOLOv5 nano model and a modified nano model with our proposed modules. Results for Parameters, GFLOPS, mAP50, and mAP50-95 are presented in Table 1. Our findings indicate a reduction in the number of parameters and computational load by about 30% for the proposed model compared to the original. However, this reduction also led to a decrease in object detection accuracy, varying from 1.66% to 5.6%. In the case of the xView dataset, the detection accuracy is increased. As shown in Fig. 3, considering that the images are satellite photos and most objects in the dataset's 60+ classes are concentrated in buildings, this appears to be an exceptional result with significantly reduced accuracy.

The results of inference on the Odroid H3+ using the same models and datasets as in Table 1 can be found in Table 2. Parameters, GFLOPS, and accuracy are omitted as they showed no significant deviation from Table 1, and the comparison focuses on model size and average inference speed per image. With the reduction in the number of parameters and GFLOPS, the model size also decreased by an average of about 29%. The inference time for the original model was already fast, showing an average performance of about 19 FPS with 50–60 ms. Although the proposed model showed a relatively small reduction in inference time compared to the decrease in parameters and model size, it demonstrated a performance improvement of about 1 FPS, averaging 20 FPS with 45–55 ms.

5   Conclusion

This paper investigates methods to achieve good performance with limited environments and data, and studies the impact of applying a deep learning model with the proposed methods on edge devices in real-world settings. We propose the FMC (Feature Maximizer Convolution) to extract as diverse features as possible from the given data, ensuring that features beneficial for performance enhancement are passed on to the next layer. FMC is applied in place of the C3 module in YOLOv5. Additionally, to maintain performance while reducing computational load, DSC (Depthwise Separable Convolution) is applied. DSC replaces the Conv module in YOLOv5, significantly reducing computational load while maintaining similar performance to 3×3 convolutions. The original YOLOv5-trained model's nano version averages 3.755 MB, but the model trained with the proposed method averages 2.7 MB, a reduction of about 28.1%. On the edge device Odroid H3+, the inference time also improved by an average of 2.5 ms. Although the object detection accuracy decreased by 6.6% based on mAP 50, the actual output results were not significantly different from the original model. Therefore, the application of FMC and DSC proposed in this paper has been proven effective for object detection in edge computing.

Acknowledgements. This result was supported by "Regional Innovation Strategy (RIS)" through the National Research Foundation of Korea(NRF) funded by the Ministry of Education(MOE)(2021RIS-003).

References

1. Perez, L., Wang, J.: The effectiveness of data augmentation in image classification using deep learning. CoRR arxiv:1712.04621 (2017)
2. Shorten, C., Khoshgoftaar, T.M.: A survey on image data augmentation for deep learning. J. Big Data **6**(1), 1–48 (2019). https://doi.org/10.1186/s40537-019-0197-0citeas
3. Sohn, K., et al.: Fixmatch: simplifying semi-supervised learning with consistency and confidence. arXiv preprint arXiv:2001.07685 (2020)
4. Sun, Q., Liu, Y., Chua, T., Schiele, B.: Meta-transfer learning for few-shot learning. In: IEEE Conference on Computer Vision and Pattern Recognition, CVPR 2019, Long Beach, CA, USA, 16–20 June 2019, pp. 403–412. Computer Vision Foundation/IEEE (2019)
5. Lin, T.-Y., et al.: Microsoft COCO: common objects in context. In: Fleet, D., Pajdla, T., Schiele, B., Tuytelaars, T. (eds.) ECCV 2014. LNCS, vol. 8693, pp. 740–755. Springer, Cham (2014). https://doi.org/10.1007/978-3-319-10602-1_48
6. Everingham, M., Van Gool, L., Williams, C.K., Winn, J., Zisserman, A.: The pascal visual object classes (voc) challenge. Int. J. Comput. Vision **88**, 303–308 (2009). https://www.microsoft.com/en-us/research/publication/the-pascal-visual-object-classes-voc-challenge/
7. Lam, D., et al.: xview: objects in context in overhead imagery (2018)
8. Zhu, P., et al.: Detection and tracking meet drones challenge. IEEE Trans. Pattern Anal. Mach. Intell. **44**(11), 7380–7399 (2021)

9. Ren, S., He, K., Girshick, R., Sun, J.: Faster r-cnn: towards real-time object detection with region proposal networks (2016)
10. Liu, W., et al.: SSD: single shot multibox detector. In: Leibe, B., Matas, J., Sebe, N., Welling, M. (eds.) ECCV 2016. LNCS, vol. 9905, pp. 21–37. Springer, Cham (2016). https://doi.org/10.1007/978-3-319-46448-0_2
11. Redmon, J., Divvala, S., Girshick, R., Farhadi, A.: You only look once: unified, real-time object detection (2015). https://arxiv.org/abs/1506.02640
12. Redmon, J., Farhadi, A.: Yolov3: an incremental improvement (2018). https://arxiv.org/abs/1804.02767
13. Jocher, G., et al.: ultralytics/yolov5: v7.0 - YOLOv5 SOTA Realtime Instance Segmentation (2022). https://doi.org/10.5281/zenodo.7347926
14. Lian, Z., Tian, F.: Deepsi: a sensitive-driven testing samples generation method of whitebox cnn model for edge computing. Tsinghua Sci. Technol. 29(3), 784–794 (2024)
15. Zeng, L., Liu, Q., Shen, S., Liu, X.: Improved double deep q network-based task scheduling algorithm in edge computing for makespan optimization. Tsinghua Sci. Technol. 29(3), 806–817 (2024)
16. Wang, G., et al.: Bed: a real-time object detection system for edge devices (2022)
17. Liu, S., Zha, J., Sun, J., Li, Z., Wang, G.: Edgeyolo: an edge-real-time object detector (2023)
18. Howard, A.G., et al.: Mobilenets: efficient convolutional neural networks for mobile vision applications. arXiv preprint arXiv:1704.04861 (2017)
19. Lin, T.-Y., Dollar, P., Girshick, R., He, K., Hariharan, B., Belongie, S.: Feature pyramid networks for object detection (2017)

Spatial Attention Network with High Frequency Component for Facial Expression Recognition

Seongmin Kim and Kanghyun Jo$^{(\boxtimes)}$

Department of Electrical, Electronic and Computer Engineering, University of Ulsan, Ulsan, Korea
asdfhdsa1234@mail.ulsan.ac.kr, acejo@ulsan.ac.kr

Abstract. Indeed, object classification is one of the most advanced fields in computer vision today, and there are ongoing efforts to classify datasets used in real-world industries, beyond just public experimental data. Facial expression recognition is indeed one of the most prominent examples of such tasks, closely related to the Human-Computer Interaction (HCI) industry. Unfortunately, facial expression classification tasks are often more challenging compared to classifying public benchmark datasets. This paper aimed to address these challenges by mimicking human facial expression recognition processes and proposed an attention network that leverages high-frequency components to recognize expressions, inspired by how humans perceive emotions. The presented attention module vectorizes the singular value matrices of the query (the high-frequency component of the 1-channel input tensor) and the key (the 1-channel input tensor) and prepares a pairwise cross-correlation matrix by performing an outer product between them to create the attention scores. The correlation matrix is transformed into an attention score by passing through a convolution layer and sigmoid function. After that, it is used for element-wise multiplication with the value (input tensor) to perform attention. This paper conducted experiments using the ResNet18 and MobileNetV2 models along with the FER2013, JAFFE, and CK+ datasets to demonstrate the significant impact of the proposed attention module. The experimental results in this study have demonstrated the effectiveness of the proposed attention network and suggest its potential significance in real-time facial expression recognition tasks.

Keywords: Facial Expression Recognition · Spatial Attention Network · Spatial Frequency-domain Filtering

1 Introduction

Image recognition (or classification) task is the most basic and important research theme of computer vision. Efforts to employ artificial intelligence

This result was supported by "Regional Innovation Strategy (RIS)" through the National Research Foundation of Korea(NRF) funded by the Ministry of Education(MOE)(2021RIS-003).

© The Author(s), under exclusive license to Springer Nature Singapore Pte Ltd. 2024
G. Irie et al. (Eds.): IW-FCV 2024, CCIS 2143, pp. 134–147, 2024.
https://doi.org/10.1007/978-981-97-4249-3_11

for object recognition in images commenced in the 20th century and, as of 2024, have demonstrated superior accuracy compared to human performance [2,3,6,8,11,23,26]. In recent times, endeavors have been undertaken to classify data from diverse industries beyond publicly available experimental datasets, such as CIFAR-100 [12]. The representative example is facial expression recognition [4,5,7,17,22]. As the demand for Human-Computer Interaction (HCI) continues to rise, the comprehension and recognition of facial expressions have emerged as pivotal tasks for facilitating more natural interactions. However, upon examination of the graph depicted in Fig. 1 below, it becomes evident that the task of recognizing facial expressions using Convolutional Neural Network (CNN) is notably challenging when contrasted with public experimental images.

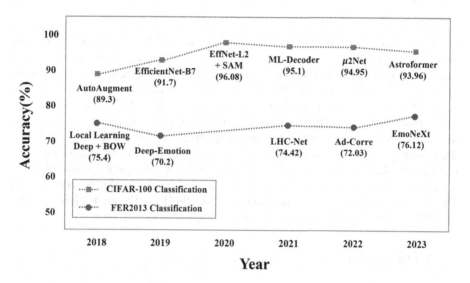

Fig. 1. The graphs of illustration depict the comparison of difficulty between CIFAR-100 classification and FER2013 classification.

On the contrary, humans can discern facial expressions significantly more effortlessly than neural networks. Because the human can recognize the tiny differences in facial expressions. This distinction signifies the variance between the orbicularis oculi muscle, orbicularis oris muscle [19], and alterations in the regions of the eyes, nose, and mouth. Hence, using just the difference of pixel values is insufficient to describe the distinction. According to this paper [20], humans rely meaningfully on the high-frequency components of facial images when classifying facial expressions.

The high frequency component of the face, Fig. 2(b), contains detailed information that is effective in recognizing human facial expressions, such as eyes, nose, mouth, and wrinkles. This image processing result can support the hypothesis that humans use not only spatial domain information but also frequency

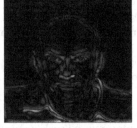

(a) Original Image   (b) High Frequency Component   (c) Low Frequency Component

Fig. 2. This illustration represents the spatial frequency domain filtering result. The face image is from CelebA dataset [13] and converted RGB to grayscale.

domain information to classify facial expressions. This paper conducted an extensive exploration of various research approaches aimed at adapting the human facial expression recognition process to CNN. Although there were many approaches to induce the model to utilize specific information intensively, the most effective one was the attention mechanism [4,18,22,27]. The attention mechanism encourages the CNN to enhance the elements in its feature map tensor on the part highly relevant to the query suggested by the network designer. This study presents a simple attention network to emphasize the high-frequency components in the feature map, aiming to enhance the performance of CNN in facial expression recognition tasks. It also demonstrates the effectiveness of the proposed network by evaluating its contributions through FER2013 [9], JAFFE [15,16], and CK+ [14] datasets.

2   Related Work

The most crucial aspect of an Attention network lies in comprehending the relationship between the query and the key. Various methodologies have been studied to grasp this relationship. They can be categorized into the following two groups.

- **Explicit Method:** The method for calculating the relationship through direct mathematical operations (e.g. Dot Product) after converting query and key data into a more manageable form such as Vector Embedding.
- **Implicit Method:** The method for calculating the relationship through an additional neural network after concatenating (or Stacking) query and key data.

Multi-head Attention [27], the most effective attention method in machine learning, is a representative example of the explicit method. Multi-head Attention [27] generates attention scores by performing a dot product operation between specific query vectors and all preprocessed key data, following the transformation of the vector-level embedded data into query, key, and value vectors. The explicit method can represent the reason for the relation between the query and keys. Because it uses a mathematical approach to measure the correspondence. However, during vector-level embedding, the purity of the original data is decreased. The human-made mathematical operation, such as dot product, has a limit to represent the complex relationship. So explicit method has low representation capacity. The well-known implicit methods are Seq2Seq+Attention [1] and Bottleneck Attention Module (BAM) [18]. Seq2Seq+Attention [1] is designed for natural language processing. This method treats the decoder state of the previous step to query and the encoder hidden state of all steps to key. It measures the attention score with additional neural networks. BAM [18] also uses additional neural networks to calculate attention scores about the channel axis and spatial axis. This attention network is designed to perform channel attention and spatial attention within a deep convolutional neural network. Because of using nonlinear neural networks, the implicit method has a high representation capacity for relationships. However, the relationship-finding process is only dependent on many hidden layers of the neural network. So, the attention network cannot produce any evidence of a relationship. Therefore, the results of the implicit method cannot be fully trusted. This paper has designed an attention network by appropriately combining both explicit and implicit methods to selectively leverage the advantages of each.

3   Proposed Method

In this chapter, a detailed description of the proposed attention network designed to accentuate the high frequency components of the face within the feature map is provided. In this paper, the feature map inputted into the attention network before creating query and key was compressed into a single-channel through pointwise convolution. This is because, as can be observed in Fig. 3, the high-frequency components are quite similar across each channel, and thus, there is no need to handle a multi-channel tensor while increasing computational complexity.

   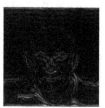

(a) 3-channel Color Image   (b) R-channel HFC   (c) G-channel HFC   (d) B-channel HFC

Fig. 3. The high pass filtering results of the 3-channel color image. HFC denotes the high frequency component.

Therefore, before performing attention, this paper undergoes pre-processing of the input tensor ($\mathbf{x} \in \mathbb{R}^{c \times n \times n}$) as shown in Eq. 1, where it is compressed through pointwise convolution.

$$\tilde{\mathbf{x}} = \mathcal{C}_{1 \times 1}(\mathbf{x}) \tag{1}$$

where $\mathcal{C}_{1 \times 1}(\cdot)$ denotes pointwise convolution. For the query used in performing attention, the high frequency component ($\mathbf{h}_{\tilde{x}}$) of a 1-channel tensor ($\tilde{\mathbf{x}} \in \mathbb{R}^{n \times n}$) was selected. To obtain $\mathbf{h}_{\tilde{x}}$, $\tilde{\mathbf{x}}$ is first mapped into the frequency domain through Fourier transformation ($\mathfrak{F}$) as described in Eq. 2, followed by the execution of a high pass filtering process.

$$\tilde{\mathbf{x}}_h = \mathfrak{F}\{\tilde{\mathbf{x}}\}\mathcal{H}_{HPF} \tag{2}$$

where $\mathcal{H}_{HPF}$ is high pass filter on frequency domain. Subsequently, by employing the inverse Fourier transformation ($\mathfrak{F}^{-1}$) as in Eq. 3, $\mathbf{h}_{\tilde{x}}$ is obtained by remapping it back into the spatial domain.

$$\mathbf{h}_{\tilde{x}} = \mathfrak{F}^{-1}\{\tilde{\mathbf{x}}_h\} \tag{3}$$

It was decided to use $\tilde{\mathbf{x}}$ as the key data. This paper attempted to obtain evidence for the relationship between query and key through mathematical operations, similar to explicit methods. In this case, the Kronecker product between two tensors(e.g. $\mathbf{A} \in \mathbb{R}^{m \times n}$, $\mathbf{B} \in \mathbb{R}^{p \times q}$) is computed as shown in Eq. 4.

$$\mathbf{A} \otimes \mathbf{B} = \begin{bmatrix} a_{11}b_{11} & a_{11}b_{12} & \cdots & a_{11}b_{1q} & \cdots & a_{1n}b_{11} & a_{1n}b_{12} & \cdots & a_{1n}b_{1q} \\ \vdots & \vdots & \ddots & \vdots & \ddots & \vdots & \vdots & \ddots & \vdots \\ a_{11}b_{p1} & a_{11}b_{p2} & \cdots & a_{11}b_{pq} & \cdots & a_{1n}b_{p1} & a_{1n}b_{p2} & \cdots & a_{1n}b_{pq} \\ \vdots & \vdots & \ddots & \vdots & \ddots & \vdots & \vdots & \ddots & \vdots \\ a_{m1}b_{11} & a_{m1}b_{12} & \cdots & a_{m1}b_{1q} & \cdots & a_{mn}b_{11} & a_{mn}b_{12} & \cdots & a_{mn}b_{1q} \\ \vdots & \vdots & \ddots & \vdots & \ddots & \vdots & \vdots & \ddots & \vdots \\ a_{m1}b_{p1} & a_{m1}b_{p2} & \cdots & a_{m1}b_{pq} & \cdots & a_{mn}b_{p1} & a_{mn}b_{p2} & \cdots & a_{mn}b_{pq} \end{bmatrix} \tag{4}$$

However, the Kronecker product between tensors required a significant amount of memory. To perform the Kronecker product between tensors with a batch size of 32, 1-channel, and a resolution of 112×112, a memory requirement of 600.25GB was needed. Therefore, this paper decided to approximate the process of creating the pairwise cross-correlation matrix. To achieve a reliable approximation, an investigation was conducted to determine which characteristics could effectively represent the unique spatial information of the images. Various characteristics were explored, and among them, this paper chose to utilize the singular values of the images. When performing Singular Value Decomposition (SVD) on an image, it can be represented as a combination of rank-1 matrices ($\mathbf{uv}^T$), obtained through the outer product of the left singular vector ($\mathbf{u}$) and the right singular vector ($\mathbf{v}$), as shown in Eq. 5.

$$\mathbf{I} = \mathbf{U}\boldsymbol{\Sigma}_I\mathbf{V}^T = \sigma_1^I\mathbf{u}_1\mathbf{v}_1^T + \sigma_2^I\mathbf{u}_2\mathbf{v}_2^T + \cdots \sigma_n^I\mathbf{u}_n\mathbf{v}_n^T \tag{5}$$

In this context, the vectors are considered as column vectors, and σ_1 represents the largest singular value. The singular values $(\sigma_1 \cdots \sigma_n)$ of an image $(\mathbf{I} \in \mathbb{R}^{n \times n})$ represent the contributions of each of the constituent elements $(\mathbf{u}\mathbf{v}^{\mathrm{T}})$ that make up the image. Therefore, the singular values of an image can be interpreted as important intrinsic information for representing the image in the spatial domain. The Fig. 4 below has been included to aid in understanding the Singular Value Decomposition (SVD) of images.

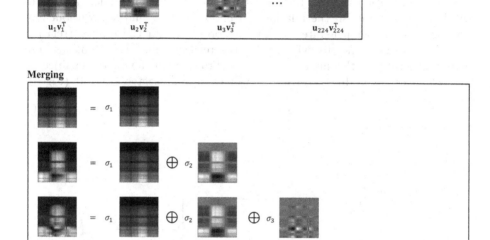

Fig. 4. The example process of singular value decomposition on grayscale image.

In this paper, the characteristics of the singular values of images are utilized to create a pairwise cross-correlation matrix by first flattening singular value matrices of the high frequency component $(\boldsymbol{\Sigma}_h)$ and the compressed tensor $(\boldsymbol{\Sigma}_x)$, as shown in Eq. 6 and 7, and then applying vector outer products as depicted in Eq. 8. Where $\mathrm{vec}(\cdot)$ is vectorization operation.

$$\boldsymbol{\Sigma}'_h = \mathrm{vec}(\boldsymbol{\Sigma}_h) \tag{6}$$

$$\boldsymbol{\Sigma}'_x = \mathrm{vec}(\boldsymbol{\Sigma}_x) \tag{7}$$

$$\boldsymbol{\Sigma}'_h \otimes \boldsymbol{\Sigma}'_x = \boldsymbol{\Sigma}'_h \boldsymbol{\Sigma}'^{\mathrm{T}}_x = \begin{bmatrix} \sigma_1^h \sigma_1^x & \sigma_1^h \sigma_2^x & \cdots & \sigma_1^h \sigma_n^x \\ \sigma_2^h \sigma_1^x & \sigma_2^h \sigma_2^x & \cdots & \sigma_2^h \sigma_n^x \\ \vdots & \vdots & \ddots & \vdots \\ \sigma_n^h \sigma_1^x & \sigma_n^h \sigma_2^x & \cdots & \sigma_n^h \sigma_n^x \end{bmatrix} \tag{8}$$

The generated cross-correlation matrix is not used directly but rather passes through a convolution layer and sigmoid function ($f_\sigma(\cdot)$) as shown in Eq. 9.

$$\mathbf{a} = f_\sigma(\mathcal{C}_{7\times7}(\boldsymbol{\Sigma}'_h \otimes \boldsymbol{\Sigma}'_x)) \tag{9}$$

The reason for passing through the convolution layer is to leverage the implicit method's approach, which involves generating an attention score matrix from the cross-correlation matrix. In contrast to the traditional implicit approach, which seeks to establish the relationship between query and key without any evidence, this paper generates attention scores through the cross-correlation matrix, providing concrete evidence for the relationship. The attention score matrix, generated in this manner, undergoes broadcasting and is then subjected to an elementwise product ($\odot$) with the value $\mathbf{x}$, as represented in Eq. 10 (Fig. 5).

$$\mathbf{x}^{\mathrm{refined}} = \mathbf{a} \odot \mathbf{x} \tag{10}$$

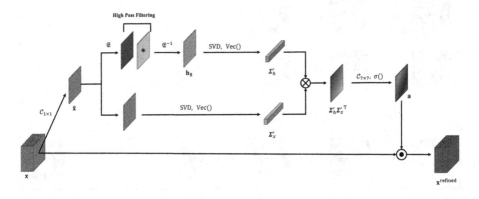

Fig. 5. This illustration depicts entire process of proposed attention network.

4   Experiment

4.1   Dataset

FER2013: FER (Facial Expression Recognition) 2013 [9] is a dataset that comprises grayscale images representing seven basic emotions: angry, disgust, fear, happy, sad, surprise, and neutral. Each image in the dataset has a resolution of 48×48 pixels, and it consists of a substantial collection of 35,887 images in total. The dataset contains facial expression data representing various races, ages, and genders. Figure 6 below illustrates examples from the FER2013 dataset. In this experiment, 28,707 images were used as the training dataset, and 7,180 images were allocated for the test dataset. For all training using this dataset, a batch size of 32 was configured.

Fig. 6. The example images of FER2013 dataset.

JAFFE: JAFFE (Japanese Female Facial Expression) [15, 16] is a dataset consisting of a total of 213 grayscale images. The dataset uses the following 7 basic emotions as class labels: Angry, Disgust, Fear, Happy, Neutral, Sad, and Surprise. In this experiment, 158 images were used as the training dataset, and 55 images were designated for the test dataset. For all training utilizing this dataset, a batch size of 8 was configured. The Fig. 7 below represents examples from the JAFFE dataset.

Fig. 7. The example images of JAFFE dataset.

CK+: The CK+ (Extended Cohn-Kanade) dataset [14] comprises 593 sequences and 123 subjects. In this experiment, the last 3 frames of each sequence were used, resulting in a total of 981 images being utilized. This dataset employs 7 emotions (anger, contempt, disgust, fear, happy, sadness, and surprise) as class labels. In this paper, 735 images were allocated for the training dataset, while 246 images were designated for the test dataset out of the 981 total images. A batch size of 16 was utilized for all training using this dataset. Figure 8 below provides examples from the CK+ dataset.

Fig. 8. The example images of CK+ dataset.

4.2   Experimental Setup

Experimental Equipment: The experiment was conducted using the equipment listed below.

– **CPU:** Intel(R) Core(TM) i9-10900X CPU @ 3.70 GHz (1EA)
– **GPU:** NVIDIA Geforce RTX 3090 24 GB VRAM (4EA)
– **RAM:** Samsung DDR4 32 GB (6EA)

Train Setup: The models used in this experiment are ResNet18 [10] and MobileNetV2 [24]. In this experiment, all training images were upscaled to a resolution of 224 × 224 pixels before use. The loss function employed in this experiment was cross-entropy, and the number of training epochs was fixed at 100 for all experiments. The initial learning rate was assigned differently for each model. ResNet18 was set to an initial learning rate of 1e–4 for all datasets, including FER2013, JAFFE, and CK+. On the other hand, MobileNetV2 was configured with a learning rate of 1e–4 for FER2013 and 1e–3 for both JAFFE and CK+. The learning rate scheduler employed the "ReduceLROnPlateau" provided by PyTorch [21]. It updated the learning rate to 0.3 times its previous value when the validation loss did not decrease continuously for 5 epochs. ResNet18 has five big convolution block (64-channel, 64-channel, 128-channel, 256-channel, and

512-channel). The attention modules are attached between each big convolution block. It means that 4 modules are used for ResNet18. MobileNetV2 has 8 big convolution block (32-channel, 16-channel, 24-channel, 32-channel, 64-channel, 96-channel, 160-channel, and 320-channel) and one pointwise convolution (1280-channel). The attention modules are attached between each big convolution block. In other words, the 7 attention modules are used for MobileNetV2.

4.3 Ablation Study

In this section, the results of the verification of whether high frequency components can indeed provide meaningful assistance in performing attention are presented. The control groups were prepared as follows: (1) Vanilla ResNet18, (2) when the query of the attention module was provided with the high frequency component (HFC), (3) when the query of the attention module was provided with the low frequency component (LFC), (4) when both HFC and LFC were used as separate queries, and (5) when the additional cross-correlation matrix between LFC and HFC was used. In the case of control group (4), both the cross-correlation matrices obtained by using HFC and LFC as queries were concatenated, and the resulting matrix passed through a convolutional layer. Control group (5) further concatenated the cross-correlation matrix obtained by providing HFC as the query and LFC as the key to the result of control group (4). Subsequently, the combined matrix was passed through a convolutional layer. The following Table 1 presents the results of the ablation study. Looking at Table 1, it is evident that providing LFC as the query results in a decrease in performance compared to the vanilla model. When both LFC and HFC were used simultaneously, the accuracy increased compared to the Vanilla model. However, it showed lower performance compared to when HFC alone was used. These research results support the argument presented in this paper that providing HFC as the query improves classification performance. Furthermore, it can be observed that providing LFC as the query actually has a negative impact on performance.

Table 1. Ablation study results with ResNet18 and CK+.

Model	Best Epoch	Accuracy (%) @ Best Epoch
ResNet18	100	86.9
ResNet18 + HFC	41	**92.31 (+5.41)**
ResNet18 + LFC	17	86.88 (−0.02)
ResNet18 + (HFC, LFC)	38	91.7 (+4.8)
ResNet18 + (HFC, LFC, HL)	19	87.73 (+0.83)

4.4 Comparison

In this section, we verify whether the attention network proposed in this paper has a beneficial impact on ResNet18 and MobileNetV2 using the FER2013, JAFFE, and CK+ datasets. Furthermore, we compare its performance with the existing implicit method, BAM (Bottleneck Attention Module) [18]. All performance comparisons are conducted based on the models that achieved the highest validation accuracy among the entire 100 epochs. Through Table 2, it can be observed that the attention network proposed in this paper generally enhances the facial expression classification performance of ResNet18 and MobileNetV2. Especially in the case of FER2013 and CK+, it outperforms the traditional implicit method, BAM, in terms of performance. In the JAFFE dataset, while MobileNetV2 exhibited significant performance improvement, it was observed that ResNet18, on the contrary, experienced a decrease in performance. This could be interpreted as occurring due to overfitting caused by the small size of the dataset. However, in situations where the dataset is abundant, it can be observed that the performance of the Vanilla model is significantly improved, and it outperforms BAM, demonstrating superior performance. Furthermore, compared to BAM, the increase in parameters is minimal, which raises expectations for its effective use in real-time inference tasks for facial expression recognition. The following Fig. 9 shows the Grad-CAM (Gradient-weighted Class Activation Mapping) [25]extracted for Vanilla MobileNetV2 and MobileNetV2 with the attention network proposed in this paper, both trained on the CK+ dataset. By examining the figure, it can be observed that the model with the added attention network extracts more generalized features from the dataset compared to the conventional MobileNetV2. Using Contempt as an example, CK+ Contempt images commonly exhibit wrinkles around the mouth area. Vanilla MobileNetV2 tends to focus more on the eyes rather than these common features. However, in the model with the added attention network, it is evident that it concentrates more on the wrinkles around the mouth area. This paper attributed this phenomenon to the attention network's ability to highlight information inherent in HFC, such as wrinkles around the mouth and changes in lip shapes, which are essential for recognizing facial expressions within the feature map. In addition, it can be interpreted that the performance of the model has also improved due to the utilization of a feature map in which information necessary for emotion recognition is highlighted.

Spatial Attention Network with High Frequency Component for FER   145

Table 2. Comparison results about ResNet18, MobileNetV2, BAM, and ours with FER2013, JAFFE, and CK+ datasets.

Dataset	Model	Param.	Best Epoch	Accuracy (%) @ Best Epoch							
Classes				Angry	Disgust	Fear	Happy	Neutral	Sad	Surprise	Average
FER2013	ResNet18	11.17M	100	56.98	47.45	43.36	82.19	61.48	46.19	78.94	59.56
	ResNet18 + BAM	11.198M (+23,808)	30	52.71	54.05	45.7	81.29	61.15	51.16	76.41	60.35 (+0.79)
	ResNet18 + Ours	11.17M (+708)	90	54.18	54.05	41.6	81.62	59.53	54.05	77.98	**60.43** (+0.87)
	MobileNetV2	2.23M	100	41.75	54.05	38.77	80.61	58.16	46.11	73.16	56.09
	MobileNetV2 + BAM	2.24M (+11,192)	38	46.76	54.05	42.29	81.12	56.61	41.38	73.77	56.56 (+0.47)
	MobileNetV2 + Ours	2.23M (+767)	57	50.87	53.15	40.82	80.05	48.74	52.13	73.41	**57.02** (+0.93)
Classes				Angry	Disgust	Fear	Happy	Neutral	Sad	Surprise	Average
JAFFE	ResNet18	11.17M	100	100	85.71	100	87.5	100	100	100	96.17
	ResNet18 + BAM	11.198M (+23,808)	30	87.5	100	100	87.5	100	100	100	**96.43** (+0.26)
	ResNet18 + Ours	11.17M (+708)	31	75	100	100	87.5	100	100	100	94.64 (-1.53)
	MobileNetV2	2.23M	100	50	71.43	62.5	87.5	87.5	62.5	62.5	69.13
	MobileNetV2 + BAM	2.24M (+11,192)	67	75	71.43	75	75	87.5	75	75	**76.28** (+7.15)
	MobileNetV2 + Ours	2.23M (+767)	32	87.5	42.86	50	75	87.5	87.5	87.5	73.98 (+4.85)
Classes				Anger	Contempt	Disgust	Fear	Happy	Sadness	Surprise	Average
CK+	ResNet18	11.17M	100	76.47	100	100	84.21	100	47.62	100	86.9
	ResNet18 + BAM	11.198M (+23,808)	45	82.35	100	93.18	73.68	98.08	85.71	100	90.43 (+3.53)
	ResNet18 + Ours	11.17M (+708)	41	79.41	100	93.18	89.47	100	85.71	100	**92.31** (+5.41)
	MobileNetV2	2.23M	100	58.52	100	90.91	63.16	98.08	52.38	98.39	80.25
	MobileNetV2 + BAM	2.24M (+11,192)	87	76.47	100	100	94.74	94.23	57.14	95.16	88.25 (+8)
	MobileNetV2 + Ours	2.23M (+767)	50	73.53	100	93.18	84.21	100	85.71	88.71	**89.34** (+9.09)

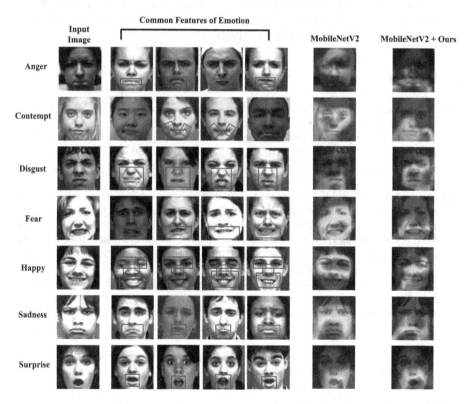

Fig. 9. This illustration represents the Grad-CAM of vanilla MobileNetV2 and ours. All the facial expression images are sourced from the CK+ dataset.

5   Conclusion

This paper introduced an attention network that encourages the utilization of high-frequency components to emulate the human process of recognizing facial expressions, aiming to enhance the facial expression recognition rate of CNN. The presented attention network combined the explicit method of mathematically calculating the relationship between query and key with the implicit method of calculation through a neural network. Rather than simply inputting query and key into a neural network, the paper first calculated the mathematical relationship between query and key, using this as evidence to guide the neural network in computing the attention score. To efficiently operate the attention network, this paper compressed the input feature map into a 1-channel tensor. Furthermore, instead of computing pixel-wise pairwise cross-correlation matrices, this paper vectorized the singular value matrices of query and key, performing outer product operations to create pairwise cross-correlation matrices. The attention network proposed in this study significantly improved the performance of ResNet18 and MobileNetV2 models trained on the FER2013, JAFFE, and CK+ datasets. Furthermore, compared to the existing implicit method, BAM, it generally demonstrated superior performance in most scenarios. And, the increase in the number of parameters was much smaller compared to BAM. The attention network proposed in this paper is expected to provide meaningful assistance in tasks that require real-time facial expression recognition.

References

1. Bahdanau, D., Cho, K., Bengio, Y.: Neural machine translation by jointly learning to align and translate. arXiv preprint arXiv:1409.0473 (2014)
2. Cubuk, E.D., Zoph, B., Mane, D., Vasudevan, V., Le, Q.V.: Autoaugment: learning augmentation policies from data. arXiv preprint arXiv:1805.09501 (2018)
3. Dagli, R.: Astroformer: more data might not be all you need for classification. arXiv preprint arXiv:2304.05350 (2023)
4. El Boudouri, Y., Bohi, A.: Emonext: an adapted convnext for facial emotion recognition. In: 2023 IEEE 25th International Workshop on Multimedia Signal Processing (MMSP), pp. 1–6 (2023). https://doi.org/10.1109/MMSP59012.2023.10337732
5. Fard, A.P., Mahoor, M.H.: Ad-corre: adaptive correlation-based loss for facial expression recognition in the wild. IEEE Access **10**, 26756–26768 (2022). https://doi.org/10.1109/ACCESS.2022.3156598
6. Foret, P., Kleiner, A., Mobahi, H., Neyshabur, B.: Sharpness-aware minimization for efficiently improving generalization. arXiv preprint arXiv:2010.01412 (2020)
7. Georgescu, M.I., Ionescu, R.T., Popescu, M.: Local learning with deep and hand-crafted features for facial expression recognition. arXiv preprint arXiv:1804.10892 (2018)
8. Gesmundo, A., Dean, J.: An evolutionary approach to dynamic introduction of tasks in large-scale multitask learning systems. arXiv preprint arXiv:2205.12755 (2022)

9. Goodfellow, I.J., et al.: Challenges in representation learning: a report on three machine learning contests. In: Lee, M., Hirose, A., Hou, Z.-G., Kil, R.M. (eds.) ICONIP 2013. LNCS, vol. 8228, pp. 117–124. Springer, Heidelberg (2013). https://doi.org/10.1007/978-3-642-42051-1_16

10. He, K., Zhang, X., Ren, S., Sun, J.: Deep residual learning for image recognition. In: Proceedings of the IEEE Conference on Computer Vision and Pattern Recognition, pp. 770–778 (2016)

11. Hu, J., Shen, L., Sun, G.: Squeeze-and-excitation networks. In: Proceedings of the IEEE Conference on Computer Vision and Pattern Recognition, pp. 7132–7141 (2018)

12. Krizhevsky, A.: Learning multiple layers of features from tiny images (2009). https://api.semanticscholar.org/CorpusID:18268744

13. Liu, Z., Luo, P., Wang, X., Tang, X.: Deep learning face attributes in the wild. In: Proceedings of International Conference on Computer Vision (ICCV) (2015)

14. Lucey, P., Cohn, J.F., Kanade, T., Saragih, J., Ambadar, Z., Matthews, I.: The extended cohn-kanade dataset (ck+): a complete dataset for action unit and emotion-specified expression. In: 2010 IEEE Computer Society Conference on Computer Vision and Pattern Recognition - Workshops, pp. 94–101 (2010). https://doi.org/10.1109/CVPRW.2010.5543262

15. Lyons, M.J.: "excavating AI" re-excavated: debunking a fallacious account of the jaffe dataset. arXiv preprint arXiv:2107.13998 (2021)

16. Lyons, M.J., Kamachi, M., Gyoba, J.: Coding facial expressions with gabor wavelets (ivc special issue). arXiv preprint arXiv:2009.05938 (2020)

17. Minaee, S., Abdolrashidi, A.: Deep-emotion: facial expression recognition using attentional convolutional network. arXiv preprint arXiv:1902.01019 (2019)

18. Park, J., Woo, S., Lee, J.Y., Kweon, I.S.: Bam: bottleneck attention module. arXiv preprint arXiv:1807.06514 (2018)

19. Park, M., Lee, J.N., Cho, J., Kim, Y.J., Yoon, J., Whang, M.: Facial vibration analysis for emotion recognition (2016). https://api.semanticscholar.org/CorpusID:137695591

20. Park, S., Jung, W.: The effect of spatial frequency filtering on facial expression recognition and age perception. Korean J. Cogn. Biol. Psychol. 18(4), 311–324 (2006)

21. Paszke, A., et al.: Pytorch: an imperative style, high-performance deep learning library. Adv. Neural Inf. Process. Syst. 32 (2019)

22. Pecoraro, R., Basile, V., Bono, V., Gallo, S.: Local multi-head channel self-attention for facial expression recognition. arXiv preprint arXiv:2111.07224 (2021)

23. Ridnik, T., Sharir, G., Ben-Cohen, A., Ben-Baruch, E., Noy, A.: Ml-decoder: scalable and versatile classification head. arXiv preprint arXiv:2111.12933 (2021)

24. Sandler, M., Howard, A., Zhu, M., Zhmoginov, A., Chen, L.C.: Mobilenetv2: inverted residuals and linear bottlenecks. In: Proceedings of the IEEE Conference on Computer Vision and Pattern Recognition, pp. 4510–4520 (2018)

25. Selvaraju, R.R., Cogswell, M., Das, A., Vedantam, R., Parikh, D., Batra, D.: Gradcam: visual explanations from deep networks via gradient-based localization. In: Proceedings of the IEEE International Conference on Computer Vision, pp. 618–626 (2017)

26. Tan, M., Le, Q.: Efficientnet: rethinking model scaling for convolutional neural networks. In: International Conference on Machine Learning, pp. 6105–6114. PMLR (2019)

27. Vaswani, A., et al.: Attention is all you need. Adv. Neural Inf. Process. Syst. 30 (2017)

Minor Object Recognition from Drone Image Sequence

Duy-Linh Nguyen⬤, Xuan-Thuy Vo⬤, Adri Priadana⬤,
and Kang-Hyun Jo$^{(\boxtimes)}$⬤

Department of Electrical, Electronic and Computer Engineering, University of Ulsan,
Ulsan 44610, South Korea
{ndlinh301,priadana}@mail.ulsan.ac.kr, xthuy@islab.ulsan.ac.kr,
acejo@ulsan.ac.kr

Abstract. Object detection in drone imagery is an interesting topic in
the Computer Vision field. This work was widely applied in traffic analysis and control, rescue systems, smart agriculture, etc. However, many
challenges exist in developing and optimizing applications because of
object density, multi-scale objects, and blur motion. To partly solve the
above problems, this research focuses on improving the performance of
the YOLOv5m network based on the advantages of the Bi-directional
Feature Pyramid Network (BiFPN), Transformer, and Convolutional
Block Attention Module (CBAM). The experiments achieve 68.6% and
42.6% of mAP on the proposed datasets (ISLab-Drone) and VisDrone
2021, respectively. That demonstrates the outperformance of the network
comparable to other networks under the same testing conditions.

Keywords: Convolutional neural network (CNN) · BiFPN · CBAM ·
UAV imagery · YOLOv5m · ViT

1 Introduction

For a long time, researchers have focused on object detection from the air using
unmanned aerial vehicles (UAVs). AUVs can collect ground images from different
altitudes and speeds. These techniques are widely deployed in forest protection
[5], wildlife protection [9], and surveillance systems [4]. In particular, with the
rapid development of smart cities, the support tools for the operation, monitoring, and protection process become more and more necessary. The image processing and analysis techniques are also required to accommodate the mobility,
compactness, and power limitations of UAVs. An ideal choice for these applications is object detection based on the YOLO [7,8,14–16] network family. Most
object detection in drone imagery methods face some common problems, such
as object density, multi-scale objects, and blur motion. Object density caused
by the overlap of objects hinders the detection of hidden objects. UAVs capture images with variable altitudes, resulting in images that also vary in scale
from tiny, small, and medium to large. The flight speed of UAVs leads to the

© The Author(s), under exclusive license to Springer Nature Singapore Pte Ltd. 2024
G. Irie et al. (Eds.): IW-FCV 2024, CCIS 2143, pp. 148–159, 2024.
https://doi.org/10.1007/978-981-97-4249-3_12

image having a certain blurry quality, which affects the locating and detecting of objects in the image. From the above observations, this paper proposes an improved method for the YOLOv5m network used in detecting drone-captured objects. Research focuses on optimizing the backbone and neck networks based on the Bi-directional Feature Pyramid Network (BiFPN) [18], Transformer [2], and Convolutional Block Attention Module (CBAM) [19]. Besides, this work also provides a drone-captured image dataset with diverse scenarios for object detection tasks.

The main contribution is as follows:

1. Redesigns the backbone and neck networks of YOLOv5m architecture with a combination of BiFPN, Transformer, and CBAM.
2. Adds one more detection head with new anchor sets to improve the tiny object detection task.
3. Proposes a drone-captured image dataset used in the Computer Vision field.

The rest of the paper is organized as follows: Sect. 2 introduces the related works to object detection in drone imagery tasks. Section 3 explains the proposed method. Section 4 analyzes and proves the experimental results. Section 5 summarizes the important issue and future orientation.

2   Related Work

2.1   Deep Neural Network-Based Method

These methods leverage the advantage of deep learning neural networks (DNNs) to consider the differences between foreground and background to cluster and detect objects in drone-captured scenarios. The work [20] proposed a framework that combines clustering and detection by sequentially searching the clustered areas and detecting drone-captured objects belonging to these regions. Observing the issues of [20], the method [1] added an efficient self-adaptive region to build the global-local detection network to improve the accuracy of high-density and large-scale object detection. Another approach [22] used a region estimation network to find the high-density drone-captured objects in diverse areas. For drone-captured vehicle image challenges, the study [23] aligns the feature between different viewpoints, backgrounds, illumination, and weather in the domain adaptation. DNN-based methods achieved high accuracy in detecting objects but the computational cost is still a huge problem.

2.2   Convolutional Neural Network-Based Method

In recent years, the strong development of convolutional neural networks (CNNs) in object detection of drone imagery topic has attracted the attention of many researchers. The research [17] evaluated different backbone architectures, prediction heads, and model pruning techniques to select a better combination in a fast object detection network. TPH-YOLOv5 [26] combined the ideas of the transformer detection head and original detection head in the YOLOv5 network architecture to improve the accuracy in detecting large-size variation objects and high-density objects. Inheriting previous work, the work in [24] work proposed a cross-layer asymmetric transformer (CA-Trans) to replace the additional prediction head in TPH-YOLOv5 for more efficiency in tiny object detection. The outstanding advantage of CNN-based methods is achieving ideal object detection accuracy with flexible integration of other techniques such as Transformer or Attention algorithms.

3   Methodology

Figure 1 presents in detail the proposed object detection network. This method is improved from the original YOLOv5m architecture [7] with three components: Backbone, Neck, and detection head.

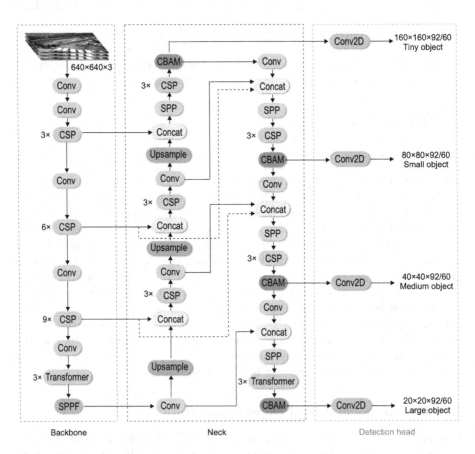

Fig. 1. The proposed object detection network in drone imagery. Numbers 92/60 are detector output coefficients for ISLab-Drone and VisDrone 2021 datasets, respectively.

3.1 Proposed Network Architecture

Backbone Module: The backbone network plays a very important role in extracting features for the entire network. Based on the existing architecture of YOLOv5, this work evaluates and replaces several components to reduce computational complexity and network parameters while still ensuring feature extraction capabilities. Specifically, the Focus module is replaced by a simpler architecture, named the Conv block. This block includes one 2D convolution (Conv2D), one batch normalization (BN), and one Sigmoid Linear Unit (SiLU) activation function. The design of the Conv block is shown in Fig. 2(a). The body of the backbone network still uses a combination of Conv blocks and Cross Stage Partial modules (CSP) with ratios of 3, 6, and 9. Figure 2(b) describes the architecture of the CSP module. The end of the backbone network adds three Transformer blocks and replaces the Spatial Pyramid Pooling (SPP) module with the Spatial Pyramid Pooling Fast (SPPF) module. The SPPF module applies all of the max pooling (MaxPooling) layers with the same kernel size (k = 5). The architecture of SPP and SPPF modules are depicted in Fig. 2(c) and Figs. 2(d).

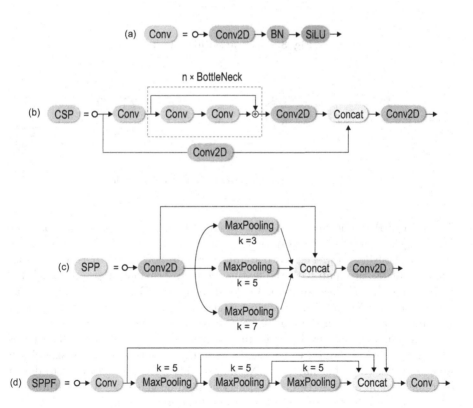

Fig. 2. The architecture of basic modules.

This block is inspired by the Vision Transformer (ViT) [2] which is used to capture global information and rich contextual information [26]. The structure of the Transformer blocks is depicted in Fig. 3. Each Transformer block is built from two sub-blocks, the Multi-head Attention (MA) layer and the Multilayer Perceptron (MLP) layer (fully connected layers). Besides, Residual connections are used between two sub-blocks. Therefore, Transformer bock also increases the ability to extract rich local information. Based on Neck's existing architecture in YOLOv5m, this work adds a CBAM at the end of each level in the multi-level feature map (small, medium, and large). On the other hand, the Neck also appends a feature map level to detect extremely small objects (Tiny). In total, this module has four feature map levels.

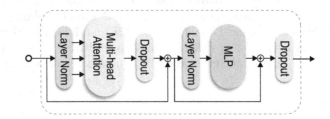

Fig. 3. The Transformer block.

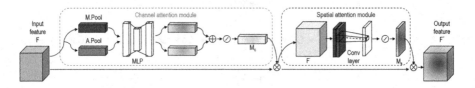

Fig. 4. The architecture of the CBAM module.

Neck Module: The Neck module is designed based on the combination of the Path Aggregation Network (PAN) [12] and the Bi-directional Feature Pyramid Network (Bi-FPN) [18]. These two architectures support each other to synthesize the current feature map with the feature maps in previous stages to enrich the information for the feature maps in the next stages. Based on Neck's existing architecture in YOLOv5m, this work stacks the SPP module and CBAM at the end of each level in the multi-level feature map (small, medium, and large). Especially in the last level, three transformer blocks are stacked between the SPP and CBAM modules to enrich the useful information for large-size object detection. On the other hand, the Neck also adds a feature map level to detect extremely small objects (tiny). In total, this module generates four feature map levels. The architecture of the CBAM module is presented in Fig. 4.

Detection Head Module: The detection head module leverages three feature map levels of the YOLOv5m architecture from the Neck module, including $80 \times 80 \times 256$, $40 \times 40 \times 512$, and $20 \times 20 \times 1024$. Besides, this study adds one more detection head at $160 \times 160 \times 128$ feature map level to increase tiny object detection ability. The number of anchor boxes is set at four and their sizes are redesigned to suit the objects in the ISLab-Drone and VisDrone 2021 datasets. The details of each detection head and the anchor size are described in Table 1.

Table 1. Detection heads and anchors.

Head	Input	Anchors	Output	Object
1 (Added)	$160 \times 160 \times 128$	(7, 9), (9, 17), (17, 15), (13, 27)	$160 \times 160 \times 92/60$	Tiny
2	$80 \times 80 \times 256$	(21, 28), (36, 18), (23, 47), (35, 33)	$80 \times 80 \times 92/60$	Small
3	$40 \times 40 \times 512$	(58, 29), (43, 60), (82, 46), (66, 88)	$40 \times 40 \times 92/60$	Medium
4	$20 \times 20 \times 1024$	(133, 77), (111, 135), (206, 137), (197, 290)	$20 \times 20 \times 92/60$	Large

3.2   Loss Function

The loss function is defined as follows:

$$Loss = \lambda_{box}\mathcal{L}_{box} + \lambda_{obj}\mathcal{L}_{obj} + \lambda_{cls}\mathcal{L}_{cls}, \tag{1}$$

in which, $\mathcal{L}_{box}$ is the bounding box regression loss using CIoU loss, $\mathcal{L}_{obj}$ is the object confidence score loss using Binary Cross Entropy loss, and L_{cls} is the classes loss also using Binary Cross Entropy loss to calculate. λ_{box}, λ_{obj}, and λ_{cls} are balancing parameters.

4   Experiments

4.1   Dataset

The experiments in this paper are trained and evaluated on two datasets, ISLab-Drone and VisDrone 2021 [25]. The ISLab-Drone dataset was proposed by the Intelligent Systems Laboratory (ISLab) at the University of Ulsan, South Korea. This dataset includes 10,000 images collected using a UAV under different weather and altitude conditions in Ulsan City and Daegu City, South Korea. It contains 18 categories: tree, person, animal, house, apartment/building, school, office, traffic sign, traffic light, streetlamp/telephone pole, banner, milestone, bridge, tower, car_vechicle, bus_vehicle, truck_vehicle, motorcycle/bike_vehicle. The number of images is divided based on the ratio 5:2.5:2.5 for the training, evaluation, and testing sets. The VisDrone Dataset 2021 is a large-scale benchmark created by the AISKYEYE team at the Lab of Machine Learning and Data Mining, Tianjin University, China. VisDrone 2021 consists of four subsets, including a training set, validation set, test-dev set, and test-challenge set. These experiments only use the training set, the validation set, and the test-dev set with 6,471, 548, and 1,610 images, respectively. The images are separated into 10 classes: pedestrian, people, bicycle, car, van, truck, tricycle, awning-tricycle, bus, motor.

4.2 Experimental Setup

This experiment applies the original YOLOv5 [7] as a code base using Python programming language and the Pytorch framework. The training and evaluation processes are conducted on a GeForce GTX 1080Ti GPU. The Adam optimization is used. The learning rate is initially set to 10^{-5} and the final by 10^{-2}. The momentum began at 0.8 and then increased to 0.937. The training process takes 300 epochs with a batch size of 32. The balancing parameters $\lambda_{cls} = 0.5$, $\lambda_{box} = 0.05$, and $\lambda_{obj} = 1$, respectively. Several data augmentation methods are applied such as mosaic, mix-up, flip left-right, and flip up-down.

4.3 Experimental Result

For the ISLab-Drone dataset, this experiment conducts training and evaluation from scratch YOLOv5 (n, s, m, l, x) series, proposed network, and then compares the performance between them. As the results are shown in Table 2, the proposed network achieves 68.6% mean Average Precision (mAP) which demonstrates that the network outperforms the whole of the YOLOv5 series. When compared with the best competitor (YOLOv5l), the proposed network achieves better performance at 2.5% of mAP while the number of parameters and GLOPS are lower nearby twice. Compared to YOLOV5m, the size and computational complexity of the proposed network are light larger than YOLOv5 but the performance is better than YOLOv5m at 6.4% of mAP.

Table 2. The comparison result of the proposed detection network with YOLOv5 series on the test set of the ISLab-Drone dataset.

Model	Parameter	GFLOPs	Weight (MB)	mAP (%)
YOLOv5x	86,287,807	204.1	173.3	65.6
YOLOv5l	46,199,823	107.9	114.3	66.1
YOLOv5m	20,921,631	48.1	42.3	62.2
YOLOv5s	7,058,671	15.9	14.5	63.6
YOLOv5n	1,783,519	4.2	3.9	55.3
Proposed method	27,377,416	67.1	55.8	68.6

In the case of the VisDrone dataset, this experiment compares the proposed network with recent work under the same conditions. As a result, Table 3 shows that the proposed network still outperforms existing studies and better best competitor by 0.5% of mAP. However, when compared to the latest version of

YOLO (YOLOv8m), the proposed network is 2.4% of mAP worse. This poses many challenges for continuously improving the proposed network in the future. The proposed network can present a better ability in object detection tasks. However, this experiment also issues several problems when detecting objects with very small scale and overlapping objects. The qualitative results of the proposed network on the test set of the ISLab-Drone and the test-dev-set of the VisDrone datasets are shown in Fig. 5.

Table 3. The comparison result of the proposed method with other networks on the test-dev set of the VisDrone dataset. The symbol "†" denotes the re-trained models.

Model	Parameter	GFLOPs	Weight (MB)	mAP (%)
YOLOv5m†	20,889,303	48.1	42.3	29.6
YOLOv8m†	25,845,550	78.8	52.0	45.0
HawkNet [11]	N/A	N/A	N/A	25.6
ClusDet [20]	N/A	N/A	N/A	28.4
DMNet[10]	N/A	N/A	N/A	29.4
Method in [22]	N/A	N/A	N/A	30.3
DSHNet [21]	N/A	N/A	N/A	30.3
CDMNet [3]	N/A	N/A	N/A	31.9
GLSAN [1]	N/A	N/A	N/A	32.5
DCRFF [13]	N/A	N/A	N/A	35.0
UFPMP-Net [6]	N/A	N/A	N/A	39.2
TPH-YOLOv5++ [24]	N/A	N/A	N/A	41.4
TPH-YOLOv5 [26]	N/A	N/A	N/A	42.1
Proposed method	27,331,208	66.9	55.7	42.6

4.4 Ablation Study

To evaluate the influence of each module in the proposed network, this study also conducts several ablation studies. By replacing the proposed modules with the original YOLOv5m network architecture, training, and evaluating on the test data set of the ISLab-Drone dataset. The results in Table 4 show that the Bi-FPN network plays an important role in enriching information for feature maps. Besides, Transformer and CBAM modules support the information capture process from local to global. That is why this work chooses the perfect combination of Bi-FPN, CBAM, and Transformer modules to improve the YOLOv5m network from 62.2% to 68.6% of mAP.

Fig. 5. The qualitative results of the proposed network on the test set of the ISLab-Drone and the test-dev-set of the VisDrone datasets.

Table 4. Ablation studies with different proposed networks on the test set of the ISLab-Drone dataset.

Module	Proposed network			
Transformer	✓			✓
Bi-FPN		✓		✓
CBAM			✓	✓
SPPF	✓	✓	✓	✓
SPP	✓	✓	✓	✓
Parameter	24,494,767	26,954,255	25,330,744	27,377,416
Weight (MB)	55.3	55.5	54.9	55.8
GFLOPs	66.5	66.9	64.7	67.1
mAP(%)	58.8	65.2	51.2	68.6

5   Conclusion

This paper conducted a technique to improve the original YOLOv5m architecture for object detection in drone imagery. Based on YOLOv5m, the proposed network contains three parts: backbone, neck, and head modules. The backbone is redesigned using simple architectures and Transformer modules. The neck is redesigned with the bi-FPN network, CBAM, and Transformer. A new head for tiny object detection is added to the detection head module and resized the anchors to fit the detection tasks. The experimental result presented the outstanding performance of the proposed network. This study will be further developed with tiny and overlapping object detection integrated with the idea in the latest YOLOv8 architecture for the future.

Acknowledgement. This result was supported by "Regional Innovation Strategy (RIS)" through the National Research Foundation of Korea (NRF) funded by the Ministry of Education (MOE)(2021RIS-003).

References

1. Deng, S., et al.: A global-local self-adaptive network for drone-view object detection. IEEE Trans. Image Process. **30**, 1556–1569 (2021). https://doi.org/10.1109/TIP.2020.3045636
2. Dosovitskiy, A., et al.: An image is worth 16x16 words: transformers for image recognition at scale. CoRR abs/2010.11929 (2020). https://arxiv.org/abs/2010.11929
3. Duan, C., Wei, Z., Zhang, C., Qu, S., Wang, H.: Coarse-grained density map guided object detection in aerial images. In: 2021 IEEE/CVF International Conference on Computer Vision Workshops (ICCVW), pp. 2789–2798 (2021). https://doi.org/10.1109/ICCVW54120.2021.00313

4. Gu, J., Su, T., Wang, Q., Du, X., Guizani, M.: Multiple moving targets surveillance based on a cooperative network for multi-UAV. IEEE Commun. Mag. **56**(4), 82–89 (2018). https://doi.org/10.1109/MCOM.2018.1700422

5. Hird, J.N., et al.: Use of unmanned aerial vehicles for monitoring recovery of forest vegetation on petroleum well sites. Remote Sens. **9**(5) (2017). https://doi.org/10.3390/rs9050413. https://www.mdpi.com/2072-4292/9/5/413

6. Huang, Y., Chen, J., Huang, D.: UFPMP-Det: toward accurate and efficient object detection on drone imagery. CoRR abs/2112.10415 (2021). https://arxiv.org/abs/2112.10415

7. Jocher, G., et al.: ultralytics/yolov5: v3.1 - Bug Fixes and Performance Improvements (2020). https://doi.org/10.5281/zenodo.4154370

8. Jocher, G., Chaurasia, A., Qiu, J.: Ultralytics yolov8 (2023). https://github.com/ultralytics/ultralytics

9. Kellenberger, B., Volpi, M., Tuia, D.: Fast animal detection in UAV images using convolutional neural networks. In: 2017 IEEE International Geoscience and Remote Sensing Symposium (IGARSS), pp. 866–869 (2017).https://doi.org/10.1109/IGARSS.2017.8127090

10. Li, C., Yang, T., Zhu, S., Chen, C., Guan, S.: Density map guided object detection in aerial images. CoRR abs/2004.05520 (2020). https://arxiv.org/abs/2004.05520

11. Lin, H., Zhou, J., Gan, Y., Vong, C.M., Liu, Q.: Novel up-scale feature aggregation for object detection in aerial images. Neurocomputing **411**, 364–374 (2020). https://doi.org/10.1016/j.neucom.2020.06.011

12. Liu, S., Qi, L., Qin, H., Shi, J., Jia, J.: Path aggregation network for instance segmentation. CoRR abs/1803.01534 (2018). http://arxiv.org/abs/1803.01534

13. Mittal, P., Sharma, A., Singh, R., Dhull, V.: Dilated convolution based RCNN using feature fusion for low-altitude aerial objects. Expert Syst. Appl. **199**, 117106 (2022). https://doi.org/10.1016/j.eswa.2022.117106

14. Redmon, J., Divvala, S.K., Girshick, R.B., Farhadi, A.: You only look once: unified, real-time object detection. CoRR abs/1506.02640 (2015). http://arxiv.org/abs/1506.02640

15. Redmon, J., Farhadi, A.: YOLO9000: better, faster, stronger. CoRR abs/1612.08242 (2016). http://arxiv.org/abs/1612.08242

16. Redmon, J., Farhadi, A.: Yolov3: an incremental improvement. CoRR abs/1804.02767 (2018). http://arxiv.org/abs/1804.02767

17. Ringwald, T., Sommer, L., Schumann, A., Beyerer, J., Stiefelhagen, R.: UAV-net: a fast aerial vehicle detector for mobile platforms. In: 2019 IEEE/CVF Conference on Computer Vision and Pattern Recognition Workshops (CVPRW), pp. 544–552 (2019). https://doi.org/10.1109/CVPRW.2019.00080

18. Tan, M., Pang, R., Le, Q.V.: Efficientdet: scalable and efficient object detection. CoRR abs/1911.09070 (2019). http://arxiv.org/abs/1911.09070

19. Woo, S., Park, J., Lee, J., Kweon, I.S.: CBAM: convolutional block attention module. CoRR abs/1807.06521 (2018). http://arxiv.org/abs/1807.06521

20. Yang, F., Fan, H., Chu, P., Blasch, E., Ling, H.: Clustered object detection in aerial images. CoRR abs/1904.08008 (2019). http://arxiv.org/abs/1904.08008

21. Yu, W., Yang, T., Chen, C.: Towards resolving the challenge of long-tail distribution in UAV images for object detection. In: 2021 IEEE Winter Conference on Applications of Computer Vision (WACV), pp. 3257–3266 (2021). https://doi.org/10.1109/WACV48630.2021.00330

22. Zhang, J., Huang, J., Chen, X., Zhang, D.: How to fully exploit the abilities of aerial image detectors. In: 2019 IEEE/CVF International Conference on Computer Vision Workshop (ICCVW), pp. 1–8 (2019).https://doi.org/10.1109/ICCVW.2019.00007

23. Zhang, R., Newsam, S., Shao, Z., Huang, X., Wang, J., Li, D.: Multi-scale adversarial network for vehicle detection in UAV imagery. ISPRS J. Photogramm. Remote. Sens. **180**, 283–295 (2021). https://doi.org/10.1016/j.isprsjprs.2021.08.002

24. Zhao, Q., Liu, B., Lyu, S., Wang, C., Zhang, H.: TPH-YOLOv5++: boosting object detection on drone-captured scenarios with cross-layer asymmetric transformer. Remote Sens. **15**(6) (2023). https://doi.org/10.3390/rs15061687. https://www.mdpi.com/2072-4292/15/6/1687

25. Zhu, P., et al.: Detection and tracking meet drones challenge. IEEE Trans. Pattern Anal. Mach. Intell. **44**(11), 7380–7399 (2021). https://doi.org/10.1109/TPAMI.2021.3119563

26. Zhu, X., Lyu, S., Wang, X., Zhao, Q.: Tph-yolov5: improved yolov5 based on transformer prediction head for object detection on drone-captured scenarios. CoRR abs/2108.11539 (2021). https://arxiv.org/abs/2108.11539

Author Index

© The Editor(s) (if applicable) and The Author(s), under exclusive license
to Springer Nature Singapore Pte Ltd. 2024
G. Irie et al. (Eds.): IW-FCV 2024, CCIS 2143, p. 161, 2024.
https://doi.org/10.1007/978-981-97-4249-3

Printed in the United States
by Baker & Taylor Publisher Services